This new edition of *The Adventures of the Man of Bronze: a Definitive Chronology* has been fully revised to make it easier to read and to include new information such as Will Murray's new Wild Adventures of Doc Savage.

The first edition of this book was the first work to include Lester Dent's original Doc Savage radio play scripts in a chronology, and to determine Doc Savage's true birthday. This new edition now includes information of the Man of Bronze's family tree, which includes Armand Chauvelin (of Scarlet Pimpernel fame), Rosa Klebb and Irma Bunt (of James Bond infamy), Wolf Larsen, Philip Marlowe and Sam Spade – as well as Frankenstein's Monster and the Phantom of the Opera!

Other Westerntainment Books

Over the Rainbow: a User's Guide to My *Dangyang* by Jeff Deischer

The Overman Paradigm by Kim Williamson

The Marvel Timeline Project, Part 1 by Jeff Deischer and Murray Ward

Brave New World: Divided We Planetfall by Lawrence V Bridgeport

The Way They Were: the Histories of Some of Adventure Fiction's Most Famous Heroes and Villains by Jeff Deischer

Spook Trail by Jeff Deischer

The Winter Wizard by Jeff Deischer

The Adventures

of the

Man of Bronze

A Definitive Chronology

Jeff Deischer

a Westerntainment Publication

Published by Westerntainment
Denver, Colorado, USA
http://westerntainment.blogspot.com
westerntainment@gmail.com

The cover to this book was provided by Frank Hamilton. It is a reproduction of a Baumhofer cover commissioned for DOC SAVAGE MAGAZINE in the 1940s but never used. I want to thank his son Brian for letting me use it once again for this new edition.

For Lester Dent, one of the great storytellers

Acknowledgments

This work would not have been possible without the help of Will Murray.

Much of my research was accomplished with the help of the Aurora and Denver Public Libraries, and through the use of *The Time Tables of History* by Bernard Grun and *The New York Public Library Book of Chronologies*. Additional material was made available by the Western Historical Manuscript Collection at the University of Missouri in Columbia, Missouri, and the Ask-A-Nurse program at Centura Health. Thanks also to numerous people who answered questions on a variety of topics, especially Lynn Ruth of the public relations office of the Empire State Building, who also sent me floor plans of the 85th floor.

I would be remiss not to thank Philip José Farmer, who started my lifelong love of books-about-books with his *Doc Savage: His Apocalyptic Life*.

Special mention goes to Jim Lannon and Jerry Nunez for their unwavering support.

Thanks also to Rick Lai. His insightful observations led to some of the changes for the 2002-2003 revision, which resulted in the 2008 second edition.

Lastly, thanks to my parents for all their help.

The Adventures

of the

Man of Bronze

A Definitive Chronology

Preface

An admirer of Philip José Farmer's *Doc Savage: His Apocalyptic Life*, I began this chronology as an attempt to place into Farmer's chronology of the Doc Savage stories those adventures which he had left out, and those added to the saga, such as the novels by Will Murray. In the early 1990s, I decided to re-read all the stories and prepare my own chronology.

As Farmer says in his introduction to the chronology in his biography of Doc, "To explain in detail [the placement of every adventure] would ... take at least twenty thousand words, and only the most zealous Savageologist would care to tackle an essay of that length". I took up this challenge. And ended up with something more than twenty thousand words.

In 1993, Will Murray was kind enough to look my chronology over and make a few suggestions, the most important of which was sending me the list of the Order of Submission for the stories. This became the keystone of this complete revision, in 1999, of my earlier attempt.

This book is chiefly a chronology of Doc Savage's adventures. It is not a Doc Savage encyclopedia, although there are numerous observations about a variety of topics concerning Doc and his aides, such as the Crime College, the Hidalgo Trading Company warehouse, etc. A familiarity with Doc Savage and his milieu is assumed.

Table of Contents

Author's Foreword to the New Edition

Apparently my criticism of Philip Jose Farmer's Wold Newton work has caused some hard feelings among some of his fans. It shouldn't. I'm one of them. Farmer possessed a great intellect and creativity and he is one of my favorite authors. His Riverworld series sits on my shelf — literally — of favorite books. My 1975 copy of *Doc Savage: His Apocalyptic Life* is dog-eared, to put it kindly. I have pored over it and pored over it, making notes in the margins, before beginning an attempt at a Doc Savage chronology myself twenty years later.

I did not, as some seem to think, set out to destroy the Wold Newton universe. I did not, in fact, set out to do anything with it. I saw errors in Farmer's Doc Savage chronology and set out to rectify them. I set out to tell the truth about Doc Savage. Along the way, I uncovered his agenda, which was counter to information in the Doc Savage series itself. Later research into ancillary literature revealed a widespread disregard for the actual texts of stories and their authors' intents.

My criticism is both simple and specific (and, I might add, not personal): Farmer distorted information to fit his own agenda and labelled it as fact. For a "scholar", this is inexcusable.

Generally speaking, Farmer fudged dates in order to connect the stories he used as the foundation for his massive Wold Newton genealogy. Among other things, he altered birth dates of some characters in order to marry them off to characters from other stories. One example of this is Professor Challenger's daughter, Enid.

In constructing a genealogy such as the Wold Newton one, it is necessary to postulate children of which there is no "official" record. Farmer does so -- and then goes on to *name* these conjectured progeny. I believe it quite possible that Monk Mayfair is related to Professor Challenger -- and even Horace Holly -- but I object to the manner in which Farmer does it. Speculation ought to be labelled as such, in order for research to retain its validity and authority.

Specifically, Farmer had a view of Doc Savage that he wanted to promote in his biography of the Man of Bronze and he ignored or distorted information in the series to do so. His research is so meticulous that this distortion can only have been intentional.

Based on his two biographies of pulp characters, Farmer was not a pulp scholar. He was an author with a point of view, or agenda, that he wanted to get across, which, at least in the case of Doc Savage, was not wholly based on evidence in the series.

Farmer is better identified as a "mythographer" -- a documenter of myths -- than as a scholar. He took stories of heroes and wove them together into a single tapestry. The research alone is staggering. The creativity is no less impressive. And pointing out errors in the weaving to correct flaws in order to make a more accurate tapestry should not be misconstrued as disrespect for the weaver.

There is nothing wrong with playing games such as Farmer's – and I have nothing against them, personally -- but they should not be offered or taken as scholarly research. They belong where I and others have put them – in fiction.

Jeff Deischer

June 2011

Foreword by Will Murray

Ever since the publication of Philip Jose Farmer's *Doc Savage: His Apocalyptic Life* in 1973, Doc Savage fans have been caught up in the Chronology Game.

The Chronology Game did not begin with Farmer, who kicked off his personal excursion into making fictitious heroes fit into the real world of men and events with *Tarzan Alive*, but with Sherlock Holmes. Specifically, with W. S. Baring-Gould's seminal *Sherlock Holmes of Baker Street*. So it's a tried and true and time-honored game.

But it is a game nonetheless. Others have played it with Doc since Farmer. Now Jeff Deischer takes a whack at it. And a good whack it is, too.

The game is tough. Let no one doubt this. Trying to fit all 190 (so far) authorized Doc Savage adventures into their proper chronological sequence with multiple writers penning the series independently of one another, harried editors scheduling books months (sometimes years!) out of sequence, editing out inconvenient internal chronology to suit the relentless monthly on-sale dates, make for a swell thicket of technical problems.

Personally, when I was writing my Doc Savage stories, I simply relied on the order of submission as my rough chronology, ignoring for the most part the ghosted books and not worrying about the niceties of contradictory internal evidence. But even that approach had its pitfalls. For example, all references to the approaching 1936 presidential campaign were excised from *The Terror in the Navy* because, although written a year before America went to the polls, it wasn't published until six months after the election. And a reference to *The Terror in the Navy* was deleted from the novel immediately following, *The Derrick Devil*, when the latter slipped into print before the former. And there's the distressing fact that Street & Smith felt readership turned over every few years, leaving Lester Dent free to recycle old plots in the belief that there were no surviving readers to complain that every so often, Doc and the boys discovered a new lost land filled with dinosaurs, each time stunned at the discovery even though by 1943, they had found dinosauria survivals on three different occasions.

As you'll discover, Jeff too relies on the order of submission as his template. But he goes beyond that, painstakingly fine-tuning it and justifying the end result with everything from lunar phases to good old-fashioned internal evidence. He's done a credible job of reconciling the near-irreconcilable. And he plays the game with exactitude, while allowing leeway for the realities of pulp publishing. Personally, I doubt very much that the Doc writers calculated the phases of the moon when writing their stories. If they needed a full moon, they just dropped one in. With Lester Dent, who early on decided that weather made a great atmospheric story quality, almost a character by itself, he made snow or rain for story purposes first, casting an eye toward the novel's probable publication date second.

I was happy to read this work in manuscript form and bring some insights and suggestions to bear on Jeff's approach. He did a great job. And I am privileged to introduce *The Adventures of the Man of Bronze: A Definitive Chronology* to you.

Will Murray
December 28, 1999

Introduction

Lester Dent was, of course, the first and best "Kenneth Robeson", the Street & Smith house name for the author of the DOC SAVAGE series. Although it was Henry Ralston and John Nanovic (a manager and editor at Street & Smith, respectively) who created Doc Savage (and his aides), it was Dent who made Doc the Man of Bronze. He even added an aide, Renny, whom he apparently based on his own father. As Murray writes, he "was a magical choice, and in the light of hindsight, would seem to have been the only choice"; "There have been several Kenneth Robesons but only one Lester Dent". These "several" other "Robesons" were Laurence Donovan, Alan Hathway, Ryerson Johnson, Harold Davis, William Bogart, and revealed here for the first time anywhere, Evelyn Coulson, one of Dent's secretaries. And as you may know, Murray himself became one with the addition of several new stories in the late 1980s.

Methodology

There are two schools of thought in preparing a chronology, one view represented by Will Murray, the other by Philip Jose Farmer.

The first can be summed up rather easily: the adventures occurred in the order they were written, at approximately the time they were written. This is similar to watching a movie or television show. There is no feeling that the events happened, someone wrote a script, and then filmed the script. It's all happening as you experience it, in the present tense. This method ignores the internal evidence, viewing it as editorial or topical references. These certainly crept into texts often enough in the 1930s for this view to be credible.

The second view is that internal references are concrete clues to when an adventure occurred, and that the occurrence of the adventures must follow historical guidelines; that is, like real events. A thing must happen before it can be written about. The inspiration for this view (whether or not it was actually Farmer's) in the Doc Savage milieu is the story *No Light to Die By*, published in 1947. In it Doc sends a cablegram to "Robeson" complaining of the publisher's treatment of him in the stories. This adds the element that the stories actually happened, and then were written about.

I prefer the second view.

The first precept of this view, naturally, is that an event must occur before it can be recorded. Finding the Last Possible Occurrence (LPO) of an adventure is the first order of business (and I should add that I am indebted to Farmer for his thoughts on this subject). The LPO is the latest date the last day of an adventure can occur. Because of the time it takes to write and prepare a manuscript for publication, and the fact the magazines were cover-dated a month later (e.g., *The Man of Bronze* was cover-dated March 1933, but on sale February 15, 1933), this interval is sixty days. But because the magazines were on the stands the third Friday of the month, the LPO is not a regular, monthly date. It would fluctuate between the 15th and 21st of a given month. Using this, the LPO of *The Man of Bronze* is December 16, 1932. The adventure, 25 days long, must therefore have started no later than November 21, 1932 (and, in fact, this is consistent with the weather mentioned in the story).

The second precept is a modification of Farmer's, combining it with Murray's view: The adventures occurred in the order they were submitted for publication unless internal evidence suggests otherwise. Internal evidence is defined as dates or days, references to known events, vegetation or weather data mentioned in the story itself. This is actually a logical extension of Farmer's occurring-in-the-order-they-were-published method (doubtless he would have used it himself if he'd had access to the order of submission information). In practice, this means that an adventure would normally follow the one before it, but in some instances, where an adventure had little or no internal evidence and was published between two adventures of radically different internal evidence, the middle one was moved to precede the latter, rather than following the former. In this way, "blocks" or sequences of adventures were preserved in order. Often adventures were placed a year earlier than a first glance might suggest. Stories were sometimes submitted for approval several months before their LPO, which is based on the publishing date. In the early years, Dent was sometimes writing two adventures a month, rather than keeping pace with the one-a-month that was being published. In the first year of the series, he wrote **fifteen** adventures.

The third precept is: When does the internal evidence suggest the adventure takes place? This is sometimes scant (Spring and Fall can have similar weather, as can Spring and Summer) and sometimes contradictory (especially when dealing with the polar weather, I found). Further, some information was inserted editorially to make the story seem current when it was published (and Dent seems to have considered this when writing adventures on many occasions). Lastly, unless there is a comment that the weather is unusual for the season, it is assumed to be typical for the season. For example, if it appears to be rainy in New York City in the story, that suggests one of the rainy months, but it doesn't rule out a Summer placement, since it rains during the summer but is not generally considered to be "rainy". Also keep in mind, for example, that although Winter doesn't officially begin as a season until late December, for most of the northern half of the continental United States, wintery weather is common a month or more earlier. We must consider seasonal weather against the season itself. So, a consensus must be reached, if possible.

"God is in the Details"

In the early adventures, there are numerous chronological "signposts" to guide us: The appearances of Pat, Habeas Corpus and Chemistry; Johnny's injured eye which Doc repairs; the Hidalgo Trading Company warehouse hangar; and others. Many later adventures are often given placement based on almost the cover date alone; if it can't take place in the current year because of the cover date, it probably took place in the previous year.

One common problem with the earlier adventures is their length (some two months long), coupled with seasonal data. Later adventures are easier to place based on their much shorter length, although dates are mentioned more frequently, giving rise to another type of problem, that of specific information contradicting the LPO.

Putting the Jigsaw Puzzle Together

After gathering as much internal evidence as possible from each adventure, this data was matched against the order of submission. What became clear was that often the adventures could be grouped in large sequences having compatible internal evidence, usually based upon a season. These sequences were interrupted by adventures with internal evidence that did not match the sequence before or after it.

The adventures are discussed in their order of submission, with the novels written by Will Murray placed where he places them in the order (the ideas for which at least two were proposed by Dent himself), except for two, which Dent worked on after *Up From Earth's-Center*, the last published Doc Savage adventure in magazine form. Some interesting tidbits of information are also mentioned along with each adventure. The length or day count of each adventure covers the actual time dealt with in the adventure, from the first day of continuous narration to the last day of continuous narration and does not describe the time of events said to occur before or after the adventure. These events are noted as a comment. Doc doesn't always get involved on the first day of an adventure. (Note: Many of my day counts don't match

Farmer's. I can only assume that he, like Rick Lai, only counted the days when Doc was involved, and our estimates of unspecified lengths of times (e.g., "many days") differed).

Doc, in the later adventures, is not nearly the superman he is portrayed as in the earlier adventures (roughly before World War II). This might lead us to consider that some of the comments made in those adventures may be closer to the truth than the unrealistic ones made in earlier tales.

I believe I can justify the placement of every adventure. You may disagree with deductions I've made and the conclusions I've drawn. The evidence is all here for you to decide for yourself.

Part 1

The Evidence

The Man of Bronze (25 days in length), has an LPO of December 16, 1932, as previously mentioned. Weather data mentioned includes rain, mist and "chill" wind, which seems to indicate Spring or Fall, during the rainy season in New York – April, November or December. Doc's skyscraper headquarters, indisputably the Empire State Building (for more information about the skyscraper, consult *Doc Savage: His Apocalyptic Life* by Philip José Farmer), seems to be open (there is an operator in an elevator). The Empire State Building opened May 1, 1931. This leaves November and December 1931, and April and November 1932 as possible likely placement candidates. It is clear from information in the story that this is the first adventure of Doc and all five of his aides.

The 86th floor, Doc's headquarters, is a "suite of offices which had been" Doc's father's, and the library is Doc's "father's great technical library". There is no mention of this here or in any other adventure that this is a medical library. The only suggestion in any adventure that Doc's father was a doctor himself occurs in this story, where it's mentioned that he saved the life of Carlos Avispa with medical treatment; however, Clark, Sr. is never referred to as "Dr. Savage" or even as "a doctor" anywhere in the series. So I believe that despite having some medical training, he was not a doctor; I will discuss this in greater detail later.

The elder Savage's "fortune had dwindled to practically nothing", obviously used up equipping Doc for his life's work; both the Fortress of Solitude and the "college" for captured criminals are in operation by 1929, at the latest (according to *The Purple Dragon*), in addition to numerous planes and automobiles Doc possesses, based on information in later novels. Doc's training must have cost a fortune by itself. Doc's father does not seem to have had access to Mayan gold, and at any rate, he would have to have had a fortune at Doc's birth, to begin his son's training, before he discovered the Valley of the Vanished.

Doc's "name was becoming a byword in the odd corners of the world", so obviously, Doc has had solo adventures prior to this one. His fame is not general knowledge, as might it be if due only to scientific accomplishments. This idea is confirmed by information in the aforementioned *The Purple Dragon*. In this adventure, both a tri-motor plane and autogyro are destroyed. The tri-motor is "about five years old". It is probably Doc's first, purchased new years earlier. This plane is likely the Ford Tri-Motor 4-AT, manufactured in 1926 and 1927 (although production continued on this model for a few years after 1927, recall that Doc's plane is "about five years old").

As Farmer discusses in his book, Doc could not have actually occupied the 86th floor, which has always been an Observation Deck. The highest floor possible would have been the 85th floor. Did Dent make a mistake? Or perhaps he chose the 86th floor symbolically: It's higher than a normal person could have. The 86th floor is attainable only by Doc, a "superman" (according to ads for the magazine, years before the later DC comic book character of the same name). Interestingly, the synopsis for *The Man Who Fell Up* names the "85th floor" as Doc's headquarters (a mistake, or a slip revealing the truth? How could Dent, who, at that point, had been writing the series for almost a decade, make such a mistake?).

The reception room is in the "west" corner of the skyscraper. The Empire State Building is not aligned with the four compass points, but very nearly so, and the "west" corner is certainly the west-by-southwest corner of the building. Doc is shot at from a neighboring skyscraper that seems to be the Chrysler Building, even though that building does not fit the given description. As Farmer notes in his book, it apparently **must** be the Chrysler Building; it is the only other building in the area which comes close to the given description, particularly its height. This identification, however, presents us with a problem. The Chrysler Building is almost due east of the Empire State Building, and the west corner of the latter could not be fired upon from the Chrysler Building. It is probably this fact which causes Farmer to place the reception room in the north (actually north-by-northwest, which just justifies the "west" description to Farmer, apparently) corner of the Empire State Building. Since comments in later adventures confirm the location of the reception room, it would seem that Doc was not shot at from the Chrysler Building. Probably the skyscraper sniper is a case of dramatic license by Dent, which is why the Chrysler Building fits neither the description (except in height) nor the location of the building in question. Doc was probably therefore fired upon from a smaller building on the west side of his headquarters.

Monk has a penthouse lab near Wall Street, and may have an "Aunt Hannah", to whom he makes reference; it is not clear if he's speaking colloquially or literally here. King Chaac speaks of Doc's father's discovery of the Valley of the Vanished "twenty years" earlier as a precise length of time. Doc and his crew are adopted into the Mayan village on the 23rd day of the adventure, and it is this day of the week ("every seventh day", at noon) that the signal is broadcast for the Mayans to send more gold to Doc; he receives "two thirds" of all the gold that comes out of the valley.

Doc mentions "training" that his aides have undergone to allow them to assist him. The most numerous reference to this throughout the series is that Doc has taught them to pilot planes. Doc states: "Tonight we begin carrying out the ideals of my father"; combined with the reference to his aides' "training", this suggests they **all** have been preparing for this time.

The Land of Terror (21 days) seems to immediately follow *The Man of Bronze*, which occurred "recently". Also, Doc's behavior is violent, not at all like it is in the later adventures; this will gradually disappear over the early issues, prominently dropping off after the third published novel,

Quest of the Spider. In this adventure, as in the previous one, Doc uses an airport on Long Island rather than his Hidalgo Trading Company warehouse hangar (which is obviously not in use yet). It is also said that Doc's offices were "formerly used by" Doc's father, echoing statements to that effect in *The Man of Bronze.*

There is a "balmy spring breeze" in this adventure. With an LPO of January 20, 1933, this adventure could be placed in the Spring of 1931 or 1932. It begins on a "Friday" and the second night seems to be moonless (it is "a black ghost").

Although it is said to be Doc's "code" to kill criminals, there is a reference to Doc's college for captured criminals. No mention is made of brain surgery, though; the place is staffed by psychologists. Perhaps testing the waters, Doc reveals information about new techniques in brain surgery to the public (via the medical establishment) "some weeks" prior to this adventure.

Doc's private elevator, which has a secret call button, is mentioned for the first time in this adventure. It is at the end of the line of passenger elevators. However, only one passenger elevator goes above the 80th floor in the Empire State Building. There are two freight elevators, however, across the hall from the passenger lift, and an alcove beyond. It is probably in this alcove that Doc's private express elevator is located (see Appendix C).

Long Tom wears a bulletproof vest, also a first. Doc seems to have developed these since *The Man of Bronze*, where they were not used. Doc's second tri-motor is destroyed in this adventure. Jerome Coffern, Doc's chemistry tutor, is killed in this adventure, and it's obvious Doc has quite an affection for him.

It is "summer" in the third recorded adventure, *Quest of the Spider* (6 days), and could very well follow *The Land of Terror*. There is a comment about Doc's plane which implies that it does; it is similar to the one destroyed in "the South Seas", where the latter tale concluded. This is the all-metal tri-motor that is sometimes called the "speed job" or said to resemble "a gray bat" (this reference probably indicates a Stinson tri-motor, according to Murray, rather than another Ford, but brand names are never mentioned by Dent). Its cruising speed is 200 MPH, and can do almost 250 MPH, carrying enough gasoline for 20 hours of flight (in an emergency).

With an LPO of February 17, 1933, this adventure could be placed in Summer 1931 or 1932. There is bright moonlight throughout this adventure, which suggests a placement near a full moon.

This adventure contains the first recorded mention of "brain operations" performed at Doc's college. The brain surgery supposedly robs the criminals of their memories and then they are trained ("conditioned" would be the correct psychological term) to be upstanding citizens. Ham believes Doc has a private retreat, but does not actually know of the Fortress of Solitude. Doc has been at there for "weeks" at the beginning of this story.

The next three recorded adventures, *The Polar Treasure* (30 days), *Pirate of the Pacific* (16 days) and *The Red Skull* (4 days), occur as a sequence. *Pirate of The Pacific* begins the day and his crew return from *The Polar Treasure*, and an account of the former is in a recent newspaper mentioned in *The Red Skull*, which must take place before August because of a reference to an "oat field ... yellowing with ripeness". Oats are harvested during the first half of July, meaning *The Red Skull* must occur no later than July 10. Between the three adventures, they take up fifty days, ending in early July at the latest. Since the LPO of *The Red Skull* is May 19, 1933, this sequence of stories must take place in 1931 or 1932. But they cannot take place in 1931, however, because *The Man of Bronze* could not then have occurred before the sequence because of the lengths of the four adventures, much less *The Land of Terror* or *Quest of the Spider*. Therefore, we have our first definite placement. *The Polar Treasure*, *Pirate of the Pacific* and *The Red Skull* must run from April 1932 to June 1932, roughly. All references to 1933 in the adventures (including "a new mayor", elected early

1933) must be considered topical, because these adventures cannot have taken place in 1933, as we have just seen.

The Man of Bronze, *The Land of Terror* and *Quest of the Spider* all therefore seem to occur in 1931. *The Man of Bronze* can be placed in May 1931, *The Land of Terror* Spring (now necessarily June) and *Quest of the Spider* Summer, probably August. However, Doc's father could not have been using the offices prior to the opening of the Empire State Building (May 1, 1931), so these placements contradict those statements about Doc's father and the offices. If *The Man of Bronze* is moved as little as a month later (to June 1931) to accommodate these facts, then *The Land of Terror* no longer occurs during Spring; it would be pushed forward to Summer. What about 1932? At 21 days in length, *The Land of Terror* could just be squeezed in ahead of *The Polar Treasure*, which we have determined probably begins in April. But this means that *Quest of the Spider* cannot directly follow *The Land of Terror*, as comments in the former story imply. It must be placed **after** the three-adventure sequence, following *The Red Skull* in Summer, because Doc has been at his Fortress of Solitude for "weeks" at the beginning of the adventure.

Further examination helps us pinpoint the dates of these adventures even closer. If the "Friday" of *The Land of Terror* is April 3, before the new moon of April 6, the adventure would end April 23 (this fits with the mention of a caterpillar in the story). It is shortly followed by *The Polar Treasure*. This puts *The Red Skull* in mid July, which hardly fits with what we have established about its placement. But, *The Land of Terror* **could** begin on Friday, March 4, just before the new moon on March 7. The "balmy spring breeze" mentioned in the story could be interpreted to mean a balmy spring-like breeze. Although this is not as direct an interpretation as could be made from this comment, it is not unreasonable; would someone call a warm breeze in early March a "balmy winter breeze"? Probably not. This allows *The Red Skull* to be moved as much as a month earlier, which fits much better with what we know about it.

The Polar Treasure takes place during the "arctic summer" (about 23 days into the adventure, anyway) and "two months" after "continuous daylight" begins, which instead suggests late May or early June (Dent says this exact same thing in *The Laugh of Death*; it may be that he considered the arctic as having only two seasons – summer and winter, and when "continuous daylight" begins in late March, it begins the six-month "summer"). If this *actually* occurs during "summer", *The Red Skull* is then pushed beyond its late June-early July placement. Whether or not Dent was speaking figuratively (and I believe he was), this must occur in Spring 1932.

Monk comments that he almost wore Doc's private express elevator out when it was first installed, implying it was added after the building was completed. So, it must have been installed between *The Man of Bronze* and *The Land of Terror*, where it is used for the first recorded time. "Completed" is probably a better word. Doc probably did not sink a new shaft down the center of the building. Doc's father doubtless foresaw this possibility and planned for it.

Johnny, who we learn had been a college professor, is writing a book about the Mayan culture (which he considered doing in *The Man of Bronze*) and it is revealed that Ham is a civil lawyer. Long Tom's "bug-zapper" is mentioned as being "perfected", projecting short wavelength rays (like ultraviolet or x-ray) and he installs sonar aboard the *Helldiver*, the villain's sub that Doc appropriates at the end of the adventure. Doc is still using "the airport" mentioned in preceding adventures. Doc and his aides now speak Mayan, and hold the honorary rank of captain on the New York police force. Doc performs a musical composition of his own at the beginning of the adventure. Doc is knocked out by his own anaesthetic gas, of which there is no mention of it dissipating after a minute as in later adventures.

In *Pirate of the Pacific*, the gas now dissipates after "two or three minutes". Obviously Doc did not improve the gas, adding this feature, between adventures because there has been no time to do so (unless he did so during the voyage home following *The Polar Treasure*, but this seems unlikely given the lack of a chemical lab aboard the vessel). Probably this was a new development that Dent had learned about just prior to writing this adventure, and included it.

Doc's front door has been replaced with one made of steel, ostensibly because Renny keeps breaking them (he did this in *The Land of Terror*, the only time we are told about to date). We learn that Johnny was not just a college professor, as mentioned in *The Polar Treasure*; he was head of the "Natural Science department of a famous university", and has published "books". The "super-firer" machine pistols do not seem to have the "single-fire" option as they do in later adventures.

We are told that "adjoining Doc's office was a suite which had been empty some months", which a villain uses to spy on Doc. This seems to be adjoining the reception room, and if true, Doc must have realized this was a potential problem and began renting the entire floor. It is worth noting that in later adventures, the lab is said to take up two-thirds of the floor; no such claim has yet been made. It may be that the lab expanded into this adjoining suite after Doc decided to rent it.

At the end of this adventure, Doc and his aides are said to have stayed until the cornerstone of a new hospital has been laid. This would take a minimum of two months, but likely three or four months. This doesn't seem to be reasonable nor feasible considering what we know about the placement of this three-adventure series. It may be that the group returns to the "Luzon Union" (read: The Philippines) some time later to attend this ceremony, possibly Fall 1932.

In *The Red Skull* it is said that Doc and each of his aides hold an honorary commission of high rank in the police department. We finally meet Monk's secretary, Lea Aster, who is mentioned in this and prior adventures as the "prettiest secretary" in the city. Doc's anaesthetic gas now dissipates after one minute, and it is possibly during the short gap between *Pirate of the Pacific* and *The Red Skull* – probably no more than two or three days – that Doc makes the improvement of limited effectiveness, if this is not a topical reference, or even a simple mistake; the longer time was only mentioned in one adventure, and then promptly changed. Doc uses a collapsible autogyro in this adventure which is small enough to take aboard his tri-motor plane (which is still kept at the Long Island airport). Ham mentions wanting to take a vacation in the Canadian woods (he gets his wish in *Brand of The Werewolf*). He is working on the plans to enlarge Doc's upstate college, using the money from *The Polar Treasure*. This story contains the first appearance of Doc's basement "special garage", which uses an elevator to lift automobiles to street level. The newspaper clipping reference mentioned earlier is about the cornerstone ceremony mentioned at the end of *Pirate of the Pacific*, which seems to suggest that Doc and his aides stayed for some sort of ceremony following that adventure. A ground-breaking ceremony could fit the time frame we have discussed.

The Lost Oasis (13 days) also seems to occur in the summer; berries "were plentiful at this time of year". Also, the first mention of the Hidalgo Trading Company warehouse (placing this story after *Quest of the Spider*) is made in this adventure, though it is an unnamed "boathouse on the Hudson side of" Manhattan Island (this also fits with Doc using the Long Island ("North Beach") airport in the last adventure). It holds "two planes" (which must be the big tri-motor (his third) and an autogyro, which is destroyed in this adventure, his second one). Because the warehouse hangar is not in use until now, and we know that Doc's father was virtually broke by *The Man of Bronze*, it seems likely that the purchase and renovation of the hangar were financed by an early shipment of gold from the Valley of the Vanished, since the money from *The Polar Treasure* was earmarked for renovation of the college.

Doc's library has a "great file of newspaper clippings, kept up to date for him by a firm engaged in such work". Doc and his aides use sign language, and it is said not to be the first time they do so, although it is the first time it has been mentioned. For the first recorded time, Doc reads lips. Prior to this adventure, Doc has been at the Fortress for "many days". With two recorded visits to the Fortress in 1932, it is obvious that Doc is gearing up for his life's work.

The Sargasso Ogre (about 32 days) starts in Egypt, where Doc and his crew are. They are on the way back to the U.S. from the Lost Oasis, placing this adventure also in Summer 1932. "The moonlight was brilliant" near the end of the adventure; this would have been near the full moon of August 16.

This story contains the first occurrence of Monk telling a woman that Ham has "a wife and thirteen children" (Ham steals this gag later in the series). They are both killed by poison, but Doc revives them. We learn that Long Tom does "atomic research". The super-firers now have the "single-fire" option, which Doc probably added during in his stay at the Fortress of Solitude prior to *The Lost Oasis*.

Renny, who has always been stated to be 6' 4", is now said to be shorter than Doc, who has been described as about six feet tall. Dent's notebook confirms Renny's height, but gives Doc's as "6 feet 8 inches". However, the "8" has been added by hand, over a handwritten "6" [inches], after the original measurement was marked out. It is impossible to read exactly what the original measurement read, but the length is too short to accommodate the word "inches", much less a numerical value accompanying it (such as "2 inches"), so may have read "even", making Doc's original height "6 feet even". Whatever it was, this is proof enough that Doc's height increased literarily over the years.

In this adventure, Doc meets one of his few physical equals, Bruze, "the Sargasso Ogre". Doc says of him: he "is the strongest man I have ever encountered". And not only is Bruze strong, he is Doc's equal in hand-to-hand combat. The text says of their struggle: "As a fight, it was virtually even". Even though it is early in Doc's career, we must assume he has fought both strong men and skilled men as part of his training, probably some of the best fighters in the world, so the statements about Bruze are impressive.

According to Dent's widow (through Will Murray), this was one of two of Dent's favorite Doc Savage stories.

The next sequence begins with the recorded adventure, *The Czar of Fear* (4 days). It is "hot" and there is "ripening grain". It obviously cannot occur in Fall 1932, but needs a Spring or Summer placement. With an LPO of August 18, 1933, *The Czar of Fear* could be placed 1933, but it likely follows *The Sargasso Ogre* in Summer 1932, in accordance with the second precept of this chronology.

The Hidalgo Trading Company warehouse is mentioned by name in this story. There are "several planes" in it, including the tri-motor, small gyros (primitive helicopters), autogyros and a "small, speedy" plane. No mention is made of the *Helldiver* sub from *The Polar Treasure*. It was left at a New York City dock at the beginning of *Pirate of the Pacific* (and may still be there).

Monk and Doc use sign language in this adventure (and Johnny reads it). Doc uses his trademark "nerve pinch" for the first time in this adventure. There is a clearing near Doc's college (almost always referred to as the "institution" in these early adventures) where a plane can land. The rehabilitation process that occurs there takes "fully a year".

As the events of *The Czar of Fear* are still in the newspapers during *The Phantom City* (24 days), the latter must surely follow that adventure by a couple of days at most, for a likely placement of Summer 1932. It's also said to be "months" after *The Polar Treasure* (not "a year" which would suggest a 1933 placement for *The Phantom City*). Occurring in April 1932, that adventure would indeed be "months" earlier. There is "brilliant moonlight" at the end of the adventure; this is probably near the full moon of September 14.

In Doc's garage are "roadsters, coupes, phaetons, and an assortment of trucks". The *Helldiver* is in the warehouse hangar, in a "partitioned part of the gigantic building", where it has been since Doc appropriated it (this partition explains why it was not mentioned in *The Czar of Fear*; the entrance to the warehouse leads into the plane section of the building).

During this adventure, Monk finds a pig that becomes his pet, Habeas Corpus. The "wife and thirteen half-wit children" joke, which Monk uses again here, is said to be a "recently acquired" gag.

It is said that Long Tom "of late ... had taken to collecting unusual objects which [Doc and his aides] encountered in their adventures. He had equipped a museum at his bachelor quarters in a high class club. His assortment already contained some interesting articles". This is a curious set of statements. In *The Man of Bronze*, *The Land of Terror*, *Quest of the Spider*, *The Polar Treasure*, *Pirate of the Pacific*, *The Red Skull*, *The Lost Oasis* and *The Sargasso Ogre* there are no such devices. The sonic brain-destroying device in *The Czar of Fear* is itself destroyed (unless there was a second device recovered that we are not told about, but this seems unlikely). Perhaps there is an unrecorded adventure wherein Long Tom begins this habit (it is never mentioned again, by the way). But it **is** referred to in Dent's notebook, which states: "Long Tom collects souvenirs of their adventures and has them in a laboratory at his house." Interestingly, this comment was pencilled in, and was not part of the original character description. Likely, the claim is dramatic license.

Doc's super-firers now fire "mercy bullets". There seems to be little time, if any, that Doc could have made this improvement between *The Czar of Fear* and this adventure; this change was probably made prior to *The Czar of Fear* at the Fortress of Solitude, during one of his two trips there this year. It is probably **not** a topical statement, unless Doc and his men are killing people in this story when they shoot them, not a very likely possibility.

This story is the first to state that Doc's skin had been bronzed by "exposure to tropical suns". It is said to be Doc's usual practice to charge a million dollar fee (to those who can afford it) to fund a charity.

In *Brand of the Werewolf* (4 days), Habeas Corpus is a "recent" addition, and it is not "winter". Doc and crew "just got back" from *The Phantom City*. Because of the active "bugs and small lizards" in Canada, it seems to be warm, and indeed, following *The Phantom City*, it could be late Summer 1932. However, Doc and his aides are taking a "fishing and hunting" vacation in Canada (Ham must have talked the others into it since *The Red Skull*, where he originally expresses his desire), so it is more likely still-warm early Fall (no later because at least some of the "leaves on the trees were still green", as well as the aforementioned reference to the summer fauna). Also, the Savage homestead is used for "part of each summer and all of the hunting seasons". This means that it is not Alex and Pat's main residence, which is never described, in this adventure or any other. This entire sequence, beginning with *The Czar of Fear*, could just be squeezed into 1933, considering the LPOs, but will still fit 1932, as well, which we would expect, according to the second precept of this chronology. The moonlight is "brilliant" and the moon looks like "a fat, milky bag" so it is likely near (probably shortly after) the full moon of October 14, 1932.

Monk uses ventriloquism for the first time in this story, and Long Tom has not heard him do it until now. We learn that the effects of Doc's "mercy bullets" usually last for more than thirty minutes. Johnny's eye is still injured in this story. It is said to be Doc's habit to use whatever treasure he finds during an adventure to fund charity hospitals.

Brand of the Werewolf contains the first appearance of Doc's "cousin" Pat Savage, who is "about eighteen" years old; "Patricia was by far the prettiest girl Monk had ever seen". Doc's "uncle" Alex has been dead for "few days" and "more than a week" by the time Doc gets to his uncle's home. Alex settled the area "forty years" earlier (circa 1890), so is probably at least sixty years old at the time of his death, and Doc's father's **older** brother, therefore (there is no reason to think that Doc's father was particularly old when Doc was born, and so was likely in his forties when he was killed). This remark also seems to suggest that Alex was born circa 1870, or perhaps earlier, and therefore about fifty when Pat was born! At no time during this adventure does Doc (or anyone else) claim that Alex and Pat are his only living relatives.

Since the Hidalgo Trading Company warehouse hangar is used in both *The Lost Oasis* and *The Czar of Fear*, those stories must follow *Quest of the Spider*, because Doc is still using the North Beach airport in that adventure, the last (chronologically speaking) adventure that he does so. If Doc is at the Fortress for about three weeks (my estimate of the probable minimum) in Summer 1932, *Quest of the Spider* could be placed in June 1932. *The Lost Oasis* would follow in July, *The Czar of Fear* would then follow in August, followed by *The Phantom City*, with *Brand of The Werewolf* occurring in early Fall 1932. These placements mean that *The Land of Terror* **must** occur in March, as there is no room later in the spring.

With the placement of *Quest of the Spider* in the last half of June, we can see that it must have begun shortly after the full moon on June 18, and end at least a week before the new moon on July 3, because of the numerous references to bright or brilliant moonlight in the story. This would put the last day no later than June 26, a Sunday. Because the second day (and the fifth) seem to be business days, that is, weekdays, the first day is likely Sunday, June 19.

"In New York, it was winter" during *The Man Who Shook the Earth* (6 days). Doc operates on Johnny's injured eye and repairs it. With an LPO of November 17, 1933, it must take place in 1932 or 1933. There is a reference to Hitler, who did not come to power until he was named chancellor on January 30, 1933, so this establishes book ends for the adventure. Habeas was acquired "recently". A February 1933 placement fits all of these criteria. The reference to Johnny's injured eye in *Brand of The Werewolf* fits with it being repaired here, if that story occurs in 1932. So that three-adventure sequence cannot take place in 1933 (in fact, on this basis, all adventures

published before *The Man Who Shook the Earth* must **occur** before it).

The exclusive club that Ham resides in is "The Midas Club", located on Park Avenue. Residents must have five million dollars that they have earned themselves, and Ham's suite consists of "half a dozen rooms". Renny, Long Tom and Johnny are said to live at "a hotel near" Doc's skyscraper, apparently in the same suite. This doesn't seem likely, given other comments made both before and after this adventure. Probably this comment is dramatic license, made to speed up the story, instead of having Doc contact them individually.

For the first time, Ham's sword cane is coated with an anaesthetic drug. Renny may be as puritanical as he looks; he tells a woman in a clinging dress that he wouldn't let his daughter dress that way (and in *The Lost Oasis* he covers himself up in a bed sheet when stranded in his underwear). A ramp has replaced the "special lift" as the entrance and exit to Doc's garage beneath the skyscraper. Doc's headquarters now seem to occupy the entire floor. Doc uses "voice scramblers" on his airplane radios. At the end of the story, Doc decides to build a hospital, which is his "usual procedure". Showing remarkable foresight, Dent casts the villains in this story as German "fanatics" who belong to a secret society that wants to conquer the world by war.

Meteor Menace (about 38 days) must occur almost immediately following *The Man Who Shook the Earth*, which was Doc and his aides' "most recent" adventure. And with an LPO of December 15, 1933, it, too, must occur in 1932 or 1933. It must follow *The Man Who Shook the Earth*, and cannot follow it by the year that is suggested by the partial construction of the hospital Doc decides to build at the end of *The Man Who Shook the Earth*. That reference is likely a topical one; perhaps the hospital was half-built when this adventure was written up as a story between April and November 1933. Doc and crew have been in Chile for some time at the beginning of the story because Saturday Loo comes there looking for Doc, so probably a week separates the two adventures, but not much more. The "brilliant moonlight" of the second night in *The Man Who Shook the Earth* is probably near the full moon of February 10, with this adventure following shortly after.

Monk calls the "Fortress of Solitude" by name in this story, though he doesn't know where it is. Doc has taught all of his aides "wrestling and jujutsu [judo]", which probably refers back to the "training" they underwent to join him in his life's work (although these skills are never referred to in any of the numerous fights in the series. Each aide seems to prefer his own personal style of combat). Doc's third tri-motor plane is destroyed during this adventure.

Johnny is said to be "unnaturally tall" in this adventure, yet in the last adventure, *The Man Who Shook the Earth*, he is "nearly six feet tall", which is hardly "unnaturally tall", even in 1933, when the national average for men was about 5'4". In *Quest of the Spider*, he is a "foot and a half" taller than the swamp dwellers. This suggests he is over six feet tall; the swamp men would have to be only four and a half feet tall for Johnny **not** to be over six feet tall. Dent's notebook states Johnny is six feet tall, which must mean that Dent considered "six feet tall" to be "unnaturally tall" – though this is unlikely since Dent himself was taller.

The Monsters (12 days) takes place in two parts. The first part, actually a prologue (8 days long) starts on the "15th" of a month during trapping season (November, December or January). The second part, which is actually the adventure (it is this part that is 12 days long), takes place "almost a year" later. It is at least "some ten weeks" after fishing season begins (the beginning of April) and probably longer. At the earliest, the prologue could start November 15, 1932, and the adventure in July 1933. But because of a reference to "dead leaves", more likely the latter part occurs in Fall (and since the events of the prologue were not "last year", it probably occurred in January of the current year). There is an article about *The Man Who Shook the Earth* in a "back issue" of a magazine which "ain't too old" in the main body of the story, which means the Fall must be that of 1933; this fits with the story's LPO of January 19, 1934.

Doc's tri-motor plane is destroyed in this adventure. It is said that "Renny permitted himself only one form of amusement", referring to his door-busting habit. This fits with comments in earlier adventures that imply he is somewhat "puritanical". Doc has "credentials signed by the highest of [federal] government officials". The super-firers now are able to shoot "mercy slugs, tracers, incendiary bullets, armor piercers, and explosives". Although current scientific thinking is that a human could not function at a height of thirty feet (the apparent size of the giants), because of structural weakness, there are a couple of comments that suggest that the giants are more solidly built than normal humans (for example, bullets don't seem to hurt them much).

In *The Mystery on the Snow* (3 days) there is a reference to "spring" being "not far along", indicating an early Spring placement. With an LPO of February 16, 1934, it could not take place in that year. A story about the events of *Meteor Menace* is the most recent clipping in a bundle of newspaper articles about Doc (the oldest is about a new surgery technique; this may be the brain surgery innovation mentioned in *The Land of Terror*, which was Doc's first big, publicly-known adventure). It is probably significant that the most recent clippings are not about *The Monsters*, which was widely covered in the press, according to that story. *The Mystery on the Snow* is therefore placed in April 1933, some months before *The Monsters*.

The "element" "benlanium" discovered prior to this adventure sounds a lot like titanium (strong, lightweight, etc., although titanium was discovered in 1791). In the warehouse hangar is a "tiny" "racing ship" [plane] capable of speeds nearly 400 MPH (this is probably the one mentioned in *The Czar of Fear*; it is destroyed in this adventure). The warehouse hangar is referred to more than once as a "vault"; its walls and ceiling are steel reinforced concrete, several feet thick. Doc's fourth tri-motor survives the adventure. Doc has apparently been watching the villain Mahal for the five days prior to this adventure. It is suggested that Renny has had boxing training (this is confirmed by comments in Dent's notebook).

Long Tom is working on his bug-zapper, using "atomic streams". Yet his bug-zapper was said to be "perfected" as far back as *The Polar Treasure*, a year earlier. An incident in *The Sargasso Ogre* may shed some light on this. In that adventure, Long Tom is lured into a trap by the information of a supposed colleague working on a bug-zapper using atomic stream projection. Long Tom, rather than thinking of suing him, instead wants to work with him. Long Tom's, then, it can be deduced, did not use "atomic streams", and this information (even though it turned out to be false) started him along this line of research. Or, the thing was falsely called "perfected" (maybe it was a topical reference, "perfected" by the time *The Polar Treasure* was written in early 1933).

For the first time, Doc's upstate criminal reform center is called the "college", and Johnny begins using big words in this adventure. This is probably not a habit he picked up suddenly. Dent or his editor John Nanovic probably thought the reading public wouldn't understand or want to read his big words. By the time this adventure was written, they must have changed their minds. Or Doc (or Johnny) insisted on greater authenticity.

"Doc occupied the entire eighty-sixth floor" now, which is in direct conflict with what is stated in *Pirate of the Pacific*. So Doc has since taken over the entire floor. Doc's lab is revealed to be on the east side of the skyscraper (the 86th floor layout is a rectangle within a rectangle: the inner rectangle consists of the corridors, stairs, elevators and building mechanicals. Doc occupies the area between the two rectangles, a torus (doughnut) with squared corners).

The King Maker (13 days) seems to take place during the summer (it is "blistering" "hot" in the Mediterranean Sea) and begins a seasonal sequence covering the warm months of 1933 (the LPOs preclude the summer of 1934 and the appearance of Habeas and Johnny's repaired eye rule out 1932), very likely starting that season in June 1933.

Doc's tri-motor is destroyed; he buys a new one and **it's** destroyed (his fifth). There is a hospital near the Hudson River that Doc has paid for and funds (anonymously, of course), possibly with the treasure from *The Sargasso Ogre*. Doc is offered the throne of Calbia, but declines. According to my research, "Calbia" seems to be Yugoslavia, based on its population and industry. The library on the 86th floor seems to be on the northwest side of the building. Doc has a Teletype that is hooked up to the police. Doc's aides each have "private planes".

There are "three trucks" in Doc's garage, one of which is a small delivery truck; and a milk truck is in use at that time (it has the license plate number "S4"). As the cab is "S3", the limousine (also "sedan", which has curtains lining the rear windows) and roadster, Doc's two most frequently used vehicles, are probably "S1" and "S2". Doc's glass anaesthetic grenades have a colored dot on them denoting their potency ("green" knocks someone out for 10-15 minutes).

Doc has informants in every European country, who keep him apprised of potential danger there. These men do not seem to be graduates of the college, but men who are already in place, and for some reason, help Doc out.

Renny has "been in a few wars". He is not speaking figuratively when he says this. Did he work as a freedom fighter or mercenary in the 1920s? In one very early adventure, Doc notes that Renny is almost retired, having enough money to last him the rest of his life.

The Thousand-Headed Man (5 days) takes place immediately following *The King Maker* (which occurred "a few weeks ago" and Doc (and his crew) is "now on his way back to America". It seems that there are leaves on trees, so it is not late Fall, Winter or early Spring in this story. It fits that it is still Summer 1933, probably July. Toward the end of the adventure, the "face of the moon" is visible, and it is "brilliant", so this adventure must end near a full moon, probably that of August 5.

Doc flies his sixth tri-motor, acquired while he was in Calbia, and it is destroyed. Doc has a Scotland Yard commission; his identification code is "SX73182". He was given it "some years ago", while working with the British Secret Service (this would therefore seem to pre-date *The Man of Bronze*, which occurred only about eighteen months before this adventure).

This adventure, according to Dent's widow (through Will Murray), was one of two of Dent's favorite Doc Savage stories.

The Squeaking Goblin (5 days) seems to follow *The Thousand-Headed Man*. "Summer visitors" are mentioned and it is "hot". There are fresh blackberries in Kentucky, so it is almost certainly July in this adventure. However, 1834 was "one hundred years ago". The adventure's LPO of May 18, 1934 precludes it from a Summer 1934 placement, as is suggested. It would seem either the summer references or the 1934 reference must be ignored. Consider that it would not be unusual for someone speaking of a 99-year period to commonly refer to it as "one hundred years". This adventure should be placed in Summer 1933, following *The Thousand-Headed Man*, which must now end near the full moon in early July, on the night of the seventh (instead of the August 5 full moon, as earlier suggested). This adventure occurs near that full moon. Doc's seventh tri-motor plane (this one is colored bronze) makes its first appearance and is destroyed.

Monk, Ham and Johnny fly Doc's "fastest plane", which neither seems to be a duplicate of the one destroyed in *The Mystery on the Snow* nor a giant tri-motor. Doc "never takes money for his services" now. He seems to have given up on the charity hospitals, or has taken to funding them with Mayan gold. Ammo drums for the super-firers are now color-coded (blue means the drum holds "tracer mercy slugs"). Monk and Johnny pull off their undercover work in this adventure as a result of their "training". Is this another reference back to the training they underwent at Doc's hands mentioned in *The Man of Bronze*?

Fear Cay (3 days) also seems to take place in 1934, as Dan Thunden, born 1803, is 131 years old "to this day". It seems to be warm.

Doc stands head and shoulders above the crowds, which suggests he is foot taller than they, well over six feet tall, which is at odds with his initial description. He is "a fully commissioned postal investigator" and has a card that "bore the postmaster general's signature". Pat appears here, during "a visit", "months" after her last appearance (in *Brand of The Werewolf*, Fall 1932). Contrary to what Farmer claims in his biography of Doc about it being a youth drug, "silphium was only a valuable medicinal herb"; "it was an amazingly efficient antiseptic and tonic". "Doc did not disillusion" Monk, who believes that silphium is a "Fountain of Youth" drug that prolongs life. Afterward, Doc and the group spend "days" on the island.

In *Death in Silver* (2 days), "last spring ... [was] five-months ... [more than] four months ago", or nine months earlier, apparently placing this adventure in winter. This fits with the "fog" noted throughout the adventure. *Fear Cay* must precede this adventure, in which Pat has relocated to New York, so this adventure seems to occur in Winter 1934. However, there are "tall flowering plants", "green" grass and a "close-cropped lawn", so the "five-months vacations" must have **ended** "last spring" rather than having begun then, making "last spring" about "four months ago". So it must be Fall, when fog can still occur, but also green flora. Its LPO of July 20, 1934 rules out a placement in that year, so it must continue the summer sequence begun by *The King Maker*. This means *Fear Cay* also occurs Summer 1933, and since *The Monsters* is a Fall story, and *Fear Cay* is a Summer story, Doc's eighth tri-motor, which appears in the former adventure (where it is destroyed), makes its first appearance in the latter adventure. The tri-motor plane now does over 300 MPH (this improvement was referred to in *The Monsters*, in which such a plane was destroyed); the plane in this adventure is his ninth.

This story includes Doc's first visit to Pat's salon, which she has purchased since *Fear Cay* (obviously). The salon is named "Park Avenue Beautician" and is located in a "modernistic skyscraper" on that street. Since the salon is up and running only a couple of months after Pat's decision to stay in New York, it seems likely that she bought an established salon. Oddly, Pat's Indian womanservant Tiny does not relocate with her, and no mention is even made of her, now or in any later adventure. This seems strange, since the two seemed close in *Brand of the Werewolf*. Perhaps Tiny has died since then, and Pat feels free to relocate.

It is said that "Doc Savage and all of his men held ... honorary commissions" "far above" lieutenant on the police force, and further, Doc has "a State Trooper commission". Doc uses a "speedboat", which he has designed or modified (also its first appearance). The *Helldiver* sub is greatly damaged in this adventure, and left lying at the bottom of New York Harbor (it is not recovered by adventure's end). It has not been used since *The Phantom City* and has been "reconditioned" since then. Long Tom is in Europe collaborating on a bug-zapper that uses "ultra-short sonic or electric waves". There is a big difference between sonic and electric waves, and neither of these seem to be the two types he has worked on so far, the ultra-short electromagnetic or the atomic stream version (unless "electric" is taken to mean "electromagnetic").

Python Isle (16 days), written by Will Murray, is said to take place "a few weeks" after *Death in Silver*, and Doc and his crew meet up with Renny in Africa, where he was during that adventure. The original tag to *Death in Silver* states that this adventure (called *Lost Island* there) occurs "within thirty days" of that adventure. Murray places this adventure in "early June" "nineteen thirty-four", but he is referring to **his** chronology of the series, and this cannot be given as much weight as other internal evidence. He also places it between

Death in Silver and *The Sea Magician*, which follows the second precept of this chronology. The hydroelectric project mentioned in both *Death in Silver* and this adventure is now one week from completion. On the first night, a "clear night", there is "no moon", and toward the end of the adventure, on the twelfth night, the moon looked "like a dime".

The Fortress of Solitude is located in a volcanic crater on an island in the Arctic. This description of the Fortress is from Dent's notebook, and in fact, was never used by Dent himself in any of the novels.

Renny has "dark eyes" and his feet are as "disproportionately large" as his hands (also taken from Dent's notebook; Dent himself never actually used this description). He is "one of the most accomplished boxers in the world", due to the insistence of his father. Ham has "black eyes". It is implied that the incidents which gave Ham his nickname (him teaching Monk off-color French words to repeat to a general, and Ham being framed for the theft of ham) occurred shortly after the two met (it does seem odd, however, that the two became such good friends **after** all the trouble each had caused the other). Long Tom's new bug-zapper, the collaboration, is referred to as "ultrasonic".

The warehouse hangar is now made of "red brick", which probably means it has a new brick facade which appears to be old. A facade of new bricks would be conspicuous, not what Doc would want; the warehouse is supposed to be a secret, after all. The *Helldiver* is in drydock there, undergoing repairs for damage sustained in *Death in Silver*.

Doc's lab on the 86th floor is said to be "fully a block long". This places the lab firmly on the northeast side of the skyscraper. It is probably "L"-shaped, with the short leg (inversed) the southeast side of the building. This leaves the northwest or southwest sides of the building as possible locations for the library. The northwest side seems more likely because of the comment in *The Mystery on the Snow* that the lab door is visible from the library door; the bookshelves in the library are arranged to form a corridor between the two

34

doors. The southwest side of the building is too narrow to accommodate the library, in my opinion (there's less than twenty feet between the interior wall of the building mechanicals and the exterior wall for some of that side, which is never wider than about twenty feet. The northwest side would allow a room of approximately thirty-five feet wide by fifty feet long). This means the lab is actually "J"-shaped, curling around to the southwest side of the skyscraper.

In addition to his State and Federal law enforcement commissions, "Doc held similar commissions all over the world". The "Captain Sampson" character is named for pulp historian and Will Murray friend Bob Sampson.

Doc buys a new tri-motor during this adventure. This seems to be the only time thus far that he has had two at the same time (two that survived an adventure, anyway). Since this not a contemporary adventure, this may be an error. There is no good reason why Doc would have two giant tri-motors. And, is there even room in the warehouse hangar for a second tri-motor, with all the other vehicles stored there? Murray maintains that this is a new tri-motor, however.

The Sea Magician (4 days) takes place "recently" after *Death in Silver*. Doc and his crew meet up with Johnny, who is still in London, as mentioned in *Death in Silver*. He has been there for "some weeks", probably since the gap between *Fear Cay* and *Death in Silver* (Pat also acquires her salon during that time, if you remember). There are "leaves" and the "moon was bright" on the third night of the adventure. Because the "moon was bright" during the adventure, and Renny does not appear, this adventure likely occurs within a week of *Python Isle*, during which Renny finishes his dam in South Africa.

Johnny, it is said, has knowledge of "gutter fighting methods". These may have been acquired while fighting school bullies; he was undoubtedly harassed as an "egghead" as a child, considering his appearance and intelligence. Doc has "an honorary inspector's commission with Scotland Yard". This may refer to his code number mentioned in *The Thousand-Headed Man*, but probably does not. That number seems to refer to him as an anonymous informant. Since their last use (apparently), Doc has created a silencer for the super-firers, probably during his stay at the Fortress prior to *Python Isle*. He buys a "new plane" during this adventure – obviously small, considering its price (it's destroyed, naturally). We learn that "Ham was [a] boxer". This is the only adventure (to date) in which no one was killed (Monk observes this, somewhat disgustedly, at adventure's end).

According to Murray, there is an unrecorded adventure that follows this one. The last two began with out-of-town Doc aides Johnny and Renny, and the last of the trio would have begun with Long Tom in Europe.

The next seasonal sequence begins with *The Annihilist* (2 days), which takes place in "Fall"; in fact, it starts on "the first chilly day of Fall". A Fall placement precludes 1934 based on the story's LPO. This places *Fear Cay* and those in its sequence in Summer 1933. Since *Fear Cay* most likely occurs in late August, or early September, the "brilliant moon" of the second night is likely the full moon of September 4. Some time prior to the beginning of this adventure, a corpse freezes when it is left exposed to the night air overnight. The first night in the Fall of 1933 when the temperature was below freezing was November 5 (the temperature was 29°). "The first chilly day of Fall", the first day of the adventure, was November 16 (the high temperature for the day was 32°, which is how I would define "chilly" in the "Fall"; besides using an absolute, this definition fits the timetable of the adventure). Because some time passes between the first victim of the Crime Annihilist and the first day of the adventure, the first victim was likely murdered on November 5.

The license plate of Doc's roadster reads "DOC 1". This is probably not the roadster he usually uses, often referred to as "inconspicuous". The license plate would defeat its casual appearance.

Doc's police commission is referred to as "Inspector" (earlier it was "Captain"; it seems Doc has been promoted since *The Red Skull*). Inspector "Hardboiled" Humbolt "was canned by the previous administration" but "the new mayor put him in charge of Manhattan". This refers to Walker, who resigned in 1932, and O'Brien, who was elected early in 1933.

Renny lives in "a penthouse overlooking Central Park"; it seems to be on the east side. Renny designed it and supervised construction, and it has a secret exit leading to a garage about a block away. How new this building is – whether or not Renny moved into it from the hotel he apparently shared with Johnny and Long Tom – is not revealed; with Renny living in this building, and Long Tom living some place where he may have had a private museum of gadgets, it seems unlikely that the trio ever shared quarters, unless it was on a temporary basis.

The upstate college consists of a building that looks like a hunting lodge, on fenced property that contains a small lake and a rocky hill. It is inside this hill that the college is located; this facility may be the expansion referred to in earlier adventures, and the college at that time may have been just the lodge building. There are about 200 inmates (or patients) there at this time. There are several camouflaged machine gun pits that fire "anti-aircraft shells" (they are operated remotely); this is the first time the college has been attacked.

This story introduces the infamous "gland" theory of crime, which states that criminal behavior is caused in individuals whose "crime gland" malfunctions; it is said to be treated with a drug the college has developed. Doc is not the only one to have this theory, according to the narrative; "many criminologists have arrived at that conclusion", we are told (interestingly, Leslie Howard's character in the 1936 movie "The Petrified Forest" thinks "glands" might be responsible for criminal behavior). This is a direct contradiction of what we have been told earlier about the treatment criminals receive. And it is wrong. That is, scientifically inaccurate. All of the glands in the human body have been identified and no such gland exists. Doc may have been doing some early gene therapy, which would not have been understood by the reading public. In 1925, the theory of gene-centers was advanced, and "The Theory of the Gene" was published in 1926. DNA was discovered in 1929. The idea of hereditary transmission of characteristics through chromosomes became accepted in 1933. It was not discovered until the early 1940s that DNA is the main controller of heredity, but Doc was often decades ahead of traditional science, and may have been in genetics. Perhaps there is a "crime gene", as yet undiscovered? Then again, maybe earlier descriptions were a little too close to reality. It is repeatedly said in earlier adventures that if the public knew what Doc was doing at the college, there would be an outcry against it. Maybe Doc **was** performing brain surgery (read: lobotomy) in an attempt to cure criminals; there is apparently nothing faulty with the repeatedly-described procedure of giving the patients amnesia and then re-retraining them. This may have motivated Doc to induce Dent to make up this obviously untrue "gland" cure for criminals, to protect the college and the real treatment process.

For the first time in the series, Monk disobeys Doc (he ignores Doc's orders to help save dying criminals).

With the specific placement of *The Annihilist*, the phases of the moon mentioned in *Python Isle* are almost certainly those of October 19 and November 3. *The Sea Magician* then follows in early November. Descriptions of moonlight in *Death in Silver* suggest it occurs near neither a full nor new moon, so therefore probably takes place about October 10, halfway between full and new moons.

The Mystic Mullah (5 days) takes place after "the leaves had fallen, for the season was well into Fall". It seems to follow *The Annihilist* therefore in Fall 1933. The "brilliant moonlight" of the fourth night is probably near the full moon of December 2; the leaves "had" fallen, not "are falling", which would be the case if the adventure occurred a month earlier. The second day is "Wednesday", which must therefore be November 29.

Doc and his aides remain in Tanan for a while after the adventure and "left Tanan as soon as they perceived conditions had attained moderate stability". The bulletproof vests worn by Doc and his aides now protect "bodies, legs, and even a portion of their necks". Doc has installed an infra-red light (usually called "infra-ray") projector on his car so he can see through fog, etc.

Red Snow (3 days) takes place in "December". Its LPO precludes it from being December 1934, so it follows *The Mystic Mullah* in 1933, as we would expect. Within the week prior to the beginning of the adventure, there has been a rash of disappearances (actually murders with the bodies not being found) and Doc has sent his luggage ahead to Florida, where he intends to do some experiments aimed at killing mosquitoes. The first day is probably Saturday or Sunday (the advertising office of a newspaper is closed), so it is not the first weekend of the month, when *The Mystic Mullah* is finishing up (it ended Saturday, December 2), and probably not one of the last two weekends, as no one mentions the seasonal holidays, so it is likely mid December, beginning on December 10 or 17. Further, since Doc and his aides remained in Tanan for some time after the adventure, and at least several **non-adventure** days precede this adventure (while Doc's luggage is en route to Miami), this effectively eliminates the 10th as the starting date.

The super-firers, for the first time, have round clips similar to Thompson submachine guns, rather than the curved clips formerly used. Doc is the silent owner of the Magnolia Chemical Products Company, which has a profit-sharing plan in use. Pat has a "private plane" at a New York airport (its first mention).

Doc's tri-motor survives this adventure only because it has been impounded by the police; the plane he rents is destroyed. Doc has lost six tri-motor planes in 1933, at a cost of ten thousand dollars each (this sum is mentioned by Monk in one story; it seems low: the Ford 5-AT sold for $50,000 in 1930, reduced after the 1929 stock market crash. The "De Luxe Club" model sold for about $68,000 in 1931, the year Doc had to begin buying new tri-motor planes after his (probable) Ford 4-AT was destroyed in *The Man of Bronze*. Although one associates Doc with utilitarian methods rather than luxury, the luxury of the "De Luxe Club" **would be** utilitarian, considering all the long flights Doc and his aides make all over the world. It had seven overstuffed chairs, a toilet compartment with running water, a kitchenette with icebox, folding berths, storage in wing compartments, a radio cabinet, a writing desk and bookcase and a two-place divan, all of which would be necessary for a mobile headquarters such as Doc needed).

The "intelligence service" mentioned in this story may be the F.B.I., which came to prominence in 1933, when F.D.R. transformed the tiny "Bureau of Investigation" into a national organization, which gunned for criminals such as Bonnie and Clyde and Dillinger (though it seems to be a "spy corps" for use abroad in this story); if so, this would make "Leslie Thorne" A.K.A. "O. Garfew Beech" J. Edgar Hoover (notice the similarity in names?), although it is hard to imagine Hoover with the personality of Beech.

Unbelievably prescient once again, Dent's villains here are Asians who plan to sneak attack the U.S. (after killing important figures, the action preceding the adventure).

Doc remains in Miami some time after the adventure to pursue the research he went there for in the first place. The tag of the story states that *Land of Always-Night* follows it.

With the placements for Fall 1933 completed, we can see that the twelve day-long *The Monsters* must precede *Death in Silver*, for there is no room for it any place later in Fall; *Death in Silver*, *Python Isle*, and *The Sea Magician* almost certainly occur in order uninterrupted, and *The Annihilist* closely follows based on weather information. *The Mystic Mullah* also uses lunar data for its placement, and is closely followed by *Red Snow*, so despite a reference to "dead leaves", *The Monsters* must be placed in early October; "dead leaves", while not particularly common in early October, are quite possible. In fact, the "brilliant moon" on the fifth night of the adventure must be the full moon of October 3.

Land of Always-Night (5 days) gives no specific internal evidence as to its time of occurrence, but "evergreen" trees provide cover, which implies that deciduous ones do not

40

because they are bare, suggesting winter. Therefore it can tentatively be placed following *Red Snow* in early January 1934. Following the adventure, Doc and his crew stay in the Land of Always-Night "nearly a month".

This is the first appearance of Doc's first dirigible, which was "only recently delivered" to Doc (reported in the newspapers). Also, the "higher addition" of a dirigible hangar to the warehouse is "quite new". Obviously, it was built shortly after the end of *The Mystic Mullah* on December 2, the last appearance of the warehouse, and the dirigible was delivered between *Red Snow* and this adventure, after Doc returns to New York City.

We learn Monk dislikes Chinese food (a "Café Oriental" restaurant is in the skyscraper building). Habeas was recently examined by "a famous psychologist", who pronounces him very intelligent (the exam lasted until the second day of the adventure). Inexplicably, a thug summons Doc's private elevator (the one with the "secret call button").

The Spook Legion (5 days) seems not to occur in winter (Doc and Monk run around outdoors nude – while invisible – for hours without a single reference to either one being cold), breaking the seasonal sequence, although it can follow *Land of Always-Night*, albeit months later in Spring 1934; there is "brush" and "high weeds" and "shrubbery". Lake water is "very chilly". There is a moon on the second night, but there are many mentions of darkness, so it may be near a new moon (just prior to it, perhaps).

No mention is made of the secret call button for Doc's private express elevator; perhaps it's gone. There is a secret staircase in the lab leading to the 85th floor corridor.

Following this adventure, Doc experiments for "weeks" with the invisibility technology (this doesn't necessarily preclude him from adventuring during that time, however). For all this study, Doc gets just an **idea** how it is accomplished and decides not to pursue the research further.

The Secret in the Sky (2 days) is the last to be published in the order it was submitted, the 27th. It is "warmer" in San Francisco than Oklahoma, so it is not summer. Although there are "dead leaves" on the ground, there are also "green leaves" and "leafy boughs", suggesting spring before dead leaves from the previous fall have decomposed. This is probably the Spring following *Land of Always-Night*. *The Spook Legion*, therefore, may have occurred in sequence on warm Spring 1934 days.

In one of the few references to hairstyle, we are told that Monk's hair "stuck up straight". Ham's sword cane blade is for the first time referred to as "Damascus steel". There is no mention of "glands" in the treatment of criminals at the college.

Doc's police "commission was a gesture of appreciation of past aid" to the city. In fact, he saved the mayor's life in an unwritten episode. We are not told which mayor he saved or which year this occurred. Since Doc has had the commission from the earliest days of his career (it was first mentioned in *The Red Skull*, Summer 1932), it is tempting to say the mayor was Walker, who resigned in that year, and the event occurred in 1932, or perhaps in 1931 after Doc and his father moved into the Empire State Building, before *The Man of Bronze* late in that year, but there is no evidence to support this idea.

The next seasonal sequence officially begins with *Spook Hole* (5 days), submitted 28th but published 30th, which occurs in "spring". It is rainy and cold, and a light snow develops. Its LPO is May 17, 1935, so it could just be squeezed in Spring 1935, but likely continues the seasonal sequence of 1934. This leads to an April placement for *Spook Hole*.

Johnny's "famous" "university ... went in for deep learning rather than athletics". This suggests Princeton, according to Murray. We learn that Ham has never been married. It is said that "all of Doc's aides were expert radiotelegraph operators"; this may refer back to their "training" at Doc's hands.

The license plate of Doc's sedan reads "Doc-3". As noted in the comments for *The Annihilist*, this is not inconspicuous (in fact, in this adventure, criminals realize Doc is on the case

because of this license plate), so he probably has a second sedan. It is probably not the case that the earlier "S" numberings were incorrect (that is, "Doc-3" being true rather than "S3"), because these plates were on different vehicles. Further, the two "S" plates mentioned were on "undercover" vehicles.

"Doc Savage had taken a considerable part in" the design of the skyscraper and "the architectural drawings had been prepared by ... Renny". This explains how Doc has secret elevators (another is revealed in this adventure, concealed inside a large aquarium in the lab, connecting to a tunnel which leads to a subway station a block away) which building inspectors seem not to know about. Or did Doc pay them off to keep silent? I don't believe that Doc bribes people, so it's probably the former. The lobby door of Doc's private express elevator is hidden behind a secret door/panel.

"Long Tom's quarters [was] a miserly room off a gloomy basement laboratory" (contradicting the earlier comment about him living in a club, collecting villain's gadgets; or has he moved? Or was that entire scenario about him living in a club collecting gadgets dramatic license? I believe the latter is true). He is in the "flyweight" class (114-125#). But Dent's notebook states Long Tom's weight is "140 pounds". At the beginning of the adventure, he is addressing Congress about his "ultrashort electro-sonic" bug-zapper, which he believes is perfected. Perhaps "electro-sonic" means the sound is generated electronically. "Ultrashort" sound waves would vibrate or pummel their target.

College "graduates" now receive ten thousand dollars to help them start their new life, "a late addition to the" treatment. This is an enormous sum in 1934, something like $100,000 in today's [2000] dollars. Following the adventure, Doc and his group spend a "few days" studying Spook Hole and vacationing.

The Roar Devil (2 days) also takes place in "spring". It is said to occur shortly before *Quest of Qui*, the next submitted adventure. The LPOs of both *The Roar Devil* and *Quest of Qui* preclude them from occurring in 1935, suggesting that *Spook*

Hole does indeed belong in 1934, as well. It "had been a wet spring" and "was hot for this portion of the spring season". Further, "apple ... trees ... were in bloom", so it is almost certainly May during this adventure, which fits with *Spook Hole* being placed in April.

Doc wears a bulletproof skullcap for the first time during this adventure. His ninth tri-motor is destroyed. Johnny is at "the museum" at the beginning of the adventure; this must be the first reference to his private museum, which is more fully described in a later adventure, *Resurrection Day*. In jest, Monk proposes to Retta Kenn at the end of the story. The bulletproof chain shorts now extend to the knee. The color green on a super-firer ammo drum denotes gas which renders the target unconscious for about half an hour. *The Roar Devil* uses a machine similar to Long Tom's bug-zapper: It emits "ultra-short sonic waves" which paralyze the eardrum (the comparison to Long Tom's device is made). The villain uses the pseudonym "April Fifth", but this not elaborated upon. Given the time frame of events described in the story, April fifth might be the day the Roar Devil began his schemes. There was also a famous racehorse with the name "April the Fifth"; in 1932 he won the Derby.

"In New York, it was early summer" in *Quest of Qui* (about 7 days). But later, it is said "most of the inhabited world called this season spring" (and Renny refers to the season as "springtime"), so it is likely early June in the story.

In the beginning of the adventure, Doc is out of town overseeing the construction of a charity hospital. Since Doc no longer charges fees to fund them, he must be building them with money from Mayan gold. Johnny's hair is not "white". Without revealing its color, Dent's notebook states it is graying at the temples. Johnny's plane, which is destroyed, is a single engine job with a bulletproof alloy hull created by Doc. Ammo drums for the super-firers are "designated with numerals". It's said that "there were windows on three sides of the laboratory", indicating its new size. Doc has almost certainly expanded the lab and now occupies the entire floor, as previously suggested, and it **is** "U"- or at least "J"-shaped.

Renny's engineering titles are revealed to be "M.S., C.E., D.S.C., C.M.H.". Monk believes Renny is a bad driver. Ham's clothing in this adventure, which is typical, includes "a dark cutaway coat" and "natty gray waistcoat" [vest], and he carries "two hundred and sixty-three dollars" in cash on his person. When he is kidnapped, and Monk says something nice about Ham, Renny comments: "First time I heard you admit Ham had anything on the ball". On the "last ... trip" Doc and his aides "took up there [to the Arctic, they] found that fantastic place underground", referring to *Land of Always-Night*, wherein the dirigible debuted.

The Hidalgo warehouse is attacked, and all of the planes therein are destroyed. There is no mention specifically of a tri-motor, and it may be that Doc has not had time to replace the one destroyed in *The Roar Devil*, less than thirty days earlier, but one would think that, with all the trouble he has keeping them intact, he would always have one on standby at a factory. The *Helldiver* and "a small dirigible which the bronze man had developed to a point where it could make stratosphere flights" both survive the fire.

"Johnny's youth had been scholastic, but he had found time for athletics, and his specialty had been distance running". A later comment implies that this was during his "college" years. He has "an unusual glandular condition", according to Doc, which "had endowed him with muscles that were more like violin strings" than muscles, giving him great endurance.

Reference is made to "the policy which [Doc] had long ago formulated, that of having nothing to do with firearms". This statement has implications. The first of these is that Doc decided this before *The Man of Bronze*, less than two and a half years earlier, which would not be "long ago". The second is that **Doc** decided this, not his father. Since Doc is an expert shot, he was trained to fire guns, and therefore decided not to use them sometime after his training (or very late in his training). Did a young Doc get himself into a situation where a gun had been taken from him, and he had felt helpless? Lastly, Doc created the super-firers prior to *The Man of Bronze*, wherein his aides use them. Why, if he planned to adventure unarmed? Did he create them specifically for his aides? How could he, if they were not yet his aides? Or, did he create them prior to his foreswearing firearms? We should remember that the mercy bullets were not created until Summer 1932, about six months after the start of Doc's career. It seems as though Doc abandoned firearms between inventing the super-firers and foreswearing firearms altogether. We may further speculate that he foreswore firearms prior to the college's opening before 1930, for if he knew that he would be able to rehabilitate criminals, surely he would have never considered killing them. He didn't create mercy bullets prior to *The Man of Bronze* because he didn't need to; he didn't use a gun. But, since his aides started doing so, beginning in *The Man of Bronze*, he created the mercy bullets for them.

Cold Death (3 days) also seems to take place in spring or summer; there is "greenery" and "leafy" "maple trees", and it is "months" after *Land of Always-Night*. It seems to follow *Quest of Qui* in June 1934.

"All of Doc's men were expert lip readers" (another reference to their "training"?). It is said that "Renny ... was more than a match for ... Monk" in a fight.

Doc uses a plane in this adventure which is probably a tri-motor similar to his earlier ones, but it is never described as such (it matches in other details, however); if so, it is his tenth. The vagueness of the description may be due to the fact that this adventure was written by Laurence Donovan (his first) and not Dent. He also claims that Long Tom's "appearance had given him the name of 'Long Tom'". How a short, thin, pale man suggests the name "Long Tom" is not explained, however.

There are "two types" of submarines in the warehouse hangar now. One is obviously the *Helldiver*, the other is not described. Is this a mistake by Donovan, or has Doc added a second sub recently? And that's not the only change at the warehouse hangar: Doc "regularly employed a crew of a dozen mechanics and others". The villain Var finds the warehouse, which is supposed to be a secret. Did one of these employees tell Var of the location of the hangar? Are these employees graduates of the crime college (who else could Doc trust?)? These questions are not answered. It is possible these employees are an invention of Donovan's. They may be employed at the time of this adventure, but they have not been "regularly employed" before now, according to preceding accounts.

The Majii (29 days) seems to occur during the summer. Although there are "dead leaves" and "heavy dew", it is "unpleasantly hot" in a Himalayan valley, and there is a prevailing northeasterly wind in New York, a summer occurrence. "Moonlight shone quite brilliantly" at the end of this adventure. This may be near the full moon of July 26.

Doc's aides can read Mayan (the first time this is mentioned), though it is said that they have been able to do so since *The Man of Bronze* (but they didn't begin **speaking** it until *The Polar Treasure*, six months after that first adventure; they may have learned the written language from Johnny, who was writing a book about the Mayans at the beginning of *The Polar Treasure*). Monk is a "practiced" knife-thrower, and downs a man using this skill.

In this adventure, we meet another of Doc's tutors. He is the head of "one of the largest hospitals devoted to psychiatric work in the city, possibly the world" (this would therefore seem to be Bellevue, which, although a regular, working hospital, is well-known for its psychiatric facilities). He is apparently an M.D. Surprisingly, we learn very little about him, not even his name. We have been told more than once that medicine was the subject Doc studied first and most intensively. This man must surely have played a bigger role in Doc's life than seems by their brief interaction. Later in the story, two doctors are killed. It is implied that Doc's tutor was one of them, but I can't believe this based upon Doc's bare acknowledgment of the murders (recall Doc's reaction to the death of Jerome Coffern, his chemistry tutor, in *The Land of Terror*). The account does not state that Doc's tutor was killed, so it must have been a subordinate who had taken over treatment from the tutor.

The Jade Ogre (14 days), written by Will Murray, refers to a "late Spring chill". It is Pat's next appearance after *Spook Hole*, according to the narrative. Again, "Spring" is a reference to Murray's chronology, and it is probably more significant that this adventure is placed after *The Majii* in his chronology than Murray's seasonal reference. None of the weather data conflicts with a Summer placement following *The Majii*. On the thirteenth night of the adventure, the moon is a "silver dollar". This is likely the full moon of August 24.

Pat's salon has been re-named "Patricia, Inc.", and has been open a "year or so" (since September 1933, according to this chronology, which fits). Because of this name change, and the speed with which she had the salon running, she most likely bought the existing "Park Avenue Beautician", re-naming it once she felt it had become her own. This is the first (chronological) reference to Pat being Doc's "only living relative".

Doc has "recently purchased" Union Airlines, and owns a controlling interest in the San Francisco "Comet" newspaper.

Doc purchases a plane, which is apparently a giant tri-motor (his eleventh), but it is destroyed before he even sees it. Doc's tri-motor is brought from New York (it debuted in *Python Isle*, if that tri-motor was indeed a redundancy, in *Cold Death* if it was an error); it is bronze colored.

The "jade ogre" in this story is virtually the same gadget used in *The Goblins*, down to its color. This would seem to be because Murray used an idea for an unwritten Curt Flagg story, the gadget from which Dent later recycled in *The Goblins*.

Mystery Under the Sea (14 days) starts on "the first Saturday of September". After the adventure, Doc and the group stay at Taz for "almost a month", sailing "from Taz on the thirtieth day".

Only one submarine is mentioned at the warehouse hangar, so it seems Donovan's "two" subs from *Cold Death*

48

can be discounted as an error. There is now an "iron doctor" in the warehouse.

The reception room of Doc's 86th floor HQ has "recently" been re-modeled, with various secret compartments having been installed. On the floor of that room is a rug that was given to Doc by the Khedive of Egypt (according to Monk). The latest Doc could have received this was in 1914, when the last of the Khedives ended his rule; it is not said, for example, that the rug was given by the "former" Khedive of Egypt.

Monk disobeys a direct order from Doc (for the second time in his life) in this adventure, this time in order to rescue Habeas Corpus. It is said to be the "first instant that any of the others remembered" Monk doing so (having apparently forgotten about that incident in *The Annihilist*).

Doc says that Monk "and Renny and Ham are probably better swimmers than" the gang of thugs, who seem to be sailors. This is quite a statement to make, and it may be that Doc has taught all his aides superior swimming techniques. The original draft of this story clearly identified the ruins of Taz as having belonged to Atlantis.

Murder Melody (2 days) occurs during the "summer season", breaking the seasonal sequence begun in *The Spook Legion*. Fishing for "spring salmon", perhaps surprisingly, does not occur in the spring; thus this reference does not contradict the season. Further, the first day is the "16th". This adventure could occur during either 1934 or 1935, and must remain unplaced for a time.

Ham, it is twice said, believes Princess Lanta is the most beautiful woman he has ever seen. Johnny comments: "I've never trusted a woman – much."

The Fantastic Island (3 days) seems to occur in the spring or fall (it's "cold" but leaves are saturated with dew; "brush" has "grown" somewhat tall). It may begin the Spring 1935 sequence but more likely continues the fall sequence interrupted by *Murder Melody*. Johnny is on an expedition to the Galapagos Islands, which seems to have left two or three weeks earlier.

Pat, Monk and Ham are taking a vacation aboard the yacht *Seven Seas* (presumably it is Doc's); it's wrecked. Doc's latest tri-motor is destroyed, his tenth. There is no mention of a dirigible in the warehouse hangar. This is somewhat surprising, for this adventure was written by Ryerson Johnson, who also wrote *Land of Always-Night*, the adventure that introduced Doc's first dirigible. It does not seem likely that Johnson would have forgotten about the dirigible, but this omission is not explained. At the warehouse, Doc employs a mechanical dummy of himself to draw the fire of a villain. Although it is said this is the fourth time it has been fired upon, it is the first recorded time.

Ham's cane is made of malacca wood. Pat understands Mayan, but does not speak it (at least during the adventure). Doc threatens Count Ramadanoff when his aides are about to be killed, and tells Johnny to kill the Count if he attempts to trip a trap. Allowing access to "uptown traffic", the ramp to Doc's basement garage appears to be located on the east side of the building, probably the southeast corner.

This is the first adventure in which Pat's eyes are described and they are described as "golden". Johnson himself later stated in an interview that Pat's eyes are blue, and his description here of them as "golden" was a mistake (unfortunately perpetuated by later authors).

Dust of Death (3 days) takes place in South America, where it is "hot, blistering" and still "hot, insufferably" so, just after sundown, so it is summer. Therefore it is cold winter in New York.

During this adventure Doc premieres his "new stratospheric dirigible" (it is damaged), and Ham finds his pet ape, Chemistry (although zoologists maintain that no South American ape exists, a convincing tale and photograph came into the public eye in the 1920s of an ape killed in the Maracaibo jungle of South America in 1920, later named *Emir Anthropoidus Loisus* ("Lois' ape") after its discoverer, Dr. Francis De Lois, a Swiss geologist; the ape was over four feet tall and had reddish hair. The similarity of this description to that of Chemistry is striking). Chemistry is not mentioned during any of the adventures so far placed in 1934, so this must occur Winter 1935. *The Fantastic Island* can precede this tale, occurring in Fall 1934. Doc and his aides remain in "Santa Amoza" (which seems to be Peru, with its capital a seaport) for "days" until "peace was restored". "Delezon" then seems to be Ecuador. But this story was based on the Chaco War between Bolivia and Paraguay, so Dent is purposely misleading us.

We are told that Doc was "ordained a son of Kukulcan, the Feathered Serpent" during *The Man of Bronze*. This probably refers to the adoption ceremony all of the group went through at the end of that adventure, unless Doc was singled out for a special honor which was not described.

There is mention of "the express elevator which carried passengers to floors eighty to ninety"; there is in fact no passenger elevator in the Empire State Building which goes from the lobby above the eightieth floor. Further, there is described an "elevator which goes only to Doc Savage's floor". This is apparently not Doc's private speed elevator (the one which makes passengers' knees buckle) because there is no mention of its tremendous speed. And the entrance to that elevator in the lobby is behind a secret panel. This elevator has a human operator (and a pneumatic cushion brake). However, its location seems to be near the location of the private lift. Probably, this was actually a normal elevator, enhanced by dramatic license.

Long Tom meets up with an old friend who was a pilot in "the Great War". And Long Tom is described as a "wizard" pilot. These comments seem to suggest that Long Tom was in the Air Service (there was no "Air Force" at that time) during the war. This does not contradict other statements that he was in the Army, because the Air Service was part of the Army at that time.

In *The Seven Agate Devils* (4 days), there is no mention of the heat in Palm Springs, the location of the adventure. So it is not likely summer, as the temperature would almost certainly be mentioned if it was. It can follow *Dust of Death* in early 1935. Chemistry appears in this adventure. Doc and his aides hitch a ride on a dirigible, although he was contacted almost "a week ago", according to one character. There is no explanation why Doc didn't fly one of his own ships, or why he waited several days to go to Los Angeles. Perhaps something kept him busy in the intervening time. Perhaps he did not have time to replace (more likely repair) the dirigible from *Dust of Death*.

Ham is knocked down once – and knocked out another time – by Kateen MacRoy, a woman, in this adventure.

Murder Mirage (5 days) begins on July 4 ("in ... minutes ... it would be ... July 5th"). This takes place out of the sequence, obviously. Its LPO will allow it to occur in 1935 (as well as 1934, of course).

Doc's dirigible is destroyed in this adventure. It is "of Doc Savage's design". It is never described as being "stratospheric" and further, does not match the description of the stratospheric dirigible in *Dust of Death*. The conclusion to be drawn is that this dirigible is Doc's **first**, the one first used in *Land of Always-Night*. Therefore, *Murder Mirage* seems to occur July 1934, between *Land of Always-Night* and *Dust of Death*. Since there is no mention of a dirigible in the warehouse hangar in *The Fantastic Island*, and the "stratospheric" model debuts in *Dust of Death*, this adventure explains why there was no dirigible in the hangar in *The Fantastic Island*; it was destroyed between the two Johnson adventures; this fits with its July placement.

But July 1934 is taken up by the 29 day-long *The Majii*.

There is a curious part in that story; in the middle of it, there is a three-week period during which Doc waits to see what the Majii will do. Interestingly enough, this slack period enables *Murder Mirage* to be placed according to what we have determined about it. It breaks down like this:

first part of *The Majii*	June 29-July 2
Murder Mirage	July 4-8
second part of *The Majii*	July 24-27

This may explain why Doc waited those three weeks: Something which seemed to be more important interrupted *The Majii*, which basically dealt with stolen jewels and political intrigue. *Murder Mirage* is said to be a "disaster [that] may menace [the] whole world" (in a telegram Doc receives on July 4).

The dirigible uses "a synthetic inflation gas. This was noninflammable and had greater lifting power than either helium or hydrogen". Nothing has greater lifting power than hydrogen, the lightest of elements, however. The gas is noninflammable and neither helium nor hydrogen, if we are to believe Donovan. This seems to be a case of dramatic license. Donovan may have been inspired by deuterium – heavy hydrogen – which was discovered in 1931. But it, too, is highly flammable. Tritium, the heaviest hydrogen isotope, is even worse. In addition to being flammable, it is radioactive.

Doc now has a "trace-back" device attached to his office telephone lines, so that he may discover the telephone number of a person calling him. Pat lives in "a luxurious apartment in the vicinity of Park Avenue"; it is not said to be in the same building as her salon.

In *The Midas Man* (5 days), Chemistry is present and it is "months" after *The Fantastic Island*. It seems to be spring (it's warm, leaves seem to be on trees and "lawn grass" is "uncut"). "Ivy vines [are] thick and green". This suggests a Spring 1935 placement, and in fact begins that seasonal sequence.

This story has the first recorded use of the speed elevator/train between the 86th floor and the Hidalgo Trading Company warehouse hangar. Since we know the Hidalgo Trading Company hangar building was not in use (and probably not purchased) until Summer 1932, construction on the "flea run" (it is unnamed here) probably did not begin before then (although Doc could, perhaps, predict the general direction the tunnel would have to run). Because it would be difficult to install a new elevator after the building had been completed, I believe that the flea run entrance does not actually go to the 86th floor, but starts in the basement garage, Doc, et al., using his private express elevator to get there. It is likely dramatic license to claim the shaft for the flea run goes all the way up to Doc's headquarters, although it is just possible the two conveyances share the same shaft.

Doc has by now a sophisticated burglar alarm system there which records the location and time of a break-in.

Doc's basement garage is on "the other side of the building" from the front, at the "freight entrance into which trucks could be backed. It was really the exit from his private basement garage." This places the exit on the southwest side of the building, on 33rd Street. This matches comments in *The Fantastic Island*, and, in fact, the loading dock area of the Empire State Building is at the west corner of the building, on 33rd Street, west of Fifth Avenue. Why Farmer had to deduce the location of the garage exit, as he asserts in his biography, is a mystery to me; its location is plainly stated in this adventure, as I have shown.

The Black Spot (4 days) also seems to take place during the spring; there's "thick shrubbery" and "blackberry bushes" (but no mention of fruit on them) and there is "rapid cooling" after sunset. And, it is "five years" after "1930", so it follows *The Midas Man* in Spring 1935.

Monk has written "chemical textbooks". And he acts jealous when Pat seems to show an interest in Red Mahoney, a newsreel cameraman. Doc owns "controlling interest in" the Electro-Chemical Research Corporation. It's implied that some of Doc's devices are tested by them.

In the warehouse hangar is "Doc's special dirigible", but there is no indication as to why it's "special". It is probably the stratospheric model salvaged from *Dust of Death*. Doc has a "new submarine", which is not the *Helldiver*; this one is said to have replaced that sub (erroneously said to have been designed by Doc; in fact, Doc originally hired the *Helldiver*, then appropriated it at the end of *The Polar Treasure*). This new sub has "lifeboats", "small, escape subs". Is this the second sub Donovan referred to in *Cold Death*? He is also the author of this story; and, again he mentions employees at the warehouse, this time "watchmen", who carry Doc's super-firers. The warehouse also has its own telephone number. Was Donovan using the most up-to-date information about the warehouse when he wrote his novels, or using inaccurate information that he made up himself?

Gangster Jingles Sporado says of Doc: "I guess he's something like me. There ain't much he can't get away with".

"Spring" is "new" in *The Men Who Smiled No More* (4 days), suggesting April. It could follow *The Black Spot* in Spring 1935.

Doc is the eleventh director on the board of World Waterways shipping lines, which owns the Domyn Islands in the south Pacific. Many of Doc's graduates live there, working in the nitrate mines.

Monk is living in a "cottage" "far out on Long Island", and has lived there "for more than a week". Doc uses his "fastest monoplane", which is apparently a duplicate of the one used in *The Mystery on the Snow*, among other adventures. It is equipped with Long Tom's aerial sonar "ground detector". The burglar alarm system for the 86th floor can be switched to an audible tone resembling the "E-string on a violin".

Doc uses "eyeprints" to identify the villain, Doctor Madren, claiming it is better than fingerprints and some day will be in wide use; he is more than sixty years ahead of his time in this claim. Of Doctor Madren, Doc says: "He gave me the toughest moments of my whole life".

This adventure was written by Donovan, of whom a pattern emerges: Pat often appears in the story; women tend to run around in negligees, or similar flimsy attire (including Pat, at least once) and their "bosoms" are mentioned; Monk says "Howlin' Calamities!" and "Goshamighty!"; often, gangsters are involved; women are bad as often as they are good; the warehouse hangar has a crew of workmen there; and Doc wears a bulletproof skullcap most of the time. Donovan's novels have a bit harder edge to them than Dent's.

In *The Metal Master* (3 days), it is "cold" and "sleeting". Chemistry, "recently acquired", has just come out of quarantine. It is said to be "a few months" after *Dust of Death*, yet Ham has pulled strings to get Chemistry released from quarantine early. Talk of a character "go[ing] to Florida for the winter" clearly places the story in Fall, and the weather November. Although the story's LPO (November 15, 1935) will allow a Fall 1935 placement, this story would seem to have to precede all those adventures in which Chemistry has appeared, such as *The Seven Agate Devils*. However, according to Murray, the quarantine comment was an editorial insertion, which is why it doesn't really make sense that after "months", Chemistry would be released **early**, and is at odds with other internal evidence. Long Tom disappeared "two weeks" earlier to assume the identity of "Punning Parker", a small-time crook. The last night of the adventure has a moon casting "white light" so bright a person can hide in a shadow it creates. This is likely the full moon of November 10, the latest in the year before the adventure's LPO.

In the lab, there is a small secret room that can only be opened by a "thermal" combination, and contains a couch. It is virtually undetectable. Contrary to what Farmer states in his biography, Doc does not rent the floor below his own (said to be the 85th in this story); Doc pays the rent if it is unrented, an entirely different thing altogether. Doc's latest tri-motor (his fourteenth) is destroyed during the adventure.

Although *White Eyes* (5 days), written by Will Murray, is said to occur during "Winter", it is the "first cold snap of the season and it had arrived prematurely", and an upcoming Christmas bonus is mentioned, pointing instead to a late Fall placement. *The Midas Man* (Spring 1935) occurred "months ago", and it is a "few years" since the U.S. went off the gold standard in 1933. Further, Chemistry appears here, and it is said to be his "first Winter" in New York. Immediately following the fall-occurring *The Metal Master* (as Murray intended it to do; he ties the activities in Cuba from that adventure to the beginning of this one), it would be his first full winter in this adventure, since we know he arrived in

New York sometime **during** Winter 1935 (prior to *The Seven Agate Devils*).

We learn that the Governor of New York gives Doc's graduates pardons so that they will not be imprisoned for crimes committed before Doc treated them. While this makes sense in one regard, it brings up more problems. Doesn't anyone notice or comment on the large number of pardons the governor is granting every month? And if the governor thinks Doc's system is such a good idea, why doesn't he arrange for other criminals, who are captured through normal channels, to go to Doc's college? Lastly, contemporary evidence from other novels doesn't support this claim. I believe it's dramatic license on Murray's part. In any case, the graduates handle the transfer of gold from Hidalgo.

The license plate of Doc's unobtrusive roadster reads "Doc 1", confirming the information in *The Annihilist*. And once again, the license plate gives the car's inconspicuous appearance away (this may be a holdover from the plot of *The Annihilist*, upon unused parts of which Murray based *White Eyes*).

The villain's death gadget in this story is a device identical to Long Tom's bug-zapper, which uses **two** beams – one of sound and one of electromagnetic radiation (this explains the earlier confusion over the functioning of the device). Long Tom's device was patented "over a year ago", sometime in 1934, apparently, probably prior to *Spook Hole* (April 1934), where he was addressing Congress on the device.

Doc flies his sixteenth tri-motor in this adventure. Doc has "a vast empire of financial holdings", which has only been hinted at thus far in the series. Long Tom masquerades as "Robert Jefferson", which may mean that the "J." in Thomas J. Roberts stands for "Jefferson". In fact, Thomas Jefferson was called "Long Tom" himself. "Harmon Cash", a villain in this story, was actually a *nom de plume* of Dent.

Haunted Ocean (4 days) occurs during "winter". It seems to follow *White Eyes* in Winter 1936. But there are three pieces of evidence – which I admit must be considered circumstantial – that cause me to instead place this adventure in Winter 1935. First, Chemistry does not appear, is not even mentioned. Second, Ham says of Habeas: "I don't like that hog but he is smarter than any ape" (referring to Monk) after Habeas has shown some usefulness. This doesn't sound like something he would say if he already had Chemistry, in my opinion. The third thing is Doc's miniature sub, used for the first (and only) time in this adventure. This adventure probably belongs early in 1935, prior to *Dust of Death*, wherein Ham finds Chemistry.

Although Donovan mistakenly states a vacuum weighs more than a particular gas (a vacuum, which is the absence of everything, weighs nothing, and is therefore lighter than anything), the sub operates by chemical reaction. Although it is never explicitly stated, it seems as though the thin chamber around the sub must contain a chemical that gives the sub buoyancy. By adding another chemical, the sub sinks; the lighter gas produced by this reaction must therefore be allowed to escape. Adding a third chemical allows the sub to rise; the heavier liquid produced by this reaction must be dumped, therefore. This sub survives the adventure (Doc's tri-motor – his twelfth – does not), and may be the second sub tantalizingly mentioned in *Cold Death*, although it seems to be too small, based on comments in *The Black Spot*. It is built and delivered by what must be the Electro-Chemical Research Corporation, though it is unnamed here (its location and function match). Is it re-designed and built to a larger scale, replacing the *Helldiver* as suggested in *The Black Spot*, which chronologically follows this adventure?

Ham speaks Norse in this story.

Johnny was apparently the head of "applied science" at a university between World War I and *The Man of Bronze*; that is, the 1920s. This is likely the same position referred to as "Natural Science" in *Pirate of the Pacific*. He represents the U.S. in a multinational commission to prevent war in this story. It is not explained why he was chosen for this post, but it is safe to assume he has high-level contacts in the State Department.

The fact that Doc's big plane was destroyed in this adventure (and his dirigible damaged in *Dust of Death* a short time later) may explain why he must hitch a ride at the beginning of *The Seven Agate Devils*, suggesting that these three adventures take place in close chronological proximity to one another. With this adventure occurring first (likely January), *Dust of Death* would follow shortly thereafter, allowing some weeks to pass between it and *The Seven Agate Devils*, wherein Chemistry makes his first recorded appearance in New York. Ham in fact probably **did** get Chemistry released early from quarantine, according the placement of these three adventures, although it wasn't mentioned until *The Metal Master*. It, being **published** before *The Seven Agate Devils*, which contained Chemistry's first **chronological** appearance, had to have the quarantine comment inserted into it to explain Chemistry's appearance therein; that comment properly belongs in *The Seven Agate Devils*.

The South Pole Terror (about 78 days) begins in "late fall" and on the 46th day, "the south pole summer was beginning", therefore about December 23, placing this roughly from early November to late January. Its LPO precludes it from occurring after 1935, and Doc's "special stratospheric dirigible, a recent addition" is "still in the experimental stage" and must be the one introduced in *Dust of Death* (Winter 1935); it is destroyed in this story. Further, on the sixth night of the adventure, there is "no moon" but also "no clouds" and therefore a new moon. This is the new moon on November 26, which puts the comment about "the south pole summer" in early January, roughly ten days after the season had begun. The placement of both *The Metal Master* and *White Eyes* earlier in November supports the placement of *The South Pole Terror* here, and specifies even further when *White Eyes* must occur: *The Metal Master* ended on November 10, and *The South Pole Terror* began on the 21st; *White Eyes* occurs between them.

It is said that Doc's aides were each "a skilled radio operator", probably a reference to their "training". For the first recorded time, Monk uses a two-tailed coin to trick Ham, who catches on at the end of the adventure, after having been suckered a couple of times in earlier adventures. Both Monk and Ham speak Italian. Doc uses his fifteenth tri-motor in this adventure. Doc's financial "holdings ...comprised transportation lines, air, sea and land, industrial plants, and innumerable other enterprises".

Doc keeps "a small amphibian" plane in a farmer's barn on Long Island in case of emergency. Could this farmer be John Scroggins, the synthetic diamond creator who had the duck farm next to Monk's Long Island cottage in *The Men Who Smiled No More*? By the way, Monk is still living in his Wall Street penthouse, so the cottage was likely a rental.

There is a peculiar description of the warehouse hangar in this story. While the place is under "police guard", a delivery man comes to "a ramshackle building on Thirty-fourth Street and mounted stairs to a musty door bearing the legend: 'Hidalgo Trading Co.'", where he is "greeted by an elderly fellow" "who did nothing but stay in the Hidalgo Trading Co. offices and perform a few simple jobs". Both the delivery man and this elderly man leave, without reference to the police. Is this office in a neighboring building as Farmer suggests in his biography? Or has Doc added a small upper office to the warehouse, that, somehow, the police weren't watching?

The idea for this story possibly didn't originate with Dent, but came from a potential ghost writer; this inexplicable scene may have survived from the original plot. Further evidence to support this idea is that Doc wears a utility belt in this story and not his usual vest. Dent, however, wrote the tale.

In *Land of Long Juju* (6 days), grass is "long" and "tender" and there are "ants" and "mosquitoes", suggesting a Spring placement. Further, based on the time of sunrise in Africa, it is likely June. Renny is said to have been in Africa for the six weeks prior to the adventure.

This is the only appearance of Doc's singular aircraft, the *Wing*. It is said to be "neither a dirigible nor an airplane", though it is "sustained by a new type of noncombustible gas of the greatest lifting capacity" (presumably Doc's gas first mentioned in *Murder Mirage*, which we have determined was fictional; both of these adventures are by Donovan, which explains the gas' use here) kept "in separate compartments". This would seem to be a jet-powered flying wing, since it is not a dirigible, despite the description giving that impression, with lighter-than-air gas in chambers. However, the ship has no propellers, and uses a chemical that mixes with air to produce thrust which is channeled through tubes. It has a metal alloy hull, is capable of flying five hundred miles an hour and can hover. It seems to be a jet-powered dirigible. It is destroyed during the adventure, and apparently not salvaged or re-built. It seems likely that design problems proved insurmountable. Its flying wing shape makes maneuvering difficult, though this not mentioned during the story. There must be some reason this ship is never revived, and this is probably it. The U.S. government experimented for decades with the "flying wing" shape before they had success with the stealth bomber. This adventure would seem not to take place in 1935, because Doc is using his special stratospheric model from *Dust of Death* that year. Or maybe the jet's single use here prompted Doc to salvage or re-construct his stratospheric model in time for *The South Pole Terror*, late in 1935.

It is said of the door to Doc's HQ: "directly opposite were the elevators". This layout has been hinted at in some earlier adventures, but unfortunately is not accurate. There **is** a door "directly opposite" of the single passenger elevator on the 85th floor of the Empire State Building (the floor plan I consulted), but it is on the northeast side of the building. The reception room has been said to be in the west corner. The freight elevators face the opposite direction, across from utility rooms. We may take some comfort in the fact that a few descriptions of the 86th floor mention that so-and-so "found" Doc's door; not a very likely description if the door was indeed directly across the hall from the elevator (*The Man of Bronze* puts it "sixty feet" down the hall, in fact). You may wonder that Doc may have changed the layout of the floor to fit his needs, thereby allowing the elevator to face his door (after all, a door is an easy thing to move). There are two things Doc **could not** have changed: The placement of the building mechanicals in the center of the 86th floor and the direction the elevator opens, for it would have to be the same as on lower floors.

There are "several secret entrances" to Doc's headquarters. So far, the ones mentioned have been one in the corridor which is heat activated and leads into the lab, the "poisonous fish" fish bowl shaft, the one in the lab to the 85th floor fire cabinet and the flea run (if you choose to count it).

Pat's salon is said to be "just off Park Avenue". Is this a Donovan mistake or a Donovan revelation? Did she move it when she re-named it (or vice-versa)? It seems unlikely that it would have been named the "Park Avenue Beautician" if it was not, indeed, on Park Avenue. And we learn that Monk "had always been infatuated with ... Pat".

At the warehouse, there are (as usual for Donovan) "hangar helpers" and "subs".

Dafydd Neal Dyar, in his article "The Switcheroo Revisited", makes a compelling argument that this adventure takes place in Latin America rather than Africa. His main points are the presence of piranha fish – native to South America, not Africa; descriptions of the "Africans" that suggest they are light-skinned; the presence of Spanish characters, and; the Mayan language being similar to one of the languages spoken by one of the "African" characters. One might add that some aspects of the "Masai" culture – particularly headhunting – are inaccurate, and better describe certain tribes of South America, such as the Jivaro, the only native tribe to resist the Spanish conquistadors. The piranha are actually pivotal to the story: They are the "long juju" of the title. Pinpointing the exact South American nation where this adventure actually occurred is a more difficult prospect, but it is certainly one of those along the western coast, as a mountain pass is also a key point in the story. And if we are to believe other comments in the text, it is also north of the equator, narrowing the possibilities to Columbia and Venezuela.

In *The Vanisher* (8 days), an "early Fall" issue of a magazine is mentioned. This is likely the September issue that went on sale mid August (as the DOC SAVAGE magazine would have done). This seems to be a current issue, and coupled with a reference to sprinklers watering a lawn, this adventure should be placed in late August or early September. Since Chemistry, "acquired not many months before", appears in this story, the adventure must occur in 1935 or 1936 (where it can just be squeezed in due to its LPO of September 18, 1936). It is tentatively placed about September first 1935.

Doc uses his fourteenth tri-motor in this adventure. The first (recorded) sign that Doc's reputation has become tarnished is mentioned in this story: "Lately, [the police] had been quick to ask questions when anything out of the way happened". However, Doc still has "a commission as Inspector on the police force".

Chemistry also appears in *Mad Eyes* (3 days), and it is "spring" during the story, which must be either 1935 or 1936. There is "rain and ... cold", at night.

Ham's club is now said to be "near Park Avenue", and for the second adventure, Donovan calls Habeas an "Australian bush hog" (and Chemistry a "baboon"). The latter two we know are mistakes, so the former is likely also (earlier adventures place it **on** Park Avenue). Doc owns Spargrove Laboratories and appears to own Twentieth Century Alloy Metal Works, which is making machinery for him (for use at Spargrove Labs).

There is mention of the training Doc's aides have received: "The bronze man had taught them a great deal of his system of training", in this instance referring to the development of the senses. However, there has never been any scene depicting any aide doing any of Doc's exercises in any adventure so far. This is probably dramatic license on Donovan's part, in my opinion.

Doc is captured on the first day of this adventure (though this is not revealed until late in the story), and impersonated very effectively; the imposter fools Doc's aides for most of the adventure. He frames Doc for a series of crimes. This probably remains in the public's memory for some time, and may be the beginning of Doc's problems with the police (as mentioned in *The Vanisher*). If so, this suggests this adventure occurs before *The Vanisher*, in Spring 1935.

He Could Stop the World (2 days) occurs in two parts. In the first part, Johnny is apparently killed, and is in fact missing for "weeks". At this time, there is "red heat" in Texas, and later, when the adventure proper takes place, it is at least "four or five weeks" later, the "season" for "snow" to "lay many feet deep on ... [upper] Mount Shasta". It seems the first part takes place in August, the latter in October or November. Its LPO confines it to 1936 or earlier.

Featured in this adventure is the *Silver Cylinder*, an aircraft much like Doc's *Wing* from *Land of Long Juju* (except for its shape), though there is no reference to this fact. The *Silver Cylinder* is cylindrical, as its name suggests, rather than wing-shaped; it was "not the balloon type of stratospheric ship" and "Doc Savage had ... [contributed] a new type of explosive air-force chambers" "which could propel it upward at tremendous speed". Compare this with the description of the motive force of the *Wing*: A chemical which mixes with air and then is directed through tubes to propel the ship. The *Silver Cylinder*, however, seems to use helium as its sustaining gas rather than Doc's special gas. So: Did Doc learn from his failure with the *Wing*, or did he let someone else test a design for him in the *Silver Cylinder*, which he carried too far in the later *Wing*? Based on the dirigibles alone, I believe this adventure occurs after *Land of Long Juju*; finding the flying wing design flaws insurmountable, Doc may have released the jet propulsion technology to someone who incorporated it into the more traditional cylindrical shape of dirigibles. This placement is supported by the order of submission, as well, and the seasonal data, if both occur in the same year.

Pat is "an expert lip reader" and lives "in an ornate Park Avenue apartment ... near ... [her beauty] parlor", and has a maid. There are "several passages leading through the walls" of Doc's HQ; another one is revealed during the story: It is located behind a large cage of tropical birds in the lab (where it leads **to** is not revealed, however). Doc mentions "an island in the South Seas" where two characters can effectively disappear. This is likely among the Domyn Islands mentioned in *The Men Who Smiled No More* (also by Donovan; he seems to have carved himself out his own little niche in the Doc Savage universe).

Monk says: "If they make me into one of them giants", as the villain is doing to people in the story, "maybe Patricia will like me better". This sounds like Monk feels more strongly about Pat than she does about him. But does this mean that Pat has no feelings for (and thus no relationship with) Monk, or that a relationship exists but Monk's feelings are stronger than Pat's? In context, it seems to suggest that Monk's feelings are unrequited.

The Terror in the Navy (4 days) seems to take place in the Spring or Fall, for although a man is mowing his lawn and there is "green shrubbery", ocean water is "bitterly cold". Prior to this adventure, Doc has been watched "for days" (also "almost a week") by the criminal gang. The moon casts an "intense shadow" the second night of the adventure, which is likely near the full moon of May 18.

It is said to take place "almost three and a half years" after the beginning of *The Man of Bronze*. This places *The Terror in the Navy* no later than Spring 1935. But it is more significant in another way: The cover dates of *The Man of Bronze* and *The Terror in the Navy* are more than four years apart, and the latter is the 49th to be submitted (not counting Dent's rejected ones that Will Murray wrote later), and was submitted late in 1935, three years after *The Man of Bronze*.

This means **Dent is aware the passage of time in the novels is not the same as either real life nor matching the publishing schedule**, because at one a month, *The Terror in the*

Navy should have been about the 41st submission ("almost three and a half" years times 12 months a year).

Let's examine another aspect of this statement: Since Chemistry appears in this story, we know that it cannot occur earlier than 1935. Yet if *The Man of Bronze* **did** occur in May 1931, as Farmer concludes, this adventure would have to occur in 1934. This is further evidence that *The Man of Bronze* occurred late in 1931 and not in the Spring of that year.

Doc is the primary designer of the Navy's new *Zephyr* dirigible, which he worked on for "months". It has an unusual shape (resembling the cross section of a wing) and uses helium. This seems to suggest that Doc's experimentation with the *Wing* from *Land of Long Juju* led to the *Zephyr*; it would make sense that Doc learned from his original *Wing*, and passed on what he had learned to the makers of both the *Zephyr* and the *Silver Cylinder* (in *He Could Stop the World*). It seems unlikely to me that Doc would design an experimental craft for someone else without first testing it himself, but this is not conclusive evidence that *Land of Long Juju* occurred in 1934.

Pat has a "streamlined" "pretty little plane", which, although equipped with a machine gun, Pat claims was "built to enter races". She can speak Mayan now.

In the reception room, "the windows along one side were so large that the wall seemed almost solidly of glass". This wall is probably the one referred to when comments have been made about a large single window, and confirms that the room is indeed in a corner, with two walls of windows. These windows have Argus ("one-way") glass. There is a niche in the corridor that allows viewing of the corridor, the reception room, and the library. I can find no place on the floor plan of the 85th floor for this to exist, however.

Doc, for one of a very few times in the recorded adventures thus far, is affected by a woman, India Allison. Doc has "a document given him by the U. S. navy as a gesture of gratitude for presenting" them with a special target-finding device. It is suggested that Renny writes an autobiography sometime after this adventure, although this may be colloquial and not a literal reference. Doc's thirteenth tri-motor, which debuted in *The Men Who Smiled No More*, is destroyed during the adventure.

The Derrick Devil (6 days) begins with Doc returning from his Fortress of Solitude. With references to "insects", "tall, dry grass", a ripe "apple" on a tree and a "haystack", it is late summer, 1935 (because of Chemistry's appearance) or 1936 (no later because of its LPO). An edited-out comment refers to this adventure taking place soon after *The Terror in the Navy*. This adventure is therefore placed in late Summer 1935.

It is said that Johnny has "a tremendous forehead". This is the first reference to it, and although it may seem to be a mistaken reference to Long Tom's bulging forehead, it is not. Dent's notebook states that Johnny's forehead is indeed "tremendous". This may mean that Johnny is balding.

Although Johnny (as well as Monk and Ham, of course) is attracted to Vida Carlaw, it is Renny who ends up with her at adventure's end. The partition in the hangar between the air vehicles and the sea vehicles seems to be gone. Doc uses a portable metal detector for the first time in this adventure. "Monk ... had ... no scruples about hitting a man when he was down"; "Doc Savage had never quite succeeded in training Monk to restrain his impulsiveness". Graduates are now taught a trade "so that there would be no pressing temptation later"; apparently giving them $10,000 didn't work out quite as well as Doc had hoped.

In *The Mental Wizard* (about 10 days), it is "winter, bitterly cold in New York", and "over a year" after *Dust of Death*, placing this adventure in February 1936.

Monk "can't hardly speak" Spanish, by his own admission. Doc "spent months in India and elsewhere learning" hypnotism. This is the first reference to Doc travelling as part of his training, and that his training was done by anyone other than "scientists". Long Tom has just published a "new book on advanced telephoto work", which seems to cover any electronic visual recording, such as X-ray or radar photography. Doc and his aides use portable microwave radios in this adventure.

The original Klantic does not match any pharaoh who lived 100 years before Tut, as Johnny claims. All the pharaohs in the time frame mentioned died, and "Klantic" may therefore have been another person of great importance, perhaps a high priest of Ikhnaton (Akenaton), Egypt's only monotheistic pharaoh, who was in fact Tut's father. This would help explain his uniqueness, and his leaving of Egypt, as Akenaton's cult was wiped out by the succeeding regime.

The mysterious woman "Z" in this story was probably named after the South American lost city postulated by the British explorer Colonel Percy Fawcett, who disappeared in 1925 searching for his Z.

The next several adventures (*The Land of Fear* through *The Forgotten Realm*) seem to form a long seasonal sequence apparently running from spring to fall (though not in strict order). In fact, it's so long – about 350 days without any gaps between the adventures – that it must be broken up into two sequences, which form the warm-months sequences for 1935 and 1936, respectively. It should be obvious that it is unlikely that many of the adventures we tentatively placed in the warm months of 1935 can remain there; they must be moved to 1934, which was always a possibility to begin with. *Murder Melody*, *Murder Mirage*, and *Mystery Under the Sea* are three that must occur in 1934. *Murder Melody* can be placed with *Murder Mirage* in the three-week gap in the middle of *The Majii*. It is worth mentioning that both of these July adventures which were submitted so far out of sequence were written by Donovan. They are followed by the September-occurring *Mystery Under the Sea*.

The first long seasonal sequence begins with *The Land of Fear* (3 days) in which it is warm. It likely begins the Summer 1935 season, prior to *The Derrick Devil* in August, or ends it following *The Vanisher* in September.

This adventure confirms that the *Seven Seas* yacht, last seen in *The Fantastic Island*, does indeed belong to Doc. It must have been salvaged following that adventure, where it was wrecked. Helping out on the yacht is "Singleton", "a Diesel expert whom Doc occasionally drafted into service as engine man when his aids were for some reason absent". He is a graduate of the college. This implies that the hangar workmen described by Donovan in his novels are probably also graduates, although no mention of them is made in this story. In the warehouse hangar is a unnamed sub which seems to be the *Helldiver*.

In Doc's 86th floor headquarters, there is a "small apartment he kept behind his elaborate offices", in which "there were books, a radio, easy-chairs and solid doors". Further, there is an "inner room", which is not described. These two rooms are likely a bedroom and kitchen, the minimum for an "apartment" (obviously, there must be at least one bathroom in Doc's headquarters elsewhere). Since the first room contains the above-mentioned items, it is likely the bedroom and the inner room a small kitchen. The entrance to the first room is through the lab. The location of this apartment is also said to be at the "back" of the headquarters. Are these rooms at the other end of the building from the reception room entrance, that is, the southeast end of the building? Or, at the end of the lab, which is J- or U-shaped? This would put them on the southwest side of the building, abutting the reception room which is at the west corner of the building. Without further information, we cannot be sure where the rooms are, but I believe that they are on the southwest side of the building, where they would be at the end of the offices, following a clockwise circle of movement through the rooms and where there is only about twenty feet width, which fits the "small" part of the description (this is the area I earlier described as being too small for the library).

The fact that Doc's anaesthetic gas has a short duration has been in the newspapers and is known by some criminals in this story. Doc is impersonated in this story.

The historical "Genlee" is actually located in South America (Brazil), and **was** founded by Confederate refugees; the sister of the philosopher Nietzsche was associated with the place, which was named "Americana".

In *Resurrection Day* (about 60 days), there is a "cold rain" and a "hot radiator" at the beginning of the story, and it is "the rainy season" (spring) in Egypt, more than halfway through the adventure. Also at about this later time, ice cream is being sold in New York and it is "very hot" in Egypt, so the adventure must have begun on a cold day in late April, and ended in late June, the only way to reconcile the various references. With an LPO of August 21, 1936 and Chemistry's appearance, this story probably occurs in Spring 1935. Other Spring 1935 adventures, such as *The Men Who Smiled No More,* must therefore precede this one. The first day of this adventure, a "Friday", is probably April 28, because the full moon implied in *The Terror in the Navy* must be that of April 18, since that adventure cannot occur in May because of this one.

In the adventure, we learn that the resurrection process took ten years to develop. If this adventure did indeed take place in 1935, this means Doc started work on the process by 1925. Since we know that Doc's "college" was in operation prior to *The Man of Bronze* (from information in *The Purple Dragon*), it seems likely that the Fortress of Solitude was also in use before Doc's first true adventure, and the research for the resurrection process was begun there. He obviously could not have done this work in his 86th floor headquarters as the Empire State Building was not completed until 1931, and the Fortress is always described as the most complete laboratory on Earth, surpassing even that on the 86th floor.

King Solomon's body was found by Johnny "not many weeks before" the beginning of the story, likely Winter 1935, in the gap between *Dust of Death* (January) and *The Seven Agate Devils* (late February or early March). Johnny's private museum is described for the first time: it is in a tall, thin building, like Johnny himself (a coincidence?), "modernistic, with a lot of windows", several minutes uptown from Doc's skyscraper. The museum itself appears to be small, occupying only a single floor, halfway up the building. Johnny's "living quarters" are there, also.

70

"Doc Savage had long ago subsidized a number [of private detective agencies], and on occasion took a hand in training their operatives", which allows them to do *pro bono* work; "The [use of the] private agencies ... was Doc Savage's method of taking care of the innumerable calls which he received from persons who were in trivial jams". This is the first recorded mention of Doc using detective agencies in this manner, however.

In *Repel* (40 days), blackberries are ripe, by the 24th day of the adventure, which must almost certainly occur in July, so it must directly follow *Resurrection Day*, as we would like.

Doc uses his fourteenth tri-motor during the story, its first appearance. It is said that "Long Tom had a weakness for slender girls", one of the few references to him liking women at all. Johnny uses "smokescreen bullets". Doc "had arranged access to the fingerprint and picture files of police departments all over the world, and he employed detective agencies continually". Doc's electrochemical-astronomy tutor is an "elderly" man "from Vienna". Doc uses "a new seaplane ... which ... was faster than anything he had ever designed". Doc did not design or build it, as far as is described; he "secured" it. The "Bad Baldwins", brother and sister criminals, undergo a two-week (!) treatment at Doc's college. However, it is clear that they do not have the routine "amnesia" other graduates have, and so did not undergo brain surgery. We are not told what did happen to them at the college, but probably the fact that neither were killers played some part in the abbreviation of their treatment.

The trouble with the police, mentioned in *The Vanisher*, has been building the entire year 1935, we can now see. In *The Seven Agate Devils* (February), Doc's face appears on the apparent murder weapons, small agate statuettes. Doc is impersonated and framed in *Mad Eyes* (April). He has a spectacular public failure in *Resurrection Day* (April-June), when the wrong man is resurrected. No wonder the police don't trust him entirely in *The Vanisher* (September).

During *The Motion Menace* (12 days), it is warm, and there is "warm ... rain", and numerous mentions of "leaves" (though corn seems to be out of season). Long Tom makes a comment about the group becoming "a zoo" which suggests that Chemistry is a recent addition, so it is likely the same year as *The Seven Agate Devils*, in which Chemistry begins his (recorded) stay with. This adventure probably does not immediately follow *Repel*, which ends in early August, because Doc is at the Fortress of Solitude prior to *The Derrick Devil*, so it therefore probably follows *The Vanisher* in early Fall; we know *The Men Who Smiled No More* and *The Terror in the Navy*, among others, must both precede *Resurrection Day* in April, and March would seem to be too cold to place this adventure there.

The Soviet Union helps Doc out during this adventure, because he "did them a favor once". This probably refers to *The Mystic Mullah*, wherein Doc helps the Soviets. The super-firers are said to have "two different secret safeties" to prevent them from being used by enemies. Their cartridges are "not much larger than a .22".

In this adventure, the origin of Long Tom's nickname is revealed: He misused a "long tom" artillery gun by loading it with a variety of debris, and the name stuck. Interestingly, there is no mention of World War I in the account, only that it happened "years earlier". And later in the tale, the text states that Long Tom "had done some high flying" in his life, which supports the idea suggested in *Dust of Death* that he served in the Air Service in World War I.

Doc says: "The American war department has an archive where they keep some things that are a little too terrible to let the rest of the world know about"; this sounds like the storage facility where the Ark of the Covenant was taken at the end of "Raiders of the Lost Ark". He suggests the device in this story be put there; why he doesn't offer to store it himself (at the Fortress of Solitude) is not explained.

Pat is on vacation as "Enola Emmel" ("Lemme Alone" reversed) until she stumbles upon some action and decides what she really needs is "diversion".

The placements of *Resurrection Day* and *Repel* also mean that *The Land of Fear* probably occurs in September following *The Vanisher*, not in late spring or early summer. These two are lengthy, and take up all of the warm part of the spring and summer. On the last night of *The Land of Fear*, there is the "dim finger nail of a new moon". This is likely near the new moon of September 29, and since it is not quite a new moon, the adventure probably ends a night or two (at most) before this new moon.

In *Ost* (about 137 days), Doc doesn't get involved until about the 43rd day, which likely occurs during the summer because it seems to be warm in San Francisco. Doc and his crew spend virtually the rest of the adventure travelling to, exploring, or leaving the city of Ost on New Guinea. In this adventure, there is a "small demountable dirigible which Doc Savage had lately acquired". The dirigible is left on the island at the end of the adventure, bereft of gas. This is its only confirmed appearance and seems to confirm this adventure does not occur during 1935, because Doc is using his special stratospheric model that year. Its LPO of May 21, 1937 precludes it from occurring later than 1936. Because all the other summers (1932-1935) are completely full, *Ost* must occur Summer 1936. Also, *The South Pole Terror*, which must occur in 1935, takes up that year's fall, when the remainder of *Ost* occurs.

Although previously said to be done by an independent company, the headline clipping "reports were made up for Doc Savage by his five aids". One of Doc's planes is identified by the call letters "WDOC"; although it is not described, this is likely the tri-motor, his most-often used plane, and his seventeenth such craft.

Since *Ost* begins the warm-months placements (if not the actual sequence), for 1936, it is time to look more closely at 1935. *Resurrection Day*, we know, occurs late April through late June, followed closely by *Repel*. The spring adventures must precede these two and the summer ones follow. *The Midas Man, The Black Spot* and *The Men Who Smiled No More* should precede *Resurrection Day*, in sequence. These three run from early April until mid April, when *The Terror in the Navy* must occur near the full moon on the 18th. *Mad Eyes* must follow before the start of *Resurrection Day* in very late April. *Repel* is followed by *The Derrick Devil*, the only other summer adventure. Johnny doesn't appear in *The Vanisher, The Land of Fear*, or *The Motion Menace*, suggesting they be grouped together between the prologue of *He Could Stop the World*, wherein Johnny is apparently killed, and its conclusion, more than a month later, wherein it's revealed he was not. Johnny's whereabouts mentioned in those three adventures must therefore be entirely fictional, or topical (accurate when they were written). *The Land of Fear*, as previously described, probably occurs at the end of September. Then there is just enough time between *The Vanisher* and *The Land of Fear* for *The Motion Menace* to occur, a few weeks prior to the harvest of corn. Then we finish the year with the main part of *He Could Stop the World* in October, followed in November by *The Metal Master*, *White Eyes* and *The South Pole Terror*, which takes us into 1936. The convoluted chronology for 1935 may in part be explained by the fact that nine of the year's seventeen adventures were written by ghost writers (not counting two of Murray's).

With 1935's placements complete, we can now see that *Land of Long Juju*, a tenth ghost-written adventure, cannot take place in that year. It must be placed in 1934, just preceding *The Majii* in late June, with Donovan's other stories; this is yet another summer-occurring Donovan adventure submitted far out of sequence. But for the first part of *The Majii*, *Land of Long Juju*, *Murder Mirage*, and *Murder Melody* all occur together. The comment in *Land of Long Juju* about Renny spending "six weeks" in "Africa" cannot, unfortunately, be true.

In *The Sea Angel* (about 17 days), "it was cold"; there is a "blizzard" in Labrador. It can follow *Ost* in late Fall 1936. Doc and his men have been on the case for "some weeks"; this is likely the length of time since they returned from *Ost*; the kidnappings may have started while they were out of the country. In the warehouse hangar is "a dirigible of small size". This is not described any further, and may or may not be a "demountable" replacement for the one in *Ost*, or perhaps even that one salvaged. The *Helldiver* is also there, by itself. The second sub, referred to by Donovan in 1935 adventures, is not mentioned. It apparently was not as successful as Doc had hoped it would be, and abandoned.

On the first day of the adventure, a "grand jury fails to indict" Monk for swindling Ham out of three million dollars, "reducing him to a pauper" (what about the $5 million he had to have to live at the Midas Club?). It is part of a plot to capture the criminals who are kidnapping financial sharks in the story. They, like Doc, attempt to cure unethical businessmen of their criminal tendencies (by hard labor, though, instead of medical means). Doc explains to Nat Piper, the head of the gang, that crime is caused by malfunctioning "glands", though if you recall, the only other time reference to this was made in *The Annihilist*. Every other time, it has been surgery to induce amnesia then conditioning (referred to as "training").

"Monk suggested to Piper that he, Monk, would willingly turn over his personal fortune to charity and reform if they would only let him drown Ham." This story was footnoted extensively (unusual in itself) in its original Street & Smith edition (Bantam cut these in theirs), explaining that the creature was first sighted Summer 1936 (and may have been an ape of some sort; it was never captured), derelict U-boats were not unusual, and hypnotism was real, all based on newspaper articles from 1936. These footnotes bolster the view that events happened, as in the case of the mysterious creature, and then were written about, exactly as Dent did himself with this adventure.

The Whistling Wraith (14 days), written by Will Murray, takes place during "summer", "weeks" after *The Motion Menace*, and *Dust of Death* is "recent". This would seem to place this adventure in very late 1935, or perhaps early 1936. But it also occurs during "summer", which would therefore seem to be that of 1936. In fact, there is further information to help us pinpoint its occurrence. The first day is "Tuesday" and on the thirteenth night "the sky was clear ... and dark as lampblack", therefore the night of a new moon. The only time these two facts match in "summer" in 1935 is Tuesday, June 17 and the new moon of June 30, and; in 1936, Tuesday, August 4, 1936 and the new moon of Monday, August 17. The June 1935 date can be eliminated because of the placements of *Resurrection Day* and *Repel*, and the fact that *The Motion Menace* had not yet occurred, leaving the August 1936 placement as the only time when all the facts fit.

Doc keeps some cars "garaged in larger cities" for his use and uses his fifteenth tri-motor in this adventure; it is bronze-colored. "The new commissioner has canceled all of them funny honorary commissions" that Doc and his crew hold, they are informed by an "Inspector Sampson" (named after Murray friend and fellow pulp historian Bob Sampson; see also the comments for *Python Isle*). Murray correctly states that, in addition to Doc's private express elevator, "three other elevators also service this floor". The flea run now has a secret entrance, behind a cabinet (previously it has been behind a blank wall panel). The red color on a super-firer cartridge means demolition, and Monk uses a "penetration cartridge", which seems to be armor-piercing (he does not use it in that capacity, however). Doc has "an honorary rank of special agent" with the F.B.I. (because of *Red Snow*?).

Although Johnny "came near to standing seven feet tall", Renny, at 6'4", is "the tallest" of the aides. I believe that Johnny's height, like Doc's, has been fictionally increased over the years, and his true height, like Doc's, is closer to his early descriptions, probably between 6' and Renny's 6'4"

(Dent's notebook states he stands six feet tall). His extreme thinness probably gives him an illusion of greater height, as well. Johnny's hair is long, probably shoulder-length. Although not usually mentioned, Murray states this description came from a reference to Johnny's hair being of scholastic length in a contemporary novel, the only such reference made to Johnny's hair by Dent. The actual description from Dent's notebook reads that Johnny's hair is "thin, carefully parted on one side in combing. Prematurely gray at the temples".

The country "Santa Bellanca" in this story is Italy, which invaded Abyssinia in 1935 (which is referred to in the story). "Merida", "across the Adriatic Sea" from Italy, is Albania, and although the geography seems to be a little off, neighboring "Carrullana", Greece. Although Yugoslavia might seem to be one possibility, it is referred to as "Calbia" in *The King Maker*, and none of the countries mentioned here are that nation, which is also referred to (though not by name).

"Pat Savage maintained an apartment in the Park Avenue building that contained her beauty establishment"; she may have moved since *He Could Stop the World*, months earlier. Or, perhaps her apartment is on Park Avenue, as stated in *He Could Stop the World*, and her beauty shop "just off Park Avenue", as mentioned in *Land of Long Juju*. Or maybe the apartment **is** in the same building, "in the vicinity of Park Avenue", as her apartment is said to be in *Murder Mirage*. Both *Murder Mirage* and *Land of Long Juju* were written by Donovan. Some of his details contradict Dent's; believe who you will. Murray has a habit of filling in continuity or factual details in his stories: Doc's evasion of the spirit of the law while fulfilling the letter of the law about the private ownership of gold in *White Eyes*; the original appearance of the Fortress of Solitude in *Python Isle*. In this adventure, he explains Doc uses a "solar health radiator" to maintain his tan; this adventure highlights his extensive knowledge of Doc lore. In a telephone conversation, Murray stated that a "solar health radiator" reference was edited out of *Red Snow*.

Personally, I believe Doc's bronze-colored skin is due to a combination of a naturally dark complexion (Pat's skin also being "bronze" supports this idea) and a tanning chemical (not a dye), that also allows his skin to shed water like a duck (which is mentioned virtually every time he gets wet in the stories).

The Desert Demons (about 2 weeks) begins in "August". This is 1936 because of the drought in California (as it was planned by Will Murray). About nine days into the story, there is "bright moonlight", which would be near the full moon of August 24, the day that Doc gets involved, because the approximately eighth day of the story is a "Monday". Doc's special "stratospheric" dirigible, which was first used in *Dust of Death*, is destroyed in this story, confirming that it was only damaged in *South Pole Terror*.

Horror in Gold (6 days) takes place in "August", and is placed following *The Desert Demons* by Murray in 1936. However, this seems to occur near the new moon ("moonlight ... was not plentiful"), which occurred on August 17. Further, Doc has his dirigible in this story, so it actually occurs just before *The Desert Demons*, not after it.

A "week" after *The Infernal Buddha* (about 2 weeks) begins, "autumn had settled in". It is "three or four years" after the latter half of 1933, so it is either Fall 1936 or 1937 here. However, both the autumns of 1936 and 1937 are completely full, with no room for a two-week adventure. So, as with other Murray stories, his seasonal data in this story must be ignored.

This is as good a place as any to explain my philosophy (or policy) in placing the **new** Will Murray stories in this chronology. When the chronology was constructed in 1998, all of the adventures were considered as a whole as well as individually; evidence in one had to be weighed against evidence in another. So I am extremely reluctant to move an already-placed adventure because of information in a new one. Another reason is, in the case of Murray's novels, specific seasonal data is included that doesn't match other information (such as that placing a story in relationship with others) because Murray is using his own chronology, and gives information to fit that chronology. Having to choose between the two (as is often the case), I prefer to maintain the relationships of his adventures to other adventures (for continuity reasons) and ignore the seasonal data (which he himself admits is not binding). This has caused me to move *The Whistling Wraith* to Fall 1935 from earlier editions of this book, ignoring the "summer" reference, so that it follows *The Motion Menace* as Murray describes (it is now placed in October). But while he places *Horror in Gold*, for example, after *The Desert Demons*, I find that it occurs before it; there is nothing specifically **in** one or the other to suggest that his preference is true, and the evidence that there is suggests otherwise. Murray's reasoning in this instance (he explained by e-mail) is that Doc would always have a dirigible at the ready, so the presence of one in *Horror in Gold* does not indicate that it precedes *The Desert Demons*. I disagree: the dirigibles are not frequently used, so I doubt that Doc would always have one on standby, as he almost certainly does the tri-motor planes.

Devil on the Moon (about 13 days) takes place "not many months" after the Italian invasion of Abyssinia in 1935 (this fact is referred to in the adventure). Although it is "pleasant" outdoors in New York, it also seems to be during the long winter of the Arctic, from about September 21 to March 20, probably just before the beginning of the six-month day, because of the perpetual twilight in the north. This adventure begins the 1936 sequence, which we know must end prior to Doc's involvement in *Ost*, already placed in Summer 1936.

"Doc had been ... encouraging the impression he no longer" lived in the Empire State Building, going so far as to have the floors re-numbered. Doc seems to have abandoned this plan, for it is not mentioned again. If this is not dramatic license, and did indeed occur, it may have been changed back because people who had legitimate business with him would have a hard time contacting him.

Pat says: "Johnny ... has the biggest heart of any man in the world".

The text states that Doc is "a young man". This may be taken to mean that his age is no more than half his life expectancy. According to my research, the life expectancy of a man born 1900-1902 was about 64 years. Doc is probably no older than 32 then in 1936, making his birth year 1904 or later.

Returning now to *The Infernal Buddha*, it cannot occur where we would like to place it. In fact, keeping the "three or four years" reference, the only time this adventure can occur is Winter 1936, and there is only one specific time that it can occur then. On the first night, there is a "moon" that causes a "shadow". On the seventh night, there is a "sliver of moon", and then on the eleventh night, a "moon". This evidence seems to suggest a new moon on the eighth night. With *The South Pole Terror* ending about February 7, *The Mental Wizard* beginning in February, and *Devil on the Moon* probably ending before March 22, *The Infernal Buddha* must occur near the new moon in February (the twenty-second), between *The South Pole Terror* and *The Mental Wizard*, which now begins (probably) on March 1.

The Golden Peril (4 days) offers no clues as to its placement. Since Doc and his crew return to the Valley of the Vanished in Central America and there is no mention of it being hot, it might be surmised that it is not summer, and can therefore follow *Devil on the Moon* early in 1936.

Long Tom's ears are "much too big", and he "could never resist the plaintive pleas of beggars". The League of Nations knows of the Valley of the Vanished and the gold there.

There is "a speedy, modern dirigible" in the warehouse hangar, presumably the one used in *Ost* only a few months later, though it is not described in further detail. Doc uses a four-motored amphibian plane in this adventure, the first time such a plane is mentioned; it is destroyed. It seems to be slower than Doc's normal tri-motors. Since this adventure is by Harold Davis, it is possible he made a mistake and this is one of Doc's tri-motors. Davis mistakenly puts glasses on Johnny in this adventure (and others), which he has not worn since Doc repaired his eye in *The Man Who Shook the Earth* (Winter 1933), over three years earlier.

The Feathered Octopus (11 days) occurs in "spring"; this helps confirm the placement of *The Golden Peril*. Its LPO allows placement in 1937 or earlier. It is said Pat's last adventure with Doc occurred "more than a month" earlier. If this adventure is placed in Spring 1936, it will in fact be "more than a month" after *Devil on the Moon* in Winter 1936.

At the end of this adventure, Johnny talks about marrying Lam Benbow (Ham tells him he's "too old"). There is no further mention in later stories of this possibility. Doc's commission with the police is still in force during the adventure. "Johnny was an excellent lock-picker". We learn Doc uses his fingerprint instead of a signature, which can be forged. Doc uses his sixteenth tri-motor in this adventure.

In use at the beginning of the story is "a private elevator" which goes up "only one floor" to a "long, narrow" "receiving chamber" manned by Monk and Ham. They use a lie detector and metal detector to screen Doc's visitors. It is not clear if this is the elevator mentioned in *Dust of Death*, but it seems likely; it is Doc's "public" private elevator.

Pat's salon is "near Park Avenue", "not on Park Avenue proper, but just off it on a side street". For the first contemporary recorded time, Pat is referred to as Doc's "one living relative", after a handful of appearances. Doc expects to have no children himself, and wants to keep Pat out of danger so she can carry on the family name.

The Living-Fire Menace (3 days) almost certainly occurs in the warm months of the year; it is "over a hundred degrees" at Palm Springs, the location of the adventure, which occurs June through September. Doc is said to have been at his Fortress of Solitude for the six months prior to the adventure.

Johnny says he "was in the army" with "an undercover agent for the Department of Justice", specifically the "F.B.I.", confirming his war service (*The Man Who Shook the Earth* states that "Johnny lost the use of his left eye in the [World] War". Johnny's rank is never referred to in any adventure. Was his rank so low it would be embarrassing to mention in the company of Doc's other aides? Or did Farmer correctly deduce from this that Johnny was a spy, and never revealed his rank because it was classified? Interestingly, Dent's notebook makes no reference to Johnny's war service, other than his eye was damaged during the war, without revealing the circumstances. This would seem to confirm that his service record was classified, and therefore he was indeed a spy during World War I. This might explain his status with the international council to prevent war in *Haunted Ocean*; he doubtless developed high-level contacts (or **future** high-level contacts) while in the spy business.

Davis also claims that "Renny was probably the poorest fighter of all Doc's aids". This contradicts statements to the contrary (such as those about his boxing skill and military experience) and numerous scenes which illustrate Renny's effectiveness in hand-to-hand combat, as well as information about Renny in Dent's notebook.

Doc believes he has a good chance of dying while attempting an experiment that will free him and his aides (it's successful, of course). In a touching scene – arguably the best in the series – Doc removes his disguise so the last image of him his aides will have is that of his true appearance.

The fifth day of *The Mountain Monster* (8 days) is "July 12".

Doc uses a "big transport plane", with four motors, and "in the rear of the plane was a small laboratory". It is also a "rocket ship", having "two powerful rockets" to propel it. Doc is in Chicago lecturing physicians when he gets involved in the adventure, so it is unclear whether he chose this plane with the lab in it as part of that lecture, or is trying out a larger "mobile headquarters"-type plane. Because of the similarities, this plane may be a replacement for the plane used in *The Golden Peril*.

A reference to "Renny's vast fighting ability" contradicts Davis' claim in the previous adventure (he wrote this one, too!). Ham has taught Chemistry "to pick pockets". "Tears were in Long Tom's eyes" when he sees what he believes to be Doc's body.

After a few Davis novels, his pattern becomes clear: The characterizations are a little off; more than once Doc tells Monk and Ham to leave their pets behind in New York; Long Tom has big ears which he is fond of tugging on; Doc uses a four-motor plane rather than his familiar tri-motor; he wears a utility belt instead of his vest; and Johnny still wears glasses.

With the specific placement of *The Mountain Monster*, we can see that it is preceded by *The Living-Fire Menace* in early July, and *The Feathered Octopus*, which occurs in "spring", likely takes place in mid-May; the comment in *The Living-Fire Menace* about Doc being at the Fortress of Solitude should read "six weeks" instead of "six months". The May placement agrees with the mention of "butterflies" in the former story.

The Forgotten Realm (about 18 days), written by Will Murray, occurs in "summer", a "few months" after *Devil on the Moon*, so it belongs in Summer 1936, where it would seem to. This adventure conveniently ends a seasonal sequence that began with *Devil on the Moon*. The sequence of *Ost* and *The Sea Angel* must follow this adventure because the length of *Ost* would push *The Forgotten Realm* out of summer if the latter followed *Ost*. The second night of the adventure has "a full moon". This would seem to be the full moon of August 3, following *The Mountain Monster* from July. This confirms that *The Whistling Wraith* belongs in 1935.

Johnny is said to stand "in the neighborhood of seven feet" and "wore his hair long"; "he had been lecturing for several weeks" in London, probably since *The Living-Fire Menace* (early July), the last adventure he participated in, which suggests that the full moon in this adventure probably is that of September 1, and not August 3. Johnny has "been knighted for outstanding accomplishments in his field"; it does not state that this is a recent title, but Monk has not heard of it so it likely is, probably received during his stay in London.

Doc's sixteenth tri-motor is destroyed during the adventure (amazingly, he has lost only two for the year 1936). It is described in detail: The third motor "was mounted ... on a pylon ... back of the cockpit" and it is bronze-colored. It is unclear from the text whether this describes all of Doc's tri-motors, or if this is a special job (and therefore his seventeenth). Murray has since stated in a private conversation that this plane **is** a special one.

"Monk ... had spent his youth in Oklahoma". The princess of the lost Roman city in this adventure is named Namora ("a Roman" reversed). In this adventure, Doc uses the "Behemoth Bell" disguise from *Devil on the Moon* (wherein the last name was omitted from the final draft).

With the placement of *The Forgotten Realm*, both *Ost* and *The Sea Angel* can be placed more accurately. The "brilliant moonlight" on (roughly) the 79th night of *Ost* is likely from the full moon of October 30, meaning the adventure begins in mid August and ends in late December, with Doc getting involved in late September, following the conclusion of *The Forgotten Realm*. The fifteenth night of *The Sea Angel*, "so full of moonlight as to be like day", must refer to the full moon of January 26, 1937. This just allows "weeks" to pass between the two adventures, as described in the latter tale.

The Pirate's Ghost (20 days) begins on "the fifteenth day of March". Its LPO precludes it from taking place in 1938, so it, too, must be placed in 1936 or 1937. If possible, it should follow the previous seasonal sequence, and we can see that Spring 1936 is full, and this does begin the Spring 1937 seasonal sequence, as we would expect. Ham sets the date for the trial of an innocent man for April 24.

Doc is the "Eastern Management" of the Hotel Surfside in Los Angeles, and owns "factories, stores, a steamship line or two, even a railroad". Doc's aides carry "credentials indicating they were special Federal agents".

Doc uses a plane in this adventure which is "famous" and "bronze-colored", and is Doc's "latest design", and it is destroyed. This is not said to be a tri-motor and may or may not be the replacement for the tri-motor described in *The Forgotten Realm* (Summer 1936), but could easily be. It may be another four-motor job, which Doc apparently experimented with in 1936, but is likely Doc's seventeenth tri-motor, the one used in *Ost*.

At the end of the adventure, after shooting 49 dimes out of the air with a pistol, Doc suggests to Sagebrush Smith that he "establish and manage a dude ranch and winter resort in the mountains back East" and implies that he will finance it.

The Red Terrors (143 days) seems to begin during an off-season for passenger liners, traditionally spring or fall, and end when it is "Sahara hot" on the Atlantic Ocean. This indicates it begins in the spring and ends in the summer. Its LPO precludes it from placement in 1938. Therefore, the sequence beginning with *Devil on the Moon* and ending with *The Forgotten Realm* must be placed in 1936, positively, and *The Pirate's Ghost* and *The Red Terrors* in 1937. Since *The Red Terrors* begins in spring, it can directly follow *The Pirate's Ghost*, starting in early April 1937. *The Red Terrors* begins with Doc on a two-month vacation ("nine weeks to the day"), apparently his first away from his aides (other than his occasional trips to the Fortress of Solitude, which cannot really be called vacations) since *The Man of Bronze*. It is obviously during this two-month vacation that the upcoming trial mentioned in *The Pirate's Ghost* takes place.

The yacht Doc uses in this adventure is never referred to as the *Seven Seas*, used in other stories, but probably is. It is "crewed by graduates" of Doc's college. Also, "all of Doc's operatives, scattered in the far corners of the earth" are graduates, working "in the information-gathering agency which Doc Savage had created"; this is its first mention.

Doc's "black sedan" has "colored police headlights and regulation siren". "Renny saw to the construction and maintenance of their mechanical equipment". Johnny has "an arm and both legs broken" during the adventure and Doc says he is "lucky to be alive". Each aide has "a secret mark" to verify a message from that aide. Monk and Ham believe they are dead during the adventure and discuss their chances of getting into heaven. Neither seems too optimistic.

Monk thinks the underwater civilization in this story is related to the one in *Mystery Under the Sea*, but this is not confirmed. However, the original title of this tale was *Terror Under the Sea*, and with the similarity of the titles, it seems it was Dent's intention that the two be related.

The Submarine Mystery (33 days) seems to take place in spring or fall, with references to "shrubbery" and "brush", but men are wearing topcoats and water in the Atlantic Ocean is "cold". There is also a reference to Japan taking territory from China and "Spanish trouble" (the Spanish Civil War, obviously). Since Japan's invasion of China began in 1937, this adventure does not occur in 1936, but follows *The Red Terrors*, which ended in Summer 1937.

"Monk buzzed. He had to be very mad before he buzzed." Monk has been "very mad before", but he has not "buzzed" until this occurrence (and never does so again). It is said that Doc's "training should have made him a ... machine ... [with] the human qualities [driven] out of him"; "some of the scientists had tried to remove" "his emotions".

In *The Giggling Ghosts* (9 days) it seems to be warm, but it is "rainy" for much of the adventure. There is also a reference to the "new ... tunnel under the Hudson River" that "had recently been completed ... some months ago"; this would be the Lincoln Tunnel, opened 1937. Further, "flowers ... were tall" and there are "thickly overgrown ... weeds", so it is likely Fall rather than Spring. Even more, a watch has been given to a character as "a Christmas bonus", and after "a couple of days", returned because it was defective. A "Christmas bonus" would not likely have been given prior to December 1, and if the watch had become defective after several months (from Christmas 1936 to Spring 1937), it would not have likely been returned to the giver, so it must be December 1937 in this adventure. *The Submarine Mystery* was a "recent" adventure, so these two stories likely occur November and December 1937.

After so many mishaps in the elevator, Doc has installed an emergency back-up system that causes the lift to rise to his floor and sound an alarm if the elevator operator releases the control button. Remember that there is only one passenger elevator servicing the upper floors (above the 80th), so it is only one elevator that Doc has had to modify; passengers using any of the other elevators servicing the second through eightieth floors may or may not be coming to see Doc.

"William Harper Littlejohn did not care for reporters, because of the joy the scribes took in exaggerating the long, lean geologist's characteristics". Is this a veiled reference to Dent and the matter of Johnny's height increasing over the years?

"In the warehouse-hangar was stored quantities of equipment", referring to things Doc takes with him when travelling. It undoubtedly duplicates some of the equipment of Doc's 86th floor headquarters that he uses while in town. Also in the hangar is a bathysphere, last seen in *The Red Terrors*, only months ago. The largest plane in the hangar is a tri-motor (his eighteenth). This seems to suggest that Davis' four-motored planes were a mistake, although they could have been a failed experiment, abandoned in 1936. Doc thinks the warehouse is not as secret as it used to be.

Doc keeps a number of residences throughout the city for his use (he uses them to ascertain the identity of the villain in this adventure). "Ham maintained a law firm of his own that was ... expertly staffed".

Doc has his police commission in the story, contradicting what we were told in *The Whistling Wraith* about its cancellation. Has the commissioner had a change of heart? I suspect the cancellation was an exaggeration (at least; perhaps it was only a suspension) by Murray. Doc also uses the combination lock on the safe to open it, again contradicting statements in *The Whistling Wraith*. Because both of these incidents in that story are related, I believe they are dramatic license by Murray.

The Munitions Master (about 6 days) contains almost no clues as to its seasonal placement; there's "heat" in West

Africa, but this is near the equator so it may be any time of
year. Since this is the one reference to temperature, and it is
not very extreme, it may be reasoned that it is not the middle
of summer, when the heat would be blistering. If it follows
The Giggling Ghosts, it would occur in January 1938, where at
least it does not disagree with the single reference, and cannot
occur much later with an LPO of May 20, 1938. At the
beginning of the adventure, Doc is attending a parade in his
honor in Paris (unusual for him, given the repeated
descriptions of his "genuine modesty") – for having
"discovered a new type of cell development that led him to
believe it might be possible to restore the health of many war
cripples, might even restore the sight of many thought
hopelessly blind". This type of healing must almost certainly
have been part of Doc's Resurrection Process, although no
mention of it is made here.

To save himself from a grisly death, Doc forces himself
"into a comatose state" which seems to be similar to the
death-like trances of Indian fakirs. Characters apparently
based on Hitler and Goering appear in this story; both are
killed (this will not be the last time such characters appear;
Hitler appears in *Violent Night*, and Goering and Goebbels
appear in *Hell Below*). Because of a brilliant frame by the
mastermind of the story, "Doc Savage was credited with
being the worst traitor in history"; of course, Doc saves the
day and clears himself.

There is a reference to Renny and Johnny being on an
"exploration trip" in the Arctic; Johnny, perhaps, as an
archaeologist, but Renny, an engineer? What could they be
exploring in the Arctic? It is a barren wilderness, with only
Eskimo settlements and the towns of Greenland. I will
address these questions in greater detail shortly.

In *Fortress of Solitude* (33 days), it is "winter" (although it is
the "six month day" in the arctic. Apparently Dent was
thinking of the season reversal south of the equator).
Matching Sunlight's personal chronology given here with
what we learn in *The Devil Genghis*, sequel to *Fortress of
Solitude*, Sunlight finds the Fortress in July, and this

adventure takes place the following winter (he found the Strange Blue Dome "last year"). Therefore, this adventure must occur in the winter of a year that Doc has not been to the Fortress since July of the previous year (or else he would have found Sunlight there, studying his devices). According to this chronology, Doc's documented stays at the Fortress leave only Winter 1935, 1937, and 1938 as possibilities. Its LPO of July 15, 1938 allows a 1938 Winter placement, but the chronology for the year 1937 has not yet been completed. Doc and his aides spend the last "three weeks" of the adventure searching for the devices Sunlight stole from the Fortress.

Although Sunlight's nationality is not revealed, he has served "in the army" of the Soviet Union, and "he could speak English with almost no accent at all" (what this accent might be is not revealed), so he is not English, Australian, Canadian or American. He is known to the governments of France and Egypt, at the very least. Although the outline for this story states that Sunlight's name is an ironic nickname given to him because of his black moods, this is not mentioned in the story itself. Sunlight's name – or nickname -- is possibly Ivan Solnyechniysvet, the Russian equivalent of "John Sunlight". Doc says of him: "John Sunlight is probably as complete a fiend as we ever met".

Doc acquired his trilling "as a habit in the Orient", we are told, in the manner of the wise men there. The library windows face the "northern sky", which confirms that room is on the northwest side of the building, as I previously suggested. The entrance to the flea run is once again behind a wall panel in the lab.

The Fortress of Solitude is "north of Hudson Bay ... near the Arctic Circle". The island would therefore seem to be a possession of Canada. It took "a long time" to build, and "was built by Eskimos", whom Doc "brought" to the Fortress so that they would not "allow anyone to enter the Strange Blue Dome ... and to take care of what was inside the Dome".

We are told that "Doc had organized" "a famous world-wide private detective agency. Its real work was to gather information for the bronze man. When not doing that, the agency did a very profitable business along regular private detective lines". This agency is composed of Doc's graduates, and is probably the same "agency" described in *The Red Terrors*.

There appears in the story "the young European ruler known as the playboy prince" of "the other Balkan nation" mentioned. This seems to be King Carol II of Rumania, according to the research of Rick Lai, to whom I'm indebted for his information on the geopolitics of the time, and who also deduces that the country ruled by "Baron Karl" is probably Hungary.

Ham has one of his front teeth knocked out by Giantia because of his attentions to Fifi, Giantia's sister (his intentions do not seem to be honorable: He is glad Fifi will shortly undergo Doc's surgery which causes amnesia; this seems to suggest that he wants to propose marriage to Fifi in order to have sex with her, then will be glad when she forgets the proposal – and the "pre-marital" sex).

The Devil Genghis (about 21 days) is a sequel to *Fortress of Solitude*, which occurred "many months ago". Specifically, this adventure takes place the Fall following *Fortress of Solitude*, after "some of the trees ... had already turned the bright colors of fall". With an LPO of September 16, 1938, it cannot take place in 1938, so *Fortress of Solitude* cannot either. This leaves only 1935 or 1937, for both adventures. While it would be possible to place this adventure in 1935 due to a lack of mention of Ham's pet ape, Chemistry, it is more reasonable to place it in 1937, along with recent adventures. The "brilliant silver moonlight" of the 13th night is probably caused by the full moon of October 19, so the adventure begins no later than October 7.

"Monk ... had [a] fortune ... every nickel of which he'd made himself", which means he did not grow up wealthy. "Johnny's private plane ... [was] a low-wing, twin-engine job with retractable wheels and a body that was both a streamlined cabin and a pontoon for water landings".

Johnny thinks Toni Lash is "unquestionably the most exquisitely tall and slender young woman he had ever seen". Even Doc is affected by her beauty ("She was probably, he thought, the most striking feminine creature he had ever seen").

Monk states (and Doc agrees): "John Sunlight escaped from the arctic, went back and got the inventions from some place where he'd hidden them", which summarizes the mastermind's activities between the two adventures. For one of the very few times in his life, Doc loses his composure when Sunlight tells him they both have the same goal ("Doc looked incredulous"). One of Sunlight's proposals is to make English the language of mankind; this was put forth as a serious suggestion in 1932, and may be where he got the idea. It may also suggest that English is his native language. All of the devices that Sunlight has with him are "ruined" by Renny and Johnny. According to Sunlight, in *Fortress of Solitude*, "no one will ever know [the] story" of his life, but piecing together information from the two adventures, it is;

1934

July?	Sunlight is sentenced to a gulag by a Soviet court.
August	Sunlight arrives at the gulag on an ice-breaker.

1935

August	Sunlight escapes from the gulag, leading all the other prisoners, on an ice-breaker.

| October | The Soviets begin their search for the ice-breaker. |

1936

January	Sunlight's ice-breaker gets stuck in the ice.
July	The Strange Blue Dome, Doc's Fortress of Solitude, is spotted by those on the ice-breaker.
October	Sunlight gains access to the Strange Blue Dome.

1937

February to March	The events of *Fortress of Solitude*.
March	Using one of Doc's devices, Sunlight afflicts the Eskimo Kummik.
July?	Sunlight afflicts Fogarty-Smith.
August	Sunlight meets with Toni Lash (from the prologue of *The Devil Genghis*; 3 days).
early to late October	The events of *The Devil Genghis*.

Sunlight therefore found the Strange Blue Dome shortly after Doc left the Fortress prior to *The Living-Fire Menace* in July 1936. It is interesting to note that Stalin's infamous purges, during which he eliminated those men he felt were a threat to him, began in December 1934, mere months after Sunlight's trial. Did Sunlight's activities, described as blackmailing his superior officers, set off Stalin's infamous paranoia?

Genghis Khan's **name** was "Genghis"; his **title** was "khan", so this story should properly have been titled *The Devil Khan*.

Let us once again consider the odd statement in *The Munitions Master* about Johnny and Renny. Sunlight had stashed some of Doc's devices stolen from the Fortress in the Arctic prior to *Fortress of Solitude*. After three weeks, Doc gives up the search for the stolen devices. Does he renew it after *The Devil Genghis*? It seems to me that Johnny and Renny might actually be looking for the rest of the devices during *The Munitions Master*. It is not stated that all of the devices were found, only that the ones Sunlight had with him were "ruined" (by Johnny and Renny; is this a coincidence?). If this is true, it places *The Munitions Master* after *The Devil Genghis*, late in 1937. Another interesting coincidence (?) is that, at the beginning of *The Munitions Master*, if you recall, Doc is being honored by France – apparently for discoveries he probably made more than two years earlier and which were known throughout the world – a country which knew of John Sunlight and considered him to be extremely dangerous. Might Doc actually be being honored for ridding the world of Sunlight? As interesting as this hypothesis is, it seems out of character for Doc to accept public acclaim for eliminating Sunlight.

The Green Death (13 days) occurs in the winter (it's "hot" in the South American jungles), and mention is made of the warm weather in South America due to the season change of crossing the equator. This is likely Winter 1938, continuing the seasonal sequence begun with *The Devil Genghis*, as a reference to the 1937 *Hindenburg* disaster suggests. Johnny has been in the jungles for at least two weeks at the beginning of the adventure. Since the eleventh night of the adventure has a "bright moon", likely a full moon, this means it cannot occur in January, with its full moon of the sixteenth. Therefore, it must occur in February 1938.

Doc's latest book, *Atomic Research Simplified*, has just been published. In Doc's skyscraper headquarters there is "an operating room", which has a door opening into the corridor, apparently near the elevator (a visitor spots the door before reaching the door to the reception room). It seems to lead into the lab. Doc's college is referred to as a "sanitarium" in this story. This may be an error by Davis, or it may be that this is the new cover for the place. Doc may have needed a good explanation for all those ambulances in the area since 1932. Doc uses an "emergency kit" fanny pack during the story rather than his usual vest. This kit is never referred to as a belt, as in previous Davis novels, by the way. Johnny "was not as susceptible to female charms as was Monk, but even Johnny thought" Gloria Delpane was "beautiful". And, "Johnny did not like to have men die" during the course of an adventure.

Doc's dirigible, his fourth, a "big airship", carries a small plane underneath (as seen in the movie "Indiana Jones and The Last Crusade"). There is also a laboratory inside and a three-man collapsible autogiro on board. This ship uses helium. Why it doesn't use Doc's special gas often described by Donovan is not explained. Perhaps Davis did not have access to Donovan's notes, or more likely, Donovan used dramatic license in describing the gas. It was always helium, in my opinion, which would still constitute a great advance for Doc in relation to the other hydrogen-using airships of the early 1930s. There is also a small secret room in the center of the gasbag, from which Doc can monitor, via closed circuit television, the entire interior of the ship. The room is unknown even to Doc's aides.

Mad Mesa (about 30 days) begins a seasonal sequence. It is "summer" at the beginning of the adventure, and there is the "fruity odor of the orchards" in the air, and still seems to be quite warm at the end. Its LPO allows it to be placed in 1938 or earlier, so it likely follows *The Red Terrors* in Summer 1937 and is placed there tentatively. Near the end of the adventure, the moon bathes everything "in soft silver" light, so it likely ends shortly after the full moon of September 20.

Doc's college is now "a cluster of grim, graystone buildings" with signs that say "Germ Research Institute". This change was likely made to explain the numerous ambulances in the area.

The Yellow Cloud (about 7 days) takes place in the summer; there are big leaves on tobacco plants in Pennsylvania, apparently near ready to be harvested. Harvest takes place in early to mid August, so this story likely takes place in July. Pat's new plastic surgeon at her salon is a refugee from Austria, which was invaded by Germany in March 1938, so this adventure must occur after that date, but in Summer of the year because of its LPO. On the last night of the adventure, "the moonlight was bright", probably from a full moon.

Doc's comment that his telephone trace-back device being "new" must refer to the fact that it acts "quickly", since it has been in use since *Murder Mirage* (July 1934). We are told Ham learned to fence at Harvard. The Hidalgo Trading Company building is about "thirty years old", putting its construction about 1908, before World War I. Doc uses a four-motor seaplane in this adventure, but it is not "his largest speed plane"; the latter is undoubtedly his latest tri-motor, even though it is not described.

Pat knows and uses sign language during the adventure, and refers to an unrecorded adventure that she was tricked out of participating in. Her salon is named "Patricia, Incorporated"; this is the first contemporary use of the new name.

Long Tom lives in a "compartment ... with his electrical experimental laboratory" (no mention of villains' gadgets being collected there is made) and drives an "old-looking" car that has "a special motor and was capable of high speed".

This may be the "flashy racer" described in *The Polar Treasure*; it would now be six years old. It has a "televisor" (portable television camera) in it.

Of Doc's training, it is said "his parents had planned from the first for him to follow his present strange career". This statement includes Doc's mother in the decision, the first recorded time such a suggestion has been made.

This story is somewhat notorious. Farmer, in his biography of Doc, says it reads "as if plotted and typed in one day and sent out by midnight messenger directly to a drunken printer with literary aspirations". He is closer to the truth than he might think. According to Murray (in a telephone conversation), this is the story written by Evelyn Coulson, one of Dent's secretaries, as he alludes to in his Afterword in *The Frightened Fish*. Did Coulson make a mistake in naming Pat's salon? Or, did its name really change? Although considered one of the poorer Docs, the opening scene, a page and a half, is pure Dent magic.

The Freckled Shark (about 8 days) occurs in summer; weeds are "five foot high" and there is "thick ... shrubbery", and "ripe blackberries". A college student is "on vacation". This must be Summer 1938 because of references to Japan's 1937 invasion of Manchuria and the 1937 Anti-Comintern Pact. There is "brilliant moonlight" near the end of the adventure.

"Pretty girls were not without their effect upon" Johnny, it is said. Ham's family is from Boston. Doc has a special pneumatic tube that runs from the post office at 38th St. and 8th Ave. and delivers his mail directly to his headquarters.

Johnny stops Monk from killing a bad guy, reminding him of Doc's code (Doc is not present), reinforcing Johnny's dislike of killing mentioned in *The Green Death*. "'Doc wouldn't know anything about it,' Monk said with cheerful reasonableness."

Doc, in the guise of "Henry Peace", vents some of his implied frustration at Monk and Ham's antics on them in this adventure. He pretends to be in love with Rhoda Haven, who is described as "Madonnalike", having "patrician features" and dressing with the severity of a "nun". Is this a clue to Doc's inner self? Johnny is described as being "by nature something of a psychologist"; it is to him that Doc turns to for advice about dealing with Rhoda Haven (Johnny thinks the situation is quite humorous). "He rather enjoyed being Henry Peace", so much so that he's afraid to continue doing it. This seems to be because of his upbringing, the stoicism that was drilled into him and the strict moral code he has. But it's also probably a reflection of the change in Doc's career. He doesn't just flit from place to place getting people out of jams, as he did in the early adventures; now he is the head of a vast financial empire and has his graduates scattered worldwide gathering information for him.

World's Fair Goblin (2 days) supposedly begins on the thirteenth day of the 1939 New York World's Fair. Its LPO of January 20, 1939 precludes it from taking place at the Fair, however. It's said that Dent got the idea for this story while touring the Fairgrounds while they were under construction. At first glance, it seems this adventure must be ignored, as being totally fictional. But I suggest that this tour reminded Dent of an adventure Doc had at the **Chicago** World's Fair a few years earlier, but wrote it up as the **New York** World's Fair in order to make it seem current. The Chicago World's Fair ("A Century of Progress") opened May 18, 1933, making the thirteenth day May 30, 1933. Naturally, all references to 1939 must be ignored, including the appearance of Chemistry (who actually does nothing significant in the story, as opposed to Habeas, whom Monk uses to try to get a message to Doc). Alternately, this adventure could have taken place at the not-yet-open 1939 Fairgrounds, but part of *The Giggling Ghosts* does, so I believe this one does not.

Ham has "dark hair" in this story, and is "proud of it". *The Man of Bronze* (and a few other adventures) states that Ham's hair is (prematurely) gray. This would seem to indicate that he has taken to dyeing it (which may explain why he's so "proud of it"). Or, Bogart, the author of this tale, made a mistake.

The statement is made that "Monk liked ... all girls, but [Pat Savage] rated far above anyone [Monk] had ever met", apparently even more so than Rae Stanley from *Meteor Menace*, where she is twice referred to as the "prettiest girl" Monk had ever seen, and this comment followed a similar about Pat in *Brand of the Werewolf*, only months earlier.

The Gold Ogre (21 days) occurs during "summer" and its LPO precludes a 1939 placement, placing it in 1938. The "brilliant moonlight" on the tenth night is probably due to the full moon of July 12, the first full moon of that summer.

It is said that "Doc Savage's assistants ... kept a clipping file". This suggests that the previously-mentioned clipping bureau probably does the clipping, and then this information is turned over to Doc's aides, who maintain the file rather than Doc, or the else aides have taken over the job from the agency since its last mention.

Doc thinks that in the future he might contact the four teenagers who help him in this adventure, if his own aides are unavailable, but this never occurred.

With the placement of *The Gold Ogre*, we can now see that *The Yellow Cloud* probably does not occur in July 1938, because of the reference to the "bright" moonlight on the last night of the adventure. A mid June 1938 placement would still fit the requirements.

The Flaming Falcons (19 days) also seems to take place in summer with references to a "sunburned" man and a "haystack". On the first night there is "bright moonlight" and the fourth day is a "Saturday". This fits August 1938 (it, too, cannot take place in 1939), so it follows *The Gold Ogre*.

Doc uses a "two-wheeled go-devil", a "motor scooter" in this adventure. The group's usual practice is to leave messages at a town's post office, because "every town has a post office", as Doc points out. Doc "rage[s] inwardly" because he thinks he has made a mistake. The **thing** in this adventure is a plant that will produce rubber that can be grown in the arid portions of the U.S. This idea was also used in *The Land of Fear*.

Doc has an "organization of part-time" "secret agents", graduates who have a job but gather information for Doc on the side. There are "scores" of them in the U.S. alone. This seems not to be the previously-described international detective agency composed of graduates.

With the placement of these two summer adventures, it becomes obvious that *The Freckled Shark* must occur between them, because of "ripe blackberries" mentioned in that adventure. This would seem to indicate a July placement, almost certainly not a June placement preceding *The Gold Ogre*, as we might like (although I personally have seen ripe blackberries as early as June 17, Doc "gathered handfuls of them", which he could not, I assure you, do in June). Since the July full moon occurs during the middle portion of *The Gold Ogre*, it cannot be the one implied toward the end of *The Freckled Shark*. Instead, it must be the approaching full moon of the first night implied in *The Flaming Falcons*. Although ripe blackberries are uncommon in August, they are not as improbable as "handfuls" of them in mid June (when that month's full moon occurred). Further, a "hurricane shutter had been put up", indicating that it is during the stormy season in the Florida Keys, late summer.

During *Merchants of Disaster* (8 days), it seems not to be winter, and it is not the "tourist ... season" (summer). Further, a man is recovering from snow blindness acquired on a skiing trip, so it is likely Spring. Its LPO of April 21, 1939 would just allow it to occur in that year, beginning placements for that year, but more likely it occurs somewhere in between *The Green Death* (February) and *The Yellow Cloud* (June) in 1938.

The villain uses a wrist microwave radio receiver that generates heat on the wrist to communicate messages. All of Doc's aides are killed (clinically dead) during the adventure, but he revives them.

Monk was "probably the best pilot of the bronze man's aids". This is the first time that this assertion has been made, and Monk has never been referred to as a "wizard" pilot as Long Tom has. Ironically, Davis also wrote the tale that reference was made in. Remember that in one adventure Davis claimed Renny was "the poorest fighter" in Doc's group, yet in the following story, praised him for his combative "ability". He seems to have trouble keeping his facts straight. And, as in other Davis tales, Doc uses a "huge, four-motored ship" with "a well-equipped workshop in the rear". In fact, the last chronological time Doc used a four-motored plane was *The Mountain Monster* (July 1936), almost two years earlier. It's unlikely that Doc would keep both a four-motor and a tri-motor plane in the hangar at the same time, so the four-motored ships are probably a "typo" by Davis. This means the plane destroyed in *The Golden Peril* is Doc's fifteenth tri-motor. His sixteenth tri-motor is then introduced in *The Feathered Octopus*, and used throughout the summer of that year until being destroyed in *The Forgotten Realm,* and in fact, this is the count I have used for his planes in the comments for the adventures. His eighteenth tri-motor debuted in *The Giggling Ghosts* and is in use in this adventure.

It is said that "at some time during each year, [Doc] slipped away to the Fortress of Solitude". He has documented stays there in 1931, 1932, 1935 and 1936, according to this chronology. And in the other years (1933, 1934 and 1937), there are periods of at least three weeks in each year he could have gone to the Fortress, so this statement seems to be true.

Doc seems to spend a few days cleaning things up after the end of the adventure.

In *The Crimson Serpent* (4 days), it is "hot and humid" in Arkansas, indicating summer. It is placed after *The Flaming Falcons* in Summer 1938, continuing that seasonal sequence, which was interrupted by *Merchants of Disaster*. Previous to the adventure, Doc had sent Renny to supervise the dam project that had gotten into trouble (this is described in the prologue).

Doc speaks about the "element" discovered in *The Living-Fire Menace* (July 1936) at the annual "Scientific Adventurers

Club" dinner. He is the guest of honor. Neither Renny nor Monk apparently speak Spanish (Monk does, but very poorly, according to a previous adventure). Ham seems to speak it fluently. The mastermind of the stolen goods ring knows that Doc protects a lost tribe of Mayans.

Doc uses his fourth dirigible, first seen in *The Green Death*. It uses helium and the cloaking "cloud", both mentioned in that adventure. This ship is never referred to as "small", as was the earlier one (in *Ost*), contrary to Farmer's comments in his biography. And, although it is shot **at** (and hit once), it is not "shot down" (as Farmer claims); rather, Doc gives the impression it is shot down to the villains in order to prevent it from **really** being shot down. The last we hear of the dirigible, it is left "parked ... in the trees", relatively unharmed.

Doc uses a wristwatch device similar to that used by the villains of *Merchants of Disaster*, which is said to be "a previous adventure" (confirming its placement earlier in 1938, and not in early 1939). Note that the text does not say "**the** previous adventure". Because chronologically, *Merchants of Disaster* was not the previous adventure. That was a Spring adventure and this is a late Summer adventure. This is a further clue that the DOC SAVAGE authors knew the adventures occurred in a different order than the one they were written in, and published in.

Hex (6 days) also occurs during "summer" and there is an "apple", a "carrot" and a "lilac flower", the latter suggesting June. This adventure probably does take place in June, between *The Yellow Cloud* and *The Gold Ogre*. The third day is "Friday", so the first day is probably Wednesday, June 22. This is the first Wednesday in "summer", and placing it on a later Wednesday would overrun *The Gold Ogre*; an earlier Wednesday would not be "summer" and would overrun *The Yellow Cloud*.

Doc is "adept at 'escape' tricks. He had once duplicated each feat of the famous magician, Houdini". Doc's "fastest plane" is a low-wing tri-motor, which seems not to be amphibian. In the past, his "fastest plane" has been said to be a small monoplane. This story is by William Bogart, who may have been thinking of the constant references to Doc's tri-motor as a "speed ship", though it was not his "fastest". So this may be his still be his eighteenth such plane.

There is an odd scene in this book, which Farmer discusses at length in his biography: "Pat had taken in the situation of Monk-holding-girl and her words were chiding". "Monk's face reddened. He blurted out, 'Now look, Pat, you got me wrong'". It is true that the situation is not what it seems (Monk has just rescued the woman) but it should be surprising if Monk wasn't holding a girl at least once during an adventure (albeit usually at the end, off-screen). This scene seems to suggest more of a two-way situation between the two than previously hinted at (as in Monk's statements in *He Could Stop the World*); we could understand his embarrassment based on those comments, but Pat's behavior doesn't make sense in a platonic context. Of course, it may be that Monk lately has been trying to get Pat into a relationship, and this situation seems to put a lie to that. Or, it may be that they are having an affair by this time. Something seems to be going on; there isn't enough evidence to know exactly what it is. Maybe Bogart didn't get the word not to reveal the situation. Or, the whole thing may be a mistake by Bogart. It is worth pointing out that all three of the scenes suggesting something may be going on between Monk and Pat (in *He Could Stop the World*, *World's Fair Goblin* and this adventure) were written by Dent ghost writers (Bogart and Donovan) and not Dent himself. Make of that what you will (personally, I doubt anything was going on, for a number of reasons). At the end of the adventure, Monk and Ham spend "several days" in town. Perhaps significantly, Pat has a date with Ham. This seems to be to pay Monk back for the earlier incident.

Poison Island (8 days) begins with a four-day prologue that begins on "September 4th". The adventure itself begins "six weeks later, approximately", or mid October. This completes the Summer seasonal sequence begun in *The Gold Ogre*. These adventures, as a group, cannot take place the same summer as *Mad Mesa*, due to their lengths. Therefore, *Mad Mesa* must

follow *The Red Terrors* in 1937, with this sequence taking
place in 1938, following *The Freckled Shark*. Because of the
specific occurrence dates of this adventure and *The Flaming
Falcons*, we can now see that *The Crimson Serpent* must take
place around or shortly after the prologue of this adventure,
before Doc gets involved in mid October; this matches the
seasonal data for *The Crimson Serpent*.

Pat has a three-masted schooner named *Patricia*, which
seems to be rather new. Ham loses a rigged bet to Monk and
must act as his chauffeur during this adventure. The
warehouse hangar now has a wind tunnel, "lately installed".
"The largest article" in Doc's vest is the ultra-violet projector,
which is slightly larger than a flat flashlight or collapsible
camera. "Doc Savage held a high commission in the Coast
Guard".

The "big" plane Doc uses (and himself destroys to fool
the mastermind villain) seems to be a tri-motor, though its
engines are not described. It is properly referred to as "being
one of the fastest craft, for its size, as yet constructed",
capable of "somewhat over three hundred and fifty miles per
hour". This matches earlier descriptions of Doc's tri-motor
planes. It may be bronze-colored, though this is not
specifically referred to. Dara Smith calls it "unusual" looking,
without explanation. This would be Doc's eighteenth tri-
motor.

The Stone Man (7 days) begins with a one-day prologue
(on a "Friday" "during the season ... of tourists") and "seven
weeks and three days" later, the adventure takes place, during
the fall. Ham says, "They bet me Harvard wouldn't win last
Saturday". This is actually a rigged bet that Monk and Renny
lose to Ham, which is apparently in retaliation for the rigged
bet Ham lost to Monk in *Poison Island*. In the fall following
Poison Island, Harvard won Saturday games on October 29,
and November 5, 12 and 19. Since Doc gave a lecture the
week prior to the adventure, it is likely not the same week

Poison Island ended, eliminating the October 29 game, so this adventure occurs in November. And because "seven weeks" ago is still tourist season, this adventure probably begins the soonest following weekend. Actually, the first day of the adventure is a "Monday", probably November 7. This puts the prologue on September 16, still summer.

Doc uses his small hospital on the West Side, near the slums, to hold his captured criminals for transportation to the college. This may have been the usual practice since *The King Maker*, the hospital's first mention, because the ambulances are probably not driving from upstate every time Doc has a pick-up for them.

Ham's hair is "ivory" colored (once again).

Pat's schooner is at the warehouse hangar, where "Doc had lately installed a large vault which held an assortment of the scientific devices which he used, these being packed in cases ready for quick transportation". This situation was first described in *The Giggling Ghosts* (November 1937, a year earlier), though no mention of the vault was made. It has obviously been installed since that adventure.

Doc's "fastest craft" is now an amphibian with "two huge motors"; it seems to have replaced the small speed plane that Doc has used from the early days of his career. The last of these was destroyed in *The Gold Ogre*, a few months earlier. However, this description may be in error, as it is claimed that "Doc had constructed" the *Helldiver*, when in fact he appropriated it from Ben O'Gard (why Dent, the author of both this adventure and *The Polar Treasure*, in which the *Helldiver* made its debut, made this mistake, I cannot explain). There is no mention of a dirigible in the hangar (and none in the previous adventure, either). The ship may be under repair at another location, but this seems unlikely; it is now two months since the craft was damaged in *The Crimson Serpent*.

In *The Angry Ghost* (7 days), it is "summer, and warm". Its LPO allows it to occur in 1939, but it probably occurs after *The Crimson Serpent* in 1938.

Doc has an "unlisted number" at his headquarters. He in fact has several telephone lines, at least one of which **is** listed.

At the beginning of the adventure, Ham is addressing Congress on the subject of no-charge hospitals (presumably these are charity hospitals, the type Doc builds and funds, although Ham may be proposing socialized medicine here). This adventure is the first to refer to Doc's skin tone "as though bronzed by tropical suns". Previously the "as though" has not appeared. This story was written by Bogart, which may explain this change in description. Doc is "an honorary member of the Secret Service" and has "a commission as a naval officer, retired". The latter may refer to the document mentioned in *The Terror in the Navy*. Doc has designed a "stratosphere plane" which "will go higher than any other plane on earth" for the army, and borrows one from them during the adventure. The "enemy ... country" in this adventure seems to be Italy.

The Dagger in The Sky (12 days) begins on a "late Fall day", and on the first night there is "bright moonlight" and a "moon-whitened sky". Its LPO of September 15, 1939 prevents it from occurring in that year, so it likely occurs in Fall 1938, following *The Stone Man*. The moonlight references are undoubtedly due to the full moon of December 7. The fourth day of the adventure is "Saturday", so the first day must be December 9, just after the full moon.

At the beginning of this adventure, Doc is starting "his first real vacation", which is going to be "a month" long. There is no reason to think that he does not go ahead with these plans following the adventure. In fact, the epilogue occurs "a few weeks" after the adventure ends, likely when Doc has just returned from his vacation.

The "Incas of Peru" are mistakenly said to have worshipped the Mayan god Kukulcan. Viracocha is in fact their equivalent god. The two cultures never shared a common border. The two South American countries in this adventure, "Hispanola" and "Cristobal" seem to be Uruguay (has a "coast" and is "not large") and Paraguay (its "last war with Hispanola was more than sixty years ago", which Cristobal "lost"; this would be the War of The Triple Alliance, 1865-1870, in which Paraguay lost to the alliance of Uruguay, Argentina and Brazil). However, Uruguay and Paraguay do not share a border, and a border dispute is at the core of this adventure. So "Hispanola" must be a nation neighboring Paraguay. Fortunately, we have a clue to help us identify this nation: A character mentions an earlier "border dispute", "settled two years ago". This would have been the Chaco War with Bolivia, 1932-1935.

This suggests then that this adventure should be placed in 1937. However, Doc refers to the annexation of the Sudetenland, which was a result of the Munich Pact (Sept. 29-30, 1938), likening the situation of Cristobal and the plot of the villains in this adventure to it; the repeated mention of Incans "living within Hispanola borders" also bolsters the Bolivia identification: The Inca were primarily situated on the western coast of South America, not the eastern. How to explain the contradictory evidence? Footnotes in the novel state that fictitious names have been given for the countries. Undoubtedly Dent furthered this deception by adding historical and geographical comments suggesting Uruguay as Hispanola.

Doc gets captured because he is distracted by the beautiful Sanda MacNamara. She is also capable and courageous. Later, he wonders what it would be like to kiss her. Monk believes Doc is "liable to fall" in love with her.

The Mayan that Doc and his aides speak is (finally) identified as "Nahuatl" (by the way, in Mayan, the "h" is silent, and used to separate two vowels which do not affect one another. The "u" and second "a" are not separated by an "h" because they **do** affect one another, the "u" almost sounding like a "w" in jaguar).

Johnny impersonates one of the villains during the story. Was the man almost seven feet tall? His height is not described. This tends to support the idea that Johnny is **not** almost seven feet tall. It would be difficult for both him and

Doc to pull off many impersonations if they are over 6'6"
when the average height was a full foot less.

We are told of "one-eyed old Prop Jackson who, if the
records had been straight, had shot down more planes than
Rickenbacker" during World War I (although he makes no
appearance). Is this Long Tom's friend Ace Jackson from
Dust of Death? It seems a large coincidence that there should
be two World War I pilots named Jackson living and working
in South America in a span of less than four years.

This adventure ends the year 1938 and fittingly ends the
placements for the year 1938.

The Other World (7 days) also seems to take place in winter
or early spring. It's "during the season" of fur-trading, there is
an "oat stubble field" and land in Canada is "snow-covered".
But there are "leaves" on trees, and "there was fog, rain" in
the U.S., so it must be early spring, probably early April.
With an LPO of October 20, 1939, it can tentatively be placed
in April 1939, beginning the Spring season.

"Doc Savage maintained on the ground floor [of his
building] the reception staff which arranged jobs for the
needy". This is a modification of the system used first in *The
Feathered Octopus* (May 1936). Those needing Doc's mystery-
solving help are passed along to one of his aides, operating
apparently in the reception room of Doc's 86th floor
headquarters. How else to explain all those people who have
come to see Doc at his office since then? We can further
reason that the job office does no further questioning than if
the person wants financial help or Doc's more usual kind of
help, because shady characters have made it to Doc's door, so
the use of the lie detector seems to have been discontinued by
the lower floor office.

Doc's "speed ship" is a "smaller, single-motored" plane;
it is destroyed. He also uses a bronze-colored tri-motor during
the adventure, his nineteenth. At one point, while in the
Other World, "Doc was probably more frightened than at any

time in his career", which is quite a statement, considering some of the jams he has been in the past ten years of his career.

The Spotted Men (3 days) takes place in the summer, referring to a "loaded hayrack" and "green lawns", indicating late June at the earliest. It can be placed in 1939, because its LPO precludes a 1940 placement and Summer 1938 is a rather full sequence. It likely continues the 1939 placements begun with *The Other World*.

Doc disguises himself as a steel worker during the adventure and "might have been any of a dozen ... strapping big men". A dozen men over 6'4" in one place in 1939? Captured thugs in this adventure are "turned over to the police", but "later ... sent to the bronze man's criminal 'college'". In the past, Doc has had his prisoners spirited away before the police even know of them.

"J. Henry Mason consulted Doc Savage ... in regard to" "T.3 ... steel", the "toughest and strongest steel known – and ... also the lightest". This alloy may have been created using benlanium from *The Mystery on the Snow*, which would explain Doc's involvement. The "T" in "T.3" may stand for "titanium", which is what benlanium seems to be.

The Evil Gnome (7 days) takes place during "early winter". It's implied that it is 1940 (and could be with an LPO of January 19, 1940) but the situation mentioned seems to describe the political climate just prior to the Winter War, which began on November 30, 1939. These events were precipitated by the German invasion of Poland in September 1939 (there is a reference to "war-torn Europe"). The "neutral nation" "that was about to be gobbled up" would then be Finland. The November placement matches "the brilliant foliage of such trees as had not yet lost their leaves" comment (which contradicts the "winter" comment, although there are some trees "naked of leaves"; more than once, Dent used "early winter" to refer to technically still-late Fall). Although the one-day prologue occurs on a "warm summer day", later comments imply that less than a week passes between this prologue and the story (the first day of the adventure is

"Thursday", and the "Monday" preceding it is when the prologue seems to occur); the "summer" is probably an editorial "correction" that is actually incorrect. Since this is almost certainly the case, the intervening days are counted in the length of the adventure. It is implied that Doc is at the Fortress prior to this story, returning Friday (he is out of town and cannot be contacted, the same description given in earlier adventures when Doc is at the Fortress).

Doc now has a "private lift in" "the back of the lobby". Over the "up" button is a plaque with his name on it. This seems not to be Doc's private express elevator, because although its rapid speed is mentioned, it does not force Lion Ellison, a woman, to her knees. Doc's private lift does this even to Monk, if you remember. And later, Doc's "private ... secret ... elevator" is mentioned. This first elevator is possibly dramatic license, because no passenger elevator runs from the lobby above the 80th floor. There would be no point for Doc to install (a very unlikely possibility) or appropriate one that only goes to the 80th floor. On the other hand, perhaps Doc has gimmicked this one elevator to deal with troublesome visitors (i.e., criminals). If so, it is likely the elevator mentioned in *Dust of Death*. It seems probable that it is also the one used in *The Feathered Octopus*, which goes to an interviewing room. But if so, why is it only apparently used these three times in nearly five years?

"There was another small door at the side of the elevator" on the 86th floor. This must be the door to the operating room, as described in *The Green Death*. The hallways are bare now; previously they were decorated (in *The Czar of Fear* (August 1932) and *The Man Who Shook the Earth* (February 1933)). This change, also mentioned in *The Angry Ghost* (September 1938), was probably part of the re-modeling Doc did prior to *Mystery Under the Sea* (September 1934), in August 1934.

The Hidalgo Trading Company hangar "from the outside looks like an ordinary brick warehouse", confirming its brick facade. Ham thinks "Doc puts more time in on memory development than anything else in that daily exercise routine" of his.

Doc says: "It has often occurred to me to wonder whether the human race might not be fundamentally evil". He tells his prime suspect this and may be saying it to draw him out, however. He must surely not believe this entirely, or else he would not attempt to rehabilitate criminals through the college.

One of Doc's graduates from his crime college helps Doc out; he believes he got his amnesia in an accident. He lies and steals to get information for Doc.

Consider that for a moment.

Doc does not explicitly tell the man to do so; he asks the graduate to get whatever information he can, and the man does so because he's grateful to Doc for saving his life after that horrible "accident" he had. And he breaks the law to do so (the information is in confidential bank files). This seems to suggest that Doc's graduates are unable to commit crimes – but only if they **believe** they are doing wrong. Since Doc would never ask them to do something wrong, anything he does ask them to do must be all right, according to their newly-instilled code of morals (remember, they are taught to hate crime at the college). Could part of their conditioning be to do whatever Doc asks them to do? Every graduate we have met thus far has been very grateful to Doc and would do anything to repay him. This is explicitly stated on more than one occasion. It is also curious that Doc, who is repeatedly said to be "a genuinely modest man", would let the graduates know they are deeply indebted to him.

The Boss of Terror (3 days) seems to take place during the fall; "It's been cold for a week" and there's a "mat of dead leaves" but there is also "foliage", and some of the trees still seem to have leaves. It is probably November in this story. With an LPO of February 16, 1940, this is almost certainly November 1939, following *The Evil Gnome*. There is "moonlight" but also "intense ... darkness" so it may be shortly after the new moon of November 11. This puts *The Evil Gnome* in the first week of November, the first day being Monday, October 30.

"The ventriloquist known as the Great Lander had taught the bronze man ... the art of 'throwing' the voice; he had taught Doc to imitate other voices, and make them seem to come from very far away".

The Flying Goblin (10 days) begins on a "warm night" but there is the "war in Europe", which started September 1, 1939. Its LPO precludes it from taking place on a warm night in Spring 1940, so it must be September 1939, probably while it is still summer (there are still leaves on trees, as well).

The warehouse hangar has "a small office that was in a corner of the large hangar building". This is not the office mentioned in *The South Pole Terror*, because it is not staffed, and it is inside the building.

The college is described as a "long, many-windowed building" which "looked like a modern city institution", a "hospital". This is viewed from a distance, so it is not clear if this building is in addition to the ones described in *Mad Mesa*, but this seems to be the likeliest explanation. There is no mention of the fence described in the latter tale, but this could be due to the distance involved; the sign itself is too far away to see, let alone read. A patient there is freed between the surgery and his "treatments", confirming that the initial surgery brings amnesia; he still has his taste for killing.

A section of wall in the lab containing windows opens up, apparently like French doors. This wall must be the southeast, the one which faces "lower New York Bay".

Bogart, the author of this tale, while producing some entertaining adventures, often seems like watered-down Dent.

The Purple Dragon (5 days) is said to begin on "August 1, 1940". This is the date that "Hiram Shalleck", one of Doc's graduates, wakes up remembering his previous life as Joe Mavrick, the right-hand man of Pal Hatrack, the "big boy" of Chicago in 1929 (who would seem to be Al Capone, therefore; note the similarity of first names). He is killed that same day. With an LPO of June 21, 1940, the adventure cannot occur in August 1940. It must be placed in 1939 – if we are to keep the "August" part of the date – despite numerous remarks to the passage of time indicating it is the year 1940. Or does it actually occur in 1940 in a month other than August? We shall have to wait and see what the placements for 1940 hold to decide. "A week" or so passes, and Doc learns of Shalleck's death on "the twelfth", the first day of the adventure.

There is reference to "the latest Doc Savage magazine" (if this adventure occurs in 1939, this would be *The Crimson Serpent*, in the August 1939 issue, which went on sale July 21. *Poison Island*, in the September issue, would not be on newsstands until August 18). Doc and his aides use an "apartment [that] was one all of Doc's aids used occasionally for sleeping quarters"; it is located on 81st Street. "A small dressing room" is part of Doc's "sleeping quarters" in or next to the lab, last mentioned in *The Land of Fear* (also by Davis).

This story makes it clear that Doc was operating solo prior to *The Man of Bronze*, and that Doc's college was in use by 1929: "Doc had been on another case" in Chicago in "1929" when he captured many of Hatrack's henchmen, sending them to the college. The graduates are "sent back into the world under new names ... far from the scene of their original crimes". There is no mention of the notorious "crime gland".

Tunnel Terror (4 days) also gives us a specific date: The third day of the adventure is "August 3rd". There is a "moon ... like a white, round face" on the first night of the adventure, a "Saturday night". The only time during Doc's career from *The Man of Bronze* until this adventure's LPO of May 17, 1940, that "August 3rd" is a Monday is 1936. So this adventure must take place just before *The Forgotten Realm*, which begins in late August (disrupting no sequence there, by the way). The full moon in August 1936 occurs on August 3, which also fits, confirming that this adventure was published far out of sequence.

Doc's perfect symmetry is mentioned, but "compared to Monk, Doc suddenly became a giant". Monk is only just over five feet tall, so this isn't much of a claim. If Doc was actually as tall as his original height is described (about six feet), he would still be "a giant" "compared to Monk".

In *The Awful Egg* (18 days), it is "hot" and not "during the winter" so it can follow *The Purple Dragon* in August 1939. Its LPO prevents a 1940 placement, also (despite the history of the *South Orion*, which "went down months ago", being "one of the first ships sunk in the war").

"All of his life, [Monk] had ... a private horror that some day someone might shoot him with a shotgun".

Johnny has "seen an old hen lay an egg when she was scared". This suggests he was raised on a farm. His "I'll be superamalgamated" catchphrase gives his identity away to a villain during the adventure. Johnny started using big words "early in his career, when he was very young". His behavior in this adventure indicates it is not difficult for him to use small words (although saying the "I'll be superamalgamated" phrase seems to be a habit which he cannot break).

There is "an elevator in the back" of the lobby, which takes Nancy to an interviewing room on the "twentieth floor". This is the elevator described in *The Evil Gnome* (which follows this adventure chronologically). Doc seems to have appropriated a normal building elevator for his use. We are not told if this elevator goes to Doc's 86th floor, but if not, Monk and Ham would have to take an elevator to the lobby, and then back up to the interviewing room, since Doc's private express elevator makes no stops between the 86th floor and the lobby. Doc uses "a filtering system whereby people with real business were separated from autograph-hunters and curiosity-lookers" and those seeking financial assistance (as described in *The Other World*). We are not told exactly how this "system" works, but we do know that:

> Visitors are sent to an office on the ground floor to determine if they seek financial help or mystery-adventure help.

If they need mystery-adventure help, they sometimes are first interviewed on a lower floor (usually by Monk and Ham, the two aides who most often appear in the adventures).

Sometimes, a visitor goes directly to the 86th floor headquarters.

Sometimes, at Doc's headquarters, they are greeted by one or more aide while Doc is busy in the lab, or otherwise unavailable.

Sometimes, they are met by Doc himself, with or without his aides.

It seems likely that Doc's headquarters are notified of someone wanting to see Doc by the financial office on the "ground floor", though this is not always described in the stories. If Doc is available (that is, not busy with an experiment and willing to see visitors), the person is sent up to the 86th floor. If any of Doc's aides are at the headquarters and Doc is **not** receiving visitors, they tell the office to send the person to the interviewing room and go there themselves. If none of Doc's aides are at headquarters, the person is sent up to see Doc himself. This system seems to describe the various events concerning Doc's visitors throughout the last several adventures. But since all the elevators must stop at the 80th floor for the transfer to the single elevator servicing the upper floors, why go to all this bother? Ordinary people – normal visitors to the Empire State Building – could take an elevator to the 80th floor to transfer to the one taking them to the Observation Deck, on the true 86th floor of the building. So, we are left with three options:

Doc uses an imperfect screening system; that is, it screens only those visitors who go through normal channels, announcing they're on their way to see Doc. People seeking to do harm to Doc can – and have, on numerous occasions – bypass this system.

Doc's headquarters are on a floor below the 80th (we already know it was not on the 86th as described), and therefore the one elevator Doc's appropriated is the only one which is able to stop at his floor.

Doc's headquarters are above the 80th floor, and the screening room is also above the 80th floor, so that no elevator (only one, at this height, remember) is able to stop at his floor without first stopping at the screening room, if Doc desires it.

There is evidence to both support and contradict each of the above scenarios. Considering all of the evidence, the first scenario fits most of the descriptions of visitors coming to see Doc. And, any unannounced visitor (those bypassing the screening process) are automatically suspect.

The Headless Men (3 days) takes place during "September" and "early Fall", which fits the placement of *The Awful Egg*. A "sliver of a moon" is visible, so this adventure would seem to take place shortly after the new moon of September 13, 1939. However, that is still technically summer, so more likely, this points to a placement in 1938, when the new moon occurred on September 23, the first day of Fall. In fact, the only other year in the series to date that all these facts match is 1935; although, "early Fall" may be used here the way "early winter" has sometimes been used to describe November, and "early summer", June" – although "early Fall" can be quite hot and thought of as "late Summer" instead.

The Life of Doc Savage book has been published (the author and publisher are not mentioned, however. Are they "Robeson" and Street & Smith, who put out the DOC SAVAGE magazine?). Lynda Ladore "left the reception room", going into "a small side room where a mirror could be seen from the door[way]", apparently a bathroom. It has "an emergency door" which opens into the corridor. Doc's police rank is now that of "commissioner", and he is addressed as such by a police officer. Doc uses his one-man speed plane which does "four hundred" miles an hour, last used in *The Gold Ogre*; it's damaged during the course of the adventure. Monk "had seen chickens race half the length of a barnyard after decapitation", which suggests he grew up on a farm.

In the reception room, there is a "big walnut" "desk in the center of the room" (it's destroyed). This seems not to be the large inlaid table mentioned in almost every description of the room, though that table is not described in this adventure. This adventure is the first written by Alan Hathway, so this may be an error on his part. In fact, there are numerous mistakes in this story: A character's eyes change color, the warehouse hangar is said to have "wood siding", and "Ham usually wound up higher in the favor of feminine acquaintances than Monk did" (this explicitly contradicts past statements and scenes), among others. It also suggests that, being written by a ghost writer, this adventure very well may belong in 1938 – where it does not disturb a sequence – not 1939, well out of sequence, and this is where I have placed it.

Doc's fourth dirigible, the "big ship" which uses helium, is destroyed in this adventure. This is the one that debuted in *The Green Death*, in early 1938. Hereafter, Doc will only use "small" dirigibles, perhaps aware that their time has passed.

The Awful Dynasty (about 36 days) occurs during a "Leap Year", and therefore begins the placements for 1940. Further, the fifth night of the adventure is "a fairly warm night", so it is not winter. On the twelfth night, the "moon" makes the landscape "almost white", and is probably very near a full moon. This day, according to the story, is a Saturday. Therefore, the full moon is probably that of April 22, a Monday, or July 19, a Friday. "It looked as if there was going to be rain"; this suggests April, but it is not conclusive. With no more evidence, we will leave this adventure temporarily unplaced.

Ham speaks Egyptian (actually Arabic), but has trouble following a conversation in that language. At the beginning of the adventure, Doc is working on "a treatise on a new type of brain surgery that was going to startle a good part of the world". Is this the surgery criminals undergo at the college? Monk is so serious about marrying Princess Amen-Amen that Ham and the others send him a telegram supposedly from his wife in New York, effectively sabotaging his relationship with the princess.

Long Tom's "eyes lighted happily" at the sight of Pat, and when she is in danger, he thinks "if anything should happen to lovely Pat --". This is the only reference to these feelings, and since this adventure was written by Bogart, this account may be inaccurate (also recall that he played up feelings between Monk and Pat, as well, in two previous adventures).

In *Devils of the Deep* (about 21 days), "it was cold in New York" City so it must be late fall, winter or early spring during this adventure. It is also "after war started" in Europe, so it continues the seasonal placements ending 1939 (or beginning 1940). An LPO of July 19, 1940 prevents a later placement. Doc has spent the "two weeks" prior to the adventure investigating in Central America "on a confidential mission for the government" which leads into the adventure.

Doc's plane is "golden-colored"; this may be a Davis "typo" for "bronze-colored". This is probably Doc's nineteenth tri-motor, chronologically last described in *The Other World*, where it debuted. Unbelievably, Monk "had never been accused of being a masher before", being falsely accused in this adventure. We learn that Doc expects to die in action during a case.

The Men Vanished (about 10 days) occurs before "November", and is not March, April, May or June, nor November or December of the previous year (because it is not the "Igapo", a type of stormy season), leaving us with July, August or September, and only the first half of September because of the adventure's LPO. Central Park is a "luxuriant green" and people are "sleeping on the grass", confirming that it is summer during this adventure. The "Explorers League" gives its medal to Doc, an occurrence which "came but once in each ten years". This also suggests it is 1940. This may or may not be the "Explorers' Club" mentioned in *The Awful Dynasty*. Since this is the first of warm-month placements for year, we'll tentatively place it in July, the beginning of the summer; this also suggests that *The Awful Dynasty* began in April rather than July.

We also learn that Doc's Fortress has been moved since *Fortress of Solitude*. This move probably occurred in early 1939, when months pass without (recorded) incident. Monk says of himself: "Liar is my middle name".

Pat's apartment is "on Park Avenue". Upon learning that the missing Daniel Stage has a sister, Pat asks: "Good-looking?" And the text states: "Pat had an inner impulse to distrust all women". No explanation is given for this feeling. Growing up without a mother might help explain this, but Pat had the mother-figure of her Indian womanservant Tiny. Ham's Midas Club seems to be down Park Avenue (southwest) from Pat's apartment.

"A rather quiet young man" who is "the proprietor" of "a small garage far uptown" (he "lived in an apartment above the place") drives an ambulance to Doc's college; he seems not to be a graduate (he knows his passengers are criminals but does not know what goes on at the college) and his relationship with Doc is not explained further.

The villain of this story, Daniel Stage (who also uses the name "Rollo Marbetti") wears a mask that gives his face the appearance of exactly half of it having been horribly disfigured. This character may have been the inspiration for Batman's foe Two-Face --similarly afflicted – whose real name was "Harvey **Dent**".

The Devil's Playground (3 days) takes place during the "summer", which fits with the July placement of the last adventure. The second night is a "moonless night". This may be the new moon on August 3, 1940. The night before is cloudy, but this is not mentioned the following night in connection to it being "moonless".

118

It also tells us the new location of the Fortress. Thugs believe they have located the Fortress "thirty minutes" (roughly 100-150 miles) beyond "the low-lying Laurentian Mountains, into the subarctic area of the Hudson Bay", apparently in the vicinity of Mansel Island. But Doc notes that this location is "five hundred miles from [the] Fortress of Solitude"; he has given them a false location. The direction is not stated, but it must surely be north of the presumed site. This would put the Fortress in the area of the Foxe Basin, perhaps on a small island, on the southern coast of Baffin Island or on Melville Peninsula. This seems to be very close to its earlier location, only a few hundred miles to the south. Mattson Kovisti "had read snatches about" the Fortress. Doubtless this referred to a nameless retreat of Doc's, since it is supposed to be a secret and its name would not be publicly known. Doc is at the Fortress at the beginning of the adventure, and has apparently been there for a short time. He had sent Monk and Ham to investigate the situation in this story "two weeks" prior to the beginning of the adventure.

"Doc's aids held honorary posts in the Civil Aeronautics Authority". Monk is sure "that [Iris Heller] was meant to be the only [woman] in his life". He speaks Ojibway during this adventure, apparently well but not fluently and he "can understand Finland talk". Dent, through the villain of the story, predicts that "our country and [Russia] might sometime be enemies". Johnny gets struck on the head and has temporary amnesia, lasting less than a day. Doc has "a new gas" which causes "slow-motion" movement.

Bequest of Evil (17 days) starts on a "Monday" in "August". It fits with the two previous Summer 1940 placements. On the following Monday night, the "land was bathed in white brightness", probably from a full moon. The full moon was Saturday, August 17, so the adventure must have begun on Monday, August 12.

Although Monk inheriting a castle and British title is a hoax in this story, he may be legitimately related to the true heirs (this is not resolved in the story). The true "Earl of Chester" looks so much like Monk that the presence of a scar on Monk must be used by the villain to tell them apart. It seems highly unlikely that a Monk-double also named "Mayfair" would not be related to Monk (he is also a "British secret agent").

The Fortress of Solitude is said to be "deep within the Arctic Circle". This does not match the location referred to in *The Devil's Playground*, but **does** match descriptions of its original location. In fact, the last adventure was written by Hathway and this one by Bogart, so it is difficult to decide whom to believe. Presumably Bogart, the most prolific of the ghost writers, would have had the more accurate information.

There is a "dressing room" apparently next to the reception room; this is probably the room described in *The Headless Men*. Doc and his aides spend what must be at least a few days ferrying scientists back to inhabited Canada from Death Island following the adventure.

The All-White Elf (4 days) also seems to place in the summer. It is after the "blitzkrieg" in September 1939 and there is "short grass", and "leaves" on trees, and a "sunburned" man, so it likely follows *Bequest of Evil* in Summer 1940.

"Renny Renwick towered alongside Doc Savage, but he lacked the bronze man's symmetrical physical build". This seems to suggest that Renny is at least not significantly shorter than Doc, if not actually taller, as the earliest descriptions state. Renny also knows quite a bit about sailing.

"Although Alec and Joe had graduated from the 'college', they had no knowledge of its real nature". The driver mentioned in *The Men Vanished* may be a graduate, after all, then.

The villain's device uses both "microlength radio waves and sonic vibration in ultrashort wave lengths", like Long Tom's bug zapper (which is not mentioned here) and various devices from other adventures (such as *White Eyes* and *The Roar Devil*, for example).

The Golden Man (about 116 days) begins on "a hot night", probably following *The All-White Elf* in mid September 1940. Its LPO precludes a 1941 placement and a reference to "war refugees" rules out 1939. The prologue is about ten days long, after which Monk and Ham spend "fourteen weeks" (also "three months and two weeks", which is actually fifteen weeks) "in jail" in South America. The adventure itself is only three days long.

During his aides' absence, Doc has "a worldwide detective agency" search for them; this sounds like his own agency composed of graduates, but it is not described as such. Ham is able to speak a little Portugese.

The "Golden Man" tells Doc, "you were born on the tiny schooner *Orion* in the shallow cove at the north end of Andros Island". This is as much as we are told about Doc's birth in the entire series. Although the "Andros Island" mentioned by the Golden Man is not specified whether it is the one in the Caribbean Sea or the one in the Mediterranean Sea, we can make an educated guess as to its location: Given Doc's father's interest in Central America – he made at least two trips there around 1910, according to *The Man of Bronze* and *They Died Twice* – the island is likely located in the Caribbean Sea.

In response to this revelation, "Doc was floored, figuratively ... by the fact that this golden man knew the exact place of his birth. It was astounding. Doc himself had known of no living man who had those facts. His five aides did not know. It was in no written record". So this raises an issue: How did Hest come by this information?

What Doc believes about the availability of the information about his birth cannot literally be true. Hest got it, somehow; he says: "The intelligence departments of most leading nations know things that apparently no one could know". Because Doc is a thorough individual, we can infer that he knows for fact that there are no eyewitnesses to his birth still alive, and that there are no official records pertaining to his birth in existence. This leaves us with three indirect methods of getting this information: An eyewitness told someone of Doc's birth, and that confidante was contacted; an eyewitness left an unofficial written account of Doc's birth, such as a diary, and this was discovered by someone and it came into Hest's hands; or a confidante of an eyewitness left an unofficial written account of Doc's birth, and it came into Hest's hands. Unfortunately, we do not have further clues to guide us, but it does not seem too unreasonable that someone like Hubert Robertson, the elder Savage's partner on his discovery of the Valley of the Vanished – now dead, fitting what Doc "had known" about "no living man" having "those facts" about his birth – might, at one time, have known of the circumstances of Doc's birth.

And this tale raises a thornier issue: What was the "unnamed nation" that the "Golden Man" – "Paul Hest ... chief of intelligence for" work for? He was sent, he claimed, to prevent "another nation" from framing his country for a U-boat attack. At first glance, the Golden Man's home country would seem to be Germany (his true name is "Hest"), with Great Britain doing the framing in order to bring America into the war. It may be Great Britain, instead, that the Golden Man works for, for the following reasons: While it is known that Great Britain, in its history, allowed at least one ship (the *Lusitania*) to be sunk by Germans in order to gain world support (particularly from America), it is quite another to do the sinking itself, and; if exposed, Great Britain had much to lose – the help it was already getting from America through lend-lease – and little to gain; Churchill knew Roosevelt believed war with Germany was inevitable (thus, Germany had little to lose by this ruse). Another theory which takes this view into account was put forth by Rick Lai; keeping Hest German, it posits that Germany framed Great Britain for framing **it** for the ship sinkings. I prefer Rick's theory to either of the other two.

Baron Orrest Karl Lestzky, Doc's "friend" who is mentioned by the Golden Man, is one of a "few great surgeons who really understands [Doc's] new brain-operating technique". Is this a reference to the surgery performed at the college? Was Lestzky, in fact, Doc's surgical tutor? The Golden Man knows of Doc's past, which Doc himself believes is known by "no living man", so it would not be beyond the Golden Man to know of the college as well.

During *The Pink Lady* (3 days), "it was hot", and the adventure takes place at "high-spring tide", which occurs on a full or new moon. Its LPO precludes a 1941 placement, so it must occur in 1940, probably after *The Awful Dynasty*, where it would not interrupt a sequence.

Monk owns "a summer place", a "shack", which "had not been used for a long time". It is located "out of the city", but in "the State" of New York, "on the [Hudson] river". Monk is wearing the fake molars that "Doc used to wear" (he has since grown "wisdom teeth" and is unable to use them).

In *The Magic Forest* (about 34 days), begins in "early spring", so it, too, occurs out of sequence. While its LPO allows a 1941 placement, it likely occurs the same spring as *The Pink Lady* in 1940, and probably precedes that adventure. On (roughly) the thirty-third night, the "moon" is "white and bright", so this is likely the full moon of April 22, putting the first day in late March, near the first day of spring.

"Renny was a charter member" "of the International Society of Master Engineers". Monk claims "Doc only sees visitors by appointment, and then only after we've completely investigated their cases", which is not exactly true.

"The elevators" are correctly said to be "down the hall" from Doc's reception room, and Doc's "high-speed, express elevator [is] farther down the hall", as I previously suggested. "It ran without stop to the ground floor of the skyscraper", correctly implying that the public passenger elevator does not.

Following the end of the adventure, Doc spends "several weeks" in Alaska. This likely takes up the better part of the month of May 1940.

123

But if we place *The Magic Forest* in spring 1940, *The Awful Dynasty* cannot occur in April, but must begin July 8, and end very near the beginning of *Bequest of Evil* on August 12. This places *The Devil's Playground* in early July, with Doc spending probably the last half of June at his Fortress of Solitude. *The Men Vanished* would then occur in the first half of that month, and *The Pink Lady* shortly before that. But *The Men Vanished* **cannot** occur in June (because of the "Igapo"), and so must be switched with *The Devil's Playground*. Then, because *The Pink Lady* occurs near a new or full moon, it probably occurs in mid May. A simpler solution would be to place *The Magic Forest* in spring 1939, where only *The Other World* is placed (it would therefore have to be moved earlier by a month). This would allow the sequence of *The Men Vanished* through *The Golden Man* (five adventures) to remain in sequence, with *The Pink Lady* preceding them, as suggested earlier, and contradicts nothing in *The Magic Forest*.

With the placements for 1940 finished, we can now see that the only time that *The Purple Dragon* could occur that year is in January. Since the year does not seem to be particularly important, and we can easily imagine Davis "updating" the file for the current year, it is probably better to leave this in August 1939.

The Mindless Monsters (2 days) takes place in "early Fall". Further, a bank is doing "month-end clearing" so it is the very end of September or the very beginning of October. A 1941 placement is ruled out on the basis of LPO. Since *The Golden Man* runs from September 1940 to January 1941, and cannot be moved to 1939, this adventure cannot be placed in 1940, either. It must occur in Fall 1939 between *The Flying_Goblin* and *The Evil Gnome* (in November).

"Monk maintained an experimental laboratory in Queens", "the existence [of which] was a secret which the bronze man and his five aids shared with no one else" (this is not Monk's Wall Street lab, needless to say). Doc is "an honorary deputy police commissioner" and uses a "four-motor transport" (which we have decided are actually tri-motors; this one is still probably his nineteenth. Hathway, the author of this story, was a friend of Davis, and must have been using the latter's notes about Doc's planes). Doc and his men use "a deaf-and-dumb sign language improved by Doc for complete expression with one hand". Doc has recently installed a prototype virtual reality chamber in his lab: It is a "corridorlike room" which uses a magnetic field and "haze gas" to disorient its victims and three-dimensional projectors to complete the effect.

The Rustling Death (4 days) takes place after the "two years" of "The World's Fair", most likely the 1939 New York City World's Fair, so it is almost certainly 1941. The third day is "the 10th" of "May", and this rules out a 1942 placement based on the story's LPO. This definitively places *The Magic Forest* earlier than 1941, as we suspected.

Doc uses a "huge four-motor transport" (which is destroyed; it is probably his nineteenth tri-motor). The references to four-motor planes have all been made by Dent ghost writers, not Dent himself. On the rare occasions that Dent does describe the planes, they are tri-motors. Usually, Dent does not bother to describe the number of motors, anymore. Doc has installed ejector seats in his planes (for the event of an uncontrolled descent).

There is a "small dirigible" in the warehouse hangar. This is Doc's fifth one, a replacement for the "big" one destroyed in *The Headless Men* (September 1938). A "dirigible" is mentioned in *The Mindless Monsters* (October 1939), but its size is not referred to; that is likely the first (published) appearance of this fifth dirigible.

"The bronze hair of Doc Savage loomed above the crowd". This height is more in line with Doc's initial description, and was probably taken from Dent's notebook by Hathway; Dent now routinely describes Doc as well over six feet tall in the adventures.

The villain's device uses "neutrons, with electrons and ultrasonic waves", in two beams. It is similar to Long Tom's second bug-zapper.

The Green Eagle (9 days) takes place in the late spring or early fall (June or September); it is "hot" during the day but "bitterly cold" at night in the mountains of Wyoming. It cannot follow *The Rustling Death* in 1941 because of its LPO, so must occur 1940 or earlier. Placing it in September 1940 would disrupt the sequence there, and it is crowded, so we will consider Spring 1940. On the first night, "the moonlight was very bright". Because of the specific lunar data in this adventure, it must occur near the full moon of June 19, placing *The Pink Lady* near the new moon on June 6. Doc is on the case for "four days" before the beginning of the adventure.

Doc recently "had discontinued the practice" of painting "his planes a distinctive bronze color" because "it had made him too conspicuous". In fact, the comment in *Devils of The Deep*, just weeks earlier, about his plane being "golden" may have been accurate, changed from its bronze color mentioned in *The Other World* (Spring 1939), a full year earlier, so this change has taken place just prior to *Devils of The Deep*, late in 1939 or early in 1940. In the past, some of his tri-motor planes have been described as being "bronze" in color, but not all of them (this has been noted in the chronology; for the record, Doc's seventh, tenth, sixteenth, seventeenth and nineteenth tri-motors have specifically described as being bronze-colored. His eighteenth one may have been, also. His nineteenth tri-motor, which debuted in *The Other World* (March 1939), survives until *The Rustling Death* (May 1941), more than two years, unbelievably, being repainted about halfway through its life. Often, the color of the tri-motors is not mentioned, but it is probably safe to assume that once Doc began painting them (with no later than his seventh one, which debuted in 1933), he did not discontinue this practice until we are told about it; therefore, I would conclude that his eighth, ninth, eleventh, et al. were also bronze-colored. Occasionally, one of Doc's other planes (such as the speed monoplane) has been referred to as "silver", but none of them as "bronze".

Mystery Island (3 days) takes place "months" after "last summer", so it is probably Spring, during "the ... war", because near Florida, although it is "excessively hot" in early afternoon, it is merely "warm" in late afternoon and "cool" and "balmy" at night. By comparison, Fall would only be "weeks" after "last summer", not "months". In New York City, there is a "cool harshness" to the night air. Its LPO is May 16, 1941, so it probably occurs shortly before this, beginning the Spring 1941 seasonal sequence.

Johnny's Uncle Ned is ill in this story. Monk "used to have" "a hound named Ponto". A super-firer "shoots seven hundred and eighty-six bullets a minute", according to Monk. As in *The Man Who Shook the Earth*, the villain uses electricity run into rock strata to create earth upheavals.

Doc and his aides have been in Charleston, South Carolina for a "few days" (on an unrelated matter) before the adventure begins (although Doc is said to be there "serving in a consulting capacity with the government engineers for that new fortified zone they're laying out around Charleston", it seems odd that all of Doc's aides are with him. Renny, probably, but what about the others? What kind of business would they have other than the type that usually brings them together? So, there may be an unrecorded adventure that ended in Charleston, and Doc was asked to stay on and consult).

During *Birds of Death* (6 days) it seems to be warm in New York but not summer because deeply tanned men are considered unusual. It is "warm" in northern Africa, not hot, so it likely takes place sometime from October to May. It probably occurs after *Mystery Island* in Spring 1941.

Monk and Ham are screening visitors "five floors" above the entrance level to Doc's skyscraper. The office is reached by using "the private ... elevator around the corner" in the lobby. This location matches earlier ones of Doc's public elevator.

Monk knows some of the Egyptian language, Arabic.

Peril in the North (3 days) seems to begin on Doc's birthday. Shortly before midnight on the first day of the adventure, his aides attempt to throw him a birthday party. It is not clear why they waited until almost midnight to do so, unless the **following** day is Doc's birthday. There is "untrimmed shrubbery and a lawn that needed mowing", and the metal of a car at night is "cold" (so is river water). But the "midnight sun" is present near Greenland, so it must be between May 25 and July 25, and likely continues the Spring 1941 sequence. Further, it is merely "mild" in the Arctic, just "a few degrees" below freezing, so not summer. It is "intensely dark" on the first night, and later, "the night was, if possible, darker than before", so it is very probably on the night of the new moon, May 25, putting this adventure after *The Rustling Death*, in May 1941. This suggests that Doc's birthday is probably May 26.

Pat has "snitched Monk's key out of his pocket" to get into Doc's headquarters. The circumstances surrounding this event are not elaborated upon. Monk makes a speech about being willing to sacrifice his life in the pursuit of rescuing some people that brings tears to Doc's eyes.

Once again prescient, Dent talks of a "dictator [who] committed suicide while besieged in his chancellory". This turns out to be a hoax, and the dictator has had a double killed in his place so he could escape. Eerily, the corpse of a Hitler double was found by the Russians outside the German chancellory before Hitler's body was found inside.

The Invisible-Box Murders (4 days) begins on a "Friday", which is a "hot" day. Since it is "warm" at night, it is probably summer (there are also "night insects"). With an LPO of August 15, 1941, it could be placed in Summer 1941, following *The Rustling Death*, possibly in June, beginning the summer sequence. Doc and his aides "started investigating this thing, three days ago", apparently "after the first three of those mysterious murders".

"The training [of Doc] was the idea of his parents". This is the first recorded mention of Doc's mother's involvement in his upbringing since *The Yellow Cloud*, the only other account thus far in the series to include Doc's mother (and that story was written by a ghost writer, if you recall).

Doc states that his police commission is "Inspector", and since Doc (and more importantly, Dent) is speaking here, we must conclude that this is his correct commission, and other comments by Dent's ghost writers (and other characters) have been in error; of course, it is also quite possible that Doc's rank has risen over the years, and he may have, in fact, been promoted from "Captain", his earliest described rank, in addition to some errors in statements.

There is now a hood on Doc's bulletproof vests. Ham has taught Chemistry to tie knots. Pat has learned to lip read "in her spare time".

Long Tom lives in a "shabby" "building ... on Amsterdam"; "few ... knew of the place", and may be the lab mentioned in *Spook Hole*. His "car was an elderly rattletrap containing ... an airplane motor". This may be the automobile from *The Polar Treasure* (Spring 1932), where it was new, now nine years old. It is almost certainly the one mentioned in *The Yellow Cloud* (Spring 1938); the descriptions are nearly identical.

Men of Fear (6 days) takes place during "hurricane season", meaning late summer – late August or September. A November 21, 1941 LPO allows a 1941 placement, so it follows *The Invisible-Box Murders* in Summer 1941. On the third night of the adventure, "the moon [was] too bright", and so is probably near the full moon of September 5.

Doc's graduates are "trained to hate crime and wrongdoing". Once again, there is no mention of treating the "crime gland". "The usual system [for transporting captured criminals to the college] was for an ambulance to come down" from the place. The incident in *The Men Vanished* must therefore be an isolated case.

In *The Man Who Fell Up* (3 days), the "temperature was low", but there are "foliage" and fog, so it is probably mid spring or mid fall. Its LPO is April 17, 1942, so it probably occurs late in 1941, possibly late October, ending a seasonal sequence begun with *The Invisible-Box Murders*. Further, although Nazis are the (unnamed) villains in the story, there is no reference to the U.S. being at war with them, so this adventure almost certainly occurs before the U.S.'s entry into the war on December 8, 1941.

Doc has a "private apartment" "a dozen floors" down from the 86th floor, and has had it "for some time"; not even his aides know of it. It may be that this apartment was the home of Doc and his father prior to *The Man of Bronze*. What little we know of the elder Savage makes it seem unlikely that he lived in Doc's Spartan quarters at the back of the lab. The reception room and library – even the hallway outside – are sumptuously decorated. In retrospect, it seems clear that the 86th floor rooms were the elder Savage's **offices**, not his living quarters. It also seems probable that Doc's small quarters in the lab were not in use in the early days of Doc's career; the villains who broke into Doc's office from an adjoining office (in *Pirate of the Pacific*) probably did so from that area. If Doc has had this apartment from the very beginning – under another name, of course, or else some villain would have attacked him there sometime during the series – that would explain how he has a secret elevator to it; we know it's very unlikely Doc was installing elevators after the skyscraper had been built. It is also interesting to note that the outline to this adventure calls the **85**th floor Doc's HQ, not the 86th. Did Dent accidentally give away **two** of Doc's secrets?

We are told that "when Ham became precise in speech, it meant he was very angry".

"The strange upbringing of Doc Savage had been the idea of his father, who had had a fixation of bringing up a son who would be a kind of modern knight"; "The fixation of the elder Savage ... was the result of some terrible thing that had happened to him, but the son had never learned exactly what it was". This is as complete an explanation of Doc's father's motive concerning his son's career as we have been given thus far in the series. As in the vast majority of such accounts, Doc's mother is not mentioned.

Bob Caston, one of Doc's graduates, "operated the newsstand in the south lobby of the building" containing Doc's headquarters. "Bob understood vaguely that, in some way, he owed a great debt to Doc Savage, although he did not know exactly what it was". "He knew that he owed his prosperity to Doc, so he was particularly anxious to please" Doc.

"Pat Savage was not supposed to understand the Mayan lingo", but she has "talked Monk into teaching it to" her. How she accomplished this is not described. However, she spoke it in *The Terror in the Navy* (April 1935) and understood it even earlier in *The Fantastic Island* (November 1934). The latter was written by Johnson, and may be a mistake. But *The Terror in the Navy* was written by Dent, as was this one.

The Too-Wise Owl (3 days) begins on a "very cold" "Tuesday" in "September". The second day is "the eighteenth of" the month. The only time in Doc's career thus far these three chronological facts are true is in September 1935 and 1940. On the first night, The "moonlight was [shining] brightly" and in fact, the full moon in 1940 occurred on September 16, Monday (it is, of course, more reasonable to place the adventure with the recent others in about 1940, rather than going all the way back to 1935).

Johnny has a "place" "on lower Max street" that he doesn't think Doc knows about (Doc does, of course). This place, therefore, is not his main residence, which is still probably his private museum (described in *Resurrection Day*).

Oliver Brooks, Ham's "older" half brother, "is an English subject" "who has always lived in Africa". He is killed near the beginning of this adventure. Since Oliver "is an English subject", his and Ham's father was probably British (explaining Ham's sometimes British epithets), and the family that Ham mentions as being Bostonian is therefore his mother's.

Long Tom's "hip bone is shattered" during the adventure. Optimistically – and we can take this to be the case since there is no later mention of a limp – Long Tom would be back on his feet, with the use of a cane, within a few days. He could discard the cane after a month, though he would still be limping for a time.

There is a one-scene epilogue "two weeks after that [last] day" of the adventure.

Both the *All-White Elf* and *The Golden Man* have been placed in September 1940. It is highly unlikely that *The Golden Man*, in particular, can be moved. This presents us with a conundrum, for *The Too-Wise Owl* cannot be moved, either, because of its precise chronological data. The most reasonable solution seems to be for the epilogue to take place two **days** rather than "two weeks" after *The Too-Wise Owl*, and placing the adventure between *The All-White Elf* and *The Golden Man* (unfortunately breaking up that sequence). This means that Monk and Ham left for Europe – where they are at the beginning of *The Golden Man* – shortly after the epilogue of *The Too-Wise Owl*, and allows Long Tom's "shattered" hip bone three months-plus to heal (the length of time Monk and Ham are missing in *The Golden Man*).

Pirate Isle (15 days) begins on "the hottest day of the summer" in the South Pacific; therefore it's winter north of the equator. It does not follow *The Too-Wise Owl*, which was recorded out of sequence, but likely begins the winter sequence for 1942. With an LPO of February 20, 1942, it likely at least **begins** in January. Further, a high tide occurs on the ninth night of the adventure and is the highest tide of the year. This is a spring tide, which occurs on a new moon or a full moon; the highest spring tide occurs in January when the Earth is at perihelion (Dent mistakenly calls this a "neap" tide, which is odd, considering that he lived for a time on a boat). In January 1942, these would be January 2 and January 16. Because there is no mention of either Christmas Day or New Year's Day, the ninth day is probably January 16 rather than January 2, putting the beginning of this adventure on January 8.

"Johnny ... vanished ... several weeks" (later referred to as "almost three months") before the beginning of the adventure, sometime (therefore) in October 1941; he appeared in *The Man*

Who Fell Up (late October), also suggesting the later January start date for this adventure.

Doc is out of town at the beginning of this adventure, and does not arrive until the fifth day, although he left New York "as soon as he got the news" of Johnny's reappearance, which was apparently the day before, because Doc has flown straight to the South Pacific without resting. This suggests he was at the Fortress of Solitude, unable to be contacted, but this is not stated.

Johnny is member "no. 341" of "the Explorers League, New York", last mentioned in *The Men Vanished* (July 1940). He is "in Who's Who. He has a writeup as long as your arm. But this Clark Savage, Jr., has a writeup as long as your leg", says one character.

"Both Doc Savage and Renny had, in fact, taught an officer's class in military parachuting technique". Renny is shot in the head during the adventure, but it is a minor wound that does not prevent him from participating (although he does not perform up to his usual standards). "Long Tom ... was probably the most conservative" "of Doc Savage and his five" aides. In this context, conservative means "cautious". Doc's plane, which has the call letters "MCX", and is destroyed, may or may not be his giant tri-motor; its engines are not mentioned. Doc is gripped with a "fury" and nearly kills the villain of the story (by strangulation), but is stopped by Johnny and another character.

The epilogue, which seems to occur two or three days after the end of the adventure, is the beginning of the next adventure, *The Speaking Stone*.

The Speaking Stone (3 days) begins two or three days after the conclusion of the previous adventure. It picks up where the last adventure left off, on Jinx Island in the South Pacific. It is "winter" in this adventure, somewhere in the Andes Mountains, near Ecuador, north of the equator. This matches the seasonal information in *Pirate Isle*.

Long Tom speaks Spanish, French, Norwegian and Russian.

Some time in the past, Doc played a practical joke on Monk, switching another pig for Habeas Corpus, leading to an embarrassing argument between Monk and Ham, whom Monk naturally blamed.

At the end of this adventure, Doc decides to spend "a few weeks" in Arriba to study the civilization.

The Three Wild Men (2 days) begins on a "sultry evening", and thus does not follow *The Speaking Stone*. Since it occurs during the warm months of the year, its LPO of May 15, 1942 rules out a placement in that year. This adventure then likely occurs during Summer 1941.

"Doc Savage had developed the organization of late months" which is composed of graduates, who operate as a sort of detective agency. This agency has been referred to in earlier novels, notably *The Red Terrors* (1937) and *Fortress of Solitude* (also 1937; this seems to suggest he formed the organization late in 1936).

Doc is "U-93, department K", "with the Department of Justice", apparently the F.B.I. (or is this that other spy corps agency from *Red Snow*?). This entitles him to priority treatment, but what else this means is not explained. Is this a reference to his status as "special agent", described in *The Whistling Wraith*?

The "ancient safe [in Doc's reception room] was nearly the size of a boxcar". Doc is able to activate "any one of several gadgets" in his headquarters by whistling a specific code into the telephone. In this adventure, he retrieves his phone messages in this manner.

At the beginning of this adventure, Doc meets with Mustaphet Kemel, who is a spy for various governments but is ultimately working for Doc. He is not a graduate, but is grateful to Doc for saving his life and the life of his son (in undisclosed circumstances that occurred prior to the adventure), and therefore has his memory. Further, he is able to kill, something the graduates are probably not able to do (Doc warns him not to). He is assigned by Doc to get a sample of a new bulletproof fabric which may be put to the wrong use, that is, used by the wrong type of people. This man must be part of the mysterious organization mentioned in *The King Maker* (June 1933).

The Fiery Menace (3 days) takes place following *The Three Wild Men*, which occurred "last month". It's "chilly" at night off the coast of Maine, so it is probably not summer when this adventure takes place. This suggests that *The Three Wild Men* occurred in warm September with this adventure following in cooler October 1941, between *Men of Fear* and *The Man Who Fell Up*.

"The only explanation he gave the State Police was that he was Doc Savage. Normally this explanation would have been sufficient, but it did not seem quite so this time". "During the past few months, [Doc and his aides] have had some trouble with the police", particularly in the previous adventure, wherein the Justice Department revoked his Federal credentials (they were reinstated by the end of the adventure, however). Doc and his aides are hunted by "Chapman, head of the homicide squad, one-time Commissioner of the Police"; "Chapman had been demoted at least twice in his career for handling important people without gloves". Was he the Police Commissioner mentioned in *The Whistling Wraith* who revoked Doc's police commission, which was reinstated later?

Long Tom and Pat hide at the former's private lab, which the police do not know about; this is undoubtedly the one on Amsterdam mentioned in *The Invisible-Box Murders*. "Monk was ... selling [a chemical] as a preparation for people to use to keep their pets off the furniture". He is "about five feet two inches high". Ham has "taught [Chemistry] to go steal things for" him. Doc "happens to own a controlling interest" in a local cab company, and is "in the Army ... in an advisory capacity". Among the scientists who trained Doc were an unnamed "Chinese philosopher ... and the African voodoo expert" (although based on African religion, voodoo technically originated in the Caribbean among black slaves). Pat has a "meek looking dark coupe which Pat called Clarence". "She had another one named Tarzan, one named Adolph Hitler, and [a fourth] she called Churchill". No explanation is given for these odd choices of names.

At the beginning of the adventure, Doc is in Washington, trying to talk his way into "the current war". We are privy to this discussion, which is often summarized in later wartime novels. This discussion must be topical, considering the placement of this adventure. So why go into the thing in such detail when this adventure almost certainly occurs in 1941 before the U.S. got into the war? Because Doc would seem unpatriotic if this scene was held until the appropriate time in the novels (likely *The King of Terror*, cover-dated December 1942, more than six months after this one; this scene should not be placed in *Pirate Isle*, the first of the 1942 placements, because if it belonged in that adventure, Dent would surely have put it there. Therefore, it must belong in an adventure unpublished at the time this adventure was recorded and published, such as *The King of Terror*). Doc is probably in Washington on other business in this adventure.

The Laugh of Death (8 days) starts on a "hot summer afternoon" after "Pearl Harbor". Its LPO of July 17, 1942 will just allow it to begin that year's Summer placements. It seems to have been "summer" for "two months" (implying a late May placement in the Arctic, late August in the continental U.S.), but Dent once again confuses the arctic seasons (as he did in *The Polar Treasure*), so this is not clear.

We learn that the Fortress of Solitude is now "not far south" of the North Pole, in the direction of the MacKenzie River and the Beaufort Sea. This location is not very far west of its last recorded location near Baffin Island, depending upon how far north it is – perhaps as little as 1500 miles. So it seems either the Baffin Island location was wrong (remember, it was described by a Dent ghost writer, not Dent himself, as in this adventure) or it was a temporary Fortress (since *Fortress of Solitude* in Winter 1937) while Doc had a new permanent one built at the location described in this adventure. Also, it "had lately changed ... appearance", and now "resembled a chunk of ice protruding from the Arctic ice pack". The original Fortress took "a long time" to build; presumably this one did, too. The question is: Did Doc move the Fortress immediately following *Fortress of Solitude* (to the location mentioned in *The*

Devil's Playground, just a few hundred miles south of the original), or did he wait until a new one was completed (at the location mentioned in this story)? It seems more reasonable to believe the Fortress has had only two locations: Its original one, where it is found by John Sunlight (and is erroneously referred to in *The Devil's Playground* as being several hundred miles south of its true location. Hathway, the author of *The Devil's Playground* may have gotten its location confused over Doc's trick of making the **villains** think it was farther south than it was; apparently the ruse was so good it worked on Hathway as well!) and its new location, described in this adventure, which coincides with the change in its appearance. There is one other possibility, if Hathway's description was not a simple error: Doc never moved the Fortress, but only disguised it, as described in this adventure. That might explain the later discrepancies in describing its new location: They were part of a poorly-organized plan to throw off searchers for the place by giving false locations.

In his article "Strange Blue Dome", Dafydd Neal Dyar suggests the location of Doc's Fortress is over the north magnetic pole. He points out that this location would allow Doc to easily find the Fortress no matter where he was coming from; it is worth mentioning that air travel in the 1930s was nowhere near as sophisticated as it is now. Lacking modern-day radar and constant contact with flight authorities, flying over wastelands – such as the one where the Fortress is located – was risky business. Without distinguishable landmarks, finding the Fortress would have been a difficult prospect. But not if it was at the north magnetic pole. It is also worth noting that in almost the exact center of the two disparate descriptions lies the north magnetic pole.

"The place, in the beginning, had been a dome affair"; this invalidates the description of the Fortress in the prologue to *Python Isle* by Murray. I suspect Dent's original description of the Fortress in his notebook may have been what he believed the Fortress was like, prior to learning its true appearance from the adventure which would become *Fortress of Solitude*.

Doc states that "Patricia Savage [is] my only living relative" (perhaps the other possible unnamed ones have died off since *Brand of the Werewolf*). She is "five feet seven" inches tall, quite tall for a woman in 1941.

There is "a small private lift inside" "a square pillar" in "a hall" on the 86th floor. However, there doesn't seem to be room in the halls of the floor for pillars. And how many secret elevators does Doc have? Probably Doc uses one of his other (already described) secret elevators.

"It had been years since [Doc] was really scared"; the last recorded time was in *The Other World* (March 1939). "Renny Renwick's private amphibian plane", which is "big", is kept at "the uptown yacht harbor". Although "a Hindu Yogi in India had taught Doc Savage the art of emotional control early in life", Doc flies into a blind rage during this adventure. The villain's gadget in this adventure is "sonic-electrical", like Long Tom's bug-zapper.

Doc uses "a not-too-reputable building off Times Square"; "he kept the place for emergencies". He has "arranged with" "an agency which supplied theatrical talent" for it "to obtain, and keep on tap ...actors who could double for [Doc or his] associates". With Doc's life in near-constant danger, this arrangement seems somewhat reckless. Presumably, the doubles were informed of the potential danger and well paid, and/or Doc used them only when he believed their lives wouldn't be endangered, but since Doc is often attacked by surprise in unexpected places, how could he know when an event was safe for the doubles?

One of Doc's college staff talks of a "new technique" to cause amnesia, but it is not described; this is surely not the surgery which has been used for at least ten years, at the time of this adventure, at the college. Perhaps Doc is considering a non-surgical method for inducing amnesia. Earl Shelton, a graduate, had been "rather dumb", but is now "a bright fellow", and is "not an extraordinary case". Has Doc perfected the intelligence-enhancing formula from *The Too-Wise Owl*

(September 1940) and put it into use at the college? The implications of this are staggering: Imagine an army of super-geniuses loyal only to Doc. Or is a better education part of their "training"?

They Died Twice (10 days) begins on an "early Fall afternoon". It is said that Doc has "made repeated efforts to get into active combat service but had been refused". However, its LPO of August 21, 1942 places it clearly in Fall 1941, when America was not yet at war. This suggests that *The Laugh of Death*, which Dent states happened after "Pearl Harbor", actually occurred in 1941 before Pearl Harbor, as well, preserving a sequence.

Renny has written "textbooks" on engineering. "Nature had given [Doc] ... bronze skin – suns had helped darken [it]".

"Secret Stevens was once a close associate of Clark Savage, Sr.". He had "saved the elder Savage's life on two occasions", and is "past sixty, at least" in this adventure (making him, probably, a decade older than Doc's father would have been). Doc "is already known as Doc Savage" when his father finds the Valley of the Vanished in 1911, suggesting that he was already a doctor by that time, or an extremely precocious child (as we might imagine). Unless "Doc" was a precocious nickname, this means that Doc was born before the turn of the century, and contradicts statements made in other adventures. So it likely was a nickname when Doc was young.

"Doc looked slightly embarrassed" at the mention of Monja's name. Is this because of the way he knows she feels about him, or the way he feels about her? The Mayans of the Valley of the Vanished, we learn, are ruled by "the Clan of the Very Highest" who "live in a valley smaller, but more impenetrable than" the Valley of the Vanished. "It adjoins [the Valley of the Vanished] and is reached by secret passages". King Chaac "is the lowliest member of the Clan of the Very Highest".

The Devil's Black Rock (56 days) starts some time before Doc gets involved; his involvement begins the day Doc and his crew return from *They Died Twice*, "the nineteenth day of October", giving us specific dates for both adventures. *They Died Twice* therefore occurred October 7-16, 1941 (and in fact, Doc is indeed out of the city on the "tenth of October" as described in this adventure). Although Doc gets Donkey Sam Davis' message on October 19, the adventure begins much earlier. The twenty-third day of the adventure is "the seventeenth of the month" (which turns out to be September), making the first day near August 26, 1941, and the last day October 20 (this turns out to be exactly one week short of my own day count). "Nearly three weeks later" (therefore near November 7), the next adventure, *The Time Terror*, is said to begin.

Although there is a reference to "this war", as in *They Died Twice*, this adventure cannot take place in 1942 because of its LPO.

The specific ending date of this adventure tells us that Johnny disappears shortly after *The Man Who Fell Up*, which must occur after this adventure's ending date of October 20, while on his way to China, as told in *Pirate Isle* (January 1942), and means that adventure certainly did not begin prior to the full moon of January 2, but the new moon of January 16, as earlier clues led to. Sam saw Doc "a year exactly to the day" in Mile High, placing Doc there September 17, 1940. However, that day is the first day of *The Too-Wise Owl*, so Sam's memory must be off. He likely saw Doc between *The All-White Elf* and *The Too-Wise Owl* shortly before September 17.

Doc's lab takes up "more than two thirds" of the 86th floor. Doc owns "a fat slice" of "The Morning Tribune" newspaper. Everybody, including Doc, gives Monk a hard time about his bad habit of trusting pretty women regardless of their character.

The Time Terror (6 days) takes place in "summer" during the war. Its LPO allows a Summer 1942 placement. However, references to the war are at odds with other evidence such as

LPO, etc., in many of the war and post-war stories (such as *They Died Twice* and *The Devil's Black Rock*, which we just looked at), so this is a tentative placement for now. It also begins a seasonal sequence. The comment in *The Devil's Black Rock* about this adventure beginning "nearly three weeks" after that one must be an error, likely an editorial insertion, referring to the month between issues of the DOC SAVAGE magazine.

Mention is made of "special correspondents", who are possibly graduates of Doc's college, but not affiliated with the detective agency, and this would therefore refer to his part-time agents, described in *The Flaming Falcons* (this would explain why they are "special"). Alternately, it may refer to the men in the mysterious organization mentioned in *The King Maker* and suggested in *The Three Wild Men*; those men are certainly "special correspondents".

Doc uses four news condensers who report to Monk. They have been in use for "the past year" and it is not clear if they have replaced the news-clipping service Doc has used in earlier years, or are somehow working in conjunction with it.

This adventure states that Pat is "one of Doc's few living blood kin", not his "only" one. Monk knows some of the Japanese language. Murray, in his *Duende History of THE SHADOW Magazine* book, "wonders if there" was "editorial inspiration" for this story, because *The Devil Monsters*, a dinosaur-themed SHADOW novel, was published "about this time".

The Talking Devil (6 days) also takes place in the summer during "the war"; "growing corn" is shoulder high, placing it in July. Johnny "is in Alaska, where he is preparing some specimens". In fact, the "specimens" "he is preparing" are probably those of dinosaurs from *The Time Terror*, the last adventure, which ended in Alaska. That adventure therefore took place in late June or early July.

It is said that Doc was under the care of scientists for "almost twenty years", making him therefore about twenty-one when the training ended ("fourteen months" plus "almost twenty years"). "Both the army and navy had refused active service of Doc Savage", suggesting a 1942 placement (the story's LPO is February 19, 1943). "Monk ... decided to misunderstand Doc's order" in order to get in on a fight. This is not the first (nor the last) time this happens, but it is one of the few where Monk's disobedience is so clearly stated. Long Tom has an "atomic microscope", undoubtedly an electron microscope, which was first demonstrated in 1940.

Doc is "the world's leading brain surgeon" and "did most of his work" at "a small but wonderfully equipped hospital uptown, which specialized in brain cases, and which was largely supported by Doc Savage". "Doc did not ... do a great deal of surgery ... his specialty being ... new and experimental technique".

There have been "rumors" of Doc's "mysterious 'college'". The police "are convinced there is such a place" but do not know its location. This seems to contradict Murray's assertion that the Governor is in on Doc's rehabilitation (as stated in *White Eyes*) and the comments in *The Spotted Men* that the police are working **with** Doc in this endeavor. But *The Spotted Men* was written by Bogart, so both of these contradicting statements were written by Dent ghost writers and not Dent himself, and they contradict most of the contemporary mentions of the college's workings; therefore I consider them to be incorrect. It is Doc's policy not to inform a graduate of his former life because "it might saddle his mind with a worry that would hamper him through the rest of his life".

Waves of Death (3 days) begins on "Aug. 12", and can follow the previous two in Summer (tentatively 1942).

It is stated in this adventure (once again) that Doc was under the care of scientists "until he was almost twenty". Further, "Doc Savage has been, for instance, under the wing of a Yale expert on atomic phenomena, a Virginia experimenter in supersensory activity [E.S.P.? This tutor would seem to be Edgar Cayce, the famous "sleeping prophet"

142

who lived in Virginia Beach; he began giving readings in 1901], a Yogi practitioner from India, a jungle chief and tracker in Africa", among others. "The training cost a fortune, a tremendous sum, and in fact was the sole purpose for which Doc's father worked for a period of many years". Was this before or after Doc's birth? When did Doc's father come up with the idea to raise his son as he did? Doc's father was apparently absent, exploring, for much of Doc's youth (we know he made multiple expeditions to Central America around 1910, according to *They Died Twice*). Was this how he "worked"? On the other hand, this suggests that Doc's father had some money, enough to live comfortably on, but not enough to finance his son's training; he did not have to work to support himself, but only to pay for Doc's training.

"Pat had talked somebody into teaching her Mayan, which had been against Doc's wishes. No one would admit being the tutor, and Pat had never tattled". It is stated clearly in *The Man Who Fell Up* that Monk taught her Mayan. Is this a "typo", did Monk erroneously get blamed in the earlier story (and now it is known that Monk did not teach her; was it Ham hoping to score points with Pat?) or does this contradiction place this story before *The Man Who Fell Up*?

Pat keeps her airplane at an airport north of Westchester County. During this adventure, she paints "Norpen Lumber Co." on it, likely so as not arouse suspicion when she arrives in Michigan, in timber country.

The King of Terror (9 days) takes place during "winter", breaking the seasonal sequence begun with *The Time Terror*. Its LPO of January 15, 1943 just allows it to be placed in that year, though more likely it belongs in 1942. And it occurs after *They Died Twice*, so cannot occur in 1941. Further, it is during "the war", and America was not at war Winter 1941. Because *Pirate Isle* starts on January 8, 1942, and the events of *The Speaking Stone* do not end until late February, this adventure occurs in early March of that year. And since this story was submitted after those two, it makes sense that it would occur after them. And we have further information to help us place this adventure: On the fifth night, there is "semi-moonlight", suggesting it is sometime between a full moon and a new one, and near neither, and; the first day of the adventure is "Saturday". If the first day was March 14, then the fifth night of the adventure would be very near the new moon of March 16, so the adventure must instead begin on March 7.

In this story, Monk meets a distant relative, a "sixteenth cousin or something", named Handsome Mayfair. "He certainly had none of the Mayfair homeliness", indicating that it is Monk's **father's** family, the Mayfairs, who are homely. Doc "Savage is the president of the Scientific Club". Is this the "Scientific Adventurers Club" mentioned in *The Crimson Serpent*? Murray suspects that the villain "Abraham Mawson" in this story is based on Commander Ellsworth, the real-life man who tried to go under the North Pole in a submarine (which was the inspiration for Doc's *Helldiver*).

"Doc Savage's private elevator was apart from the others. Once it had been in the same bank with other elevators, but lately it had been changed, being now placed at the end of a small corridor that was a narrow thumb off the main lobby". This is his express elevator, although its location seems to match the "private" elevator which takes visitors to the interviewing room on a low floor (usually referred to as the fifth) or to the 86th floor. As mentioned before, it's not an easy thing to move an elevator – practically impossible, in fact – and this is probably a case of dramatic license. There is a secret room next to this elevator.

The Black, Black Witch (5 days) takes place "three hundred and eighty-eight years" after "1555", or 1943. But its LPO of December 18, 1942 precludes a 1943 placement entirely. This is an example, one of many in the later tales, of topical references to dates in order to make the story seem current. It is "fall" and "bitingly cold" at night, November or December. It seems to be after 1941 (it's after "Germany declared war on the United States" and it must be close to 1943 because of the times given), so it must be Fall 1942. Further, the third day is "Friday", and that night the moon is as "bright as fire", so it is probably near the full moon of November 22, a Sunday (December's full moon is beyond the story's LPO).

Monk speaks German "perfectly" because "he had studied chemistry ... for some time in one of the Leipzig schools". Since we know he grew up relatively poor in Oklahoma, probably on a farm, he almost certainly had a scholarship to attend such a school. Ham "once had" a "Park Avenue apartment" but "had to give it up because [he] couldn't pay the rent", which was about "twenty thousand [dollars] a year". Is this the Midas Club apartment?

In *The Running Skeletons* (2 days), it seems to be summer, with growing watermelons, an "untended lawn" and "untrimmed shrubbery" that "was a jungle", and in fact begins a seasonal sequence. Also, there is a reference to "the current war", indicating a 1942 placement (the story's LPO rules out a 1943 placement). Although there is a "haystack", it does not seem to be hot outside, so it may occur on warm days in June, or perhaps cool days in July.

Doc "had only two cars left ... because the other machines had been removed to defense plants, where their design could be studied". This is yet another instance of Farmer distorting what Dent says, suggesting that the vehicles are gone because Doc can no longer afford them.

In *Mystery on Happy Bones* (2 days), it's "wartime" and there is a "great deal of shrubbery" and "many roses". An April 16, 1943 LPO makes this a Summer 1942 adventure.

Monk and Ham are using a "fifth floor office" to screen visitors. It has an "adjoining room", which has its own exit. Monk knows "a little lock-picking"; Ham does not. Doc "had been taught by an old Ubangi hunter ... the facility of sleeping and yet being awake". He has "nervous perspiration" before a routine parachute jump. There have been footnotes in the last year (or so) of novels explaining that Doc's feats are not so incredible. Renny is "an artillery expert", which suggests this is where he served in World War I. However, statements in Dent's notebook imply that Renny was in the Engineering Corps during the war.

The Goblins (3 days) mentions "crisp morning mountain air" and "chokecherries", so it must be summer and it's "about six months" after the U.S. enters "the war" so it follows

Mystery on Happy Bones in Summer 1942. A closer reading of one of the character's personal chronology further pinpoints this adventure as taking place between mid July and mid August.

"The art of silent movement ... had been taught [to Doc] by jungle natives in Africa". The little green man in this story is virtually the same gadget used in *The Jade Ogre*, down to its color; Dent apparently recycled it from an unused Curt Flagg outline that Will Murray later turned into *The Jade Ogre*.

The Mental Monster (1 day) also seems to take place during summer. Lake water is very "warm", and it occurs "since the country had entered the war". Further, "there had, of course, been no fire in the fireplace for months", which suggests it has been too warm for a fire. It likely follows *The Goblins* in Summer 1942.

In this story we learn Monk owns the building on (or near) Wall Street where he lives. "Almost a year ago" Doc had installed an "escape set-up" consisting of "the manholes and grating around the building with connecting passages". "Doc Savage had honorary commissions in both the police and fire departments". A "very young" "Doc had acquired the habit" of trilling from "an old Hindu, a specialist in mental discipline".

"The short life of the [anaesthetic gas Doc uses] was something that Doc Savage, despite plenty of experimenting, had not been able to overcome". This is a direct contradiction of earlier comments, and of the gas' first use in *The Polar Treasure*. And it is it's limited effectiveness which makes it so valuable: Doc and his men can hold their breaths for its duration. Many have been the circumstances that they couldn't have used the gas if it didn't have a limited duration.

Hell Below (5 days) mentions "the war" and "the heat" in Washington, D.C., which fits with a Summer 1942 placement. There is "bright moonlight" on the first night of the adventure, probably from the full moon on July 27, 1942. This means that *Mystery on Happy Bones*, *The Goblins* and *The Mental Monster* all occur in the last half of July, ending just before the beginning of *Hell Below* on about July 27.

Doc's grenades are color-coded: "black and white checkered ... meant smoke"; "red for gas, yellow for explosive, white for shrapnel". Renny speaks "good German".

Doc and "Vogel Plattenheber" (Josef Goebbels) were students "at a Vienna university" together "some years ago". In fact, Goebbels never attended "a Vienna university". He attended a several universities in Germany from 1917-1920, but none in Vienna. Doc is undoubtedly younger than his classmates, suggesting his birth year as somewhere between 1904 and 1907, which agrees with earlier comments. Plattenheber, whose nickname is "the Hare", is killed during the adventure. Herman Goering appears as "the Seal". The two are abandoning Germany in this adventure.

The Secret of the Su (5 days) takes place during "hurricane" season, late August or September. An LPO of August 20, 1943 precludes a 1943 placement, so it, too, must occur in Summer 1942. There is a "dark moon shadow", so it is late August. This means fits with the placement of *Hell Below* in late July.

The Su are supposedly the descendants of Atlantis, but apparently have no connection with the beings in *The Red Terrors* (at least it is not mentioned). Renny says Ham has "big blue eyes". If so, they must be dark blue eyes, because Ham's eyes have always been referred to as "dark". Renny is probably speaking figuratively here. Doc and his aides spend "not less than a week" with the Su at the end of this adventure.

It seems to be warm in *The Spook of Grandpa Eben* (3 days); a man is mowing his lawn and trees are "thick". It is not "winter". "There's a war", placing it in 1942. Doc has been undercover for "two weeks", and "the moonlight was silver bright" on the second night, so it fits that this is near the full moon of September 24, a Thursday. Although the first day is "Monday", the second day is "Friday"! With Doc's stay with the Su following the last adventure, three weeks separate these two adventures; this means that *Hell Below* cannot occur in late August, with *The Secret of the Su* following it. *Hell Below* **must** occur in late July.

"Doc Savage owns a share of the capital stock in ... the Copeland Chemical Co." which "he bought ... recently" (also "some time ago"). Ham teaches a law class in the evenings "during the winters". How he has time for this with all the adventuring he does with Doc is not explained.

The Whisker of Hercules (3 days) also takes place during "summer". There are "no blackberries now", so it is not late June, July, or early August. It also occurs near a full moon that casts shade that is "quite black". This would seem to be at the full moon of September 24, following *The Spook of Grandpa Eben*. However, if this adventure does begin on September 24 or shortly thereafter, it would begin in **Fall**, not "summer". While it might seem feasible to simply switch *The Whisker of Hercules* and *The Spook of Grandpa Eben*, Doc spends many days prior to the latter tale investigating. Therefore, *The Whisker of Hercules* must occur even earlier in the summer (unfortunately breaking up our long summer sequence). The only time it can do so is in late August, which fits with the absence of blackberries; with *Hell Below* beginning so close to July's full moon, *The Whisker of Hercules* probably does not immediately follow it, but precedes *The Secret of the Su* in late August. These two adventures may, in fact, straddle the August full moon. This also allows the beginning of *The Spook of Grandpa Eben* to fall on Thursday, the first day of the full moon, making its second day being "Friday", as described in the tale.

According to Plan of a One-Eyed Mystic (5 days) begins on "a fall day, crisp and bright", "Thursday ... the first week of October", after "the war broke". Although an October 15, 1943 LPO allows placement in that year, this adventure ends the seasonal sequence begun in *The Running Skeletons*.

Renny "had learned about fingerprinting technique as part of his training under Doc".

The placement of the sequence from *The Running Skeletons* to *According to Plan of a One-Eyed Mystic* in 1942 means *Waves of Death*, *The Laugh of Death*, *The Time Terror* and *The Talking Devil* all therefore probably occur in Summer 1941, not 1942. The trouble with the police mentioned in *The Three Wild Men* (October 1941), which we know refers to *Pirate Isle*, immediately preceding it, also refers to *The Invisible-Box Murders*, wherein Doc is suspected of multiple murders, and

The Talking Devil, wherein Doc is falsely accused of botching surgery; both of these occurred within "the past few months" before *The Three Wild Men*. This also means that Doc did not know who had taught Pat the Mayan language in August 1941 (as stated in *Waves of Death*), but found out it was Monk by Fall 1941 (as stated in *The Man Who Fell Up*). What about the comments in *The Fantastic Island* and *The Terror in the Navy*? Those are probably errors, because Doc, always trying to keep Pat out of adventures, would probably not want Pat to know Mayan, and there was no fuss made over her supposed knowledge of the language in those two instances. What may have happened is that Johnson made an honest mistake in attributing this talent to her (as he did with her "golden" eyes, as he admitted), and Dent, recalling that she had spoken Mayan earlier, included it in *The Terror in the Navy*, without checking his facts.

Death Had Yellow Eyes (3 days) occurs during "spring". It is "crisp" and there is "rain", so it is probably April. "The war" is more than "four months" old, so it is probably Spring 1943 rather than Spring 1942.

Monk is still living in his Wall Street penthouse and Ham is living in an "apartment on Park Avenue". This seems to be the Midas Club apartment, because it has an adjoining courtyard (to the "north"), which has been previously mentioned. What about that comment in *The Black, Black Witch* (November 1942) that Ham has had to move out of a Park Avenue apartment due to high rent? Either that comment was erroneous, or this move occurred before *The Man of Bronze*, since Ham has been living at the Midas Club since that time. Probably, then, this occurred when Ham was just starting out as a lawyer. One of Ham's ancestor's was Colonel Blackstone Brooks, also a lawyer.

We learn that one of Doc's bulletproof "undershirt[s] of ... chain mail ... weighed only four pounds". Johnny's eyes are described as a "sort of a vague blue". Although he is in disguise, there is no reference to colored contact lenses like Doc often uses, so this may be the true color of his eyes. Ham knows "a few words of Hindu". Monk cannot read lips, contradicting the statement in *Cold Death* (written by Donovan, remember) that all of Doc's aides can read lips.

With this adventure, Moran replaced Nanovic as editor of the DOC SAVAGE series. Murray states in his Afterword in *Omnibus* #13: "his editorial dictates forever changed the tone of the Doc Savage stories"; Moran decreed: "Doc should always be the plausible man ... not a superman".

The Derelict of Skull Shoal (5 days) occurs after Italy's surrender during the war (September 3, 1943), but it is "warm and clammy" south of Bermuda. An LPO of December 17, 1943 places it late Summer or early Fall 1943. Doc has been on the case for at least "two days" before the adventure begins, and was probably contacted a few days prior to that.

Moran's view of Doc is seen full force here. Doc's crime fighting operation is now referred to as "an enormous business".

"Doc ... had enough weight with the Navy Department to take command of a submarine". The submarine in question is the *Triggerfish*, which was last mentioned in *The Submarine Mystery* (Fall 1937), where it was stationed at Panama under the name *Swordfish*. Due to events early in that adventure, its name is changed to *Trigger fish* (two words). It comes to the rescue in this adventure, and is nearly captured by the villains. Oddly, the female lead in this adventure is nicknamed "Trigger" (this raises the question: Did the sub's name get changed back after *The Submarine Mystery*, and Dent got mixed up because of the woman's name?).

Doc suffers a concussion and at the end of the adventure, four days later, is still feeling "the effect of the rap over the head he had received in the beginning of the affair". At the time the injury occurred, he "became alarmed about his condition" and suffered from "delirium", in his expert medical opinion. This may explain some of the behavioral aberrations he displays in later tales (although he hasn't been his superhuman self for at least the last year or so of published adventures).

Doc spent "many months exploring the jungle of northern Brazil, and in the Guineas"; the last is doubtless a typo for "Guyanas", which are north of Brazil. New Guinea is in the Pacific Ocean near Australia, and this passage clearly refers to the area north of the Amazon Basin. Doc has "done a short book" on "the native dialects" of the area. This exploring may have been part of Doc's training, or at least prior to *The Man of Bronze*, as Doc has rarely had "many months" free since then.

We learn that Ham, somewhat unsurprisingly, has at some time in the past been "sued ... for breach of promise" to marry a "chorus girl".

The Three Devils (2 days) also occurs during a "spring" during the "war". It likely follows *Death Had Yellow Eyes*. Further, "July" is referred to, but not as **next month** so it is probably not June in this tale, but April or May.

"Monk and Ham and Johnny" are so badly burned by acid during the adventure that it will take "a good plastic surgeon" to "fix them up as good as new in time".

Murray observes that there are apparently three pages missing from the published version of this story, at the end of a chapter. They were somehow lost between the manuscript (where they remain) and the published account. It seems unlikely that the pages were purposely edited out.

The Pharaoh's Ghost (4 days) occurs "near the rainy season" in Egypt (spring), for a tentative Spring 1943 placement, following *The Three Devils*. It is probably late May or early June, because it is "hot" at night, and 104° during the day. Doc and his aides "had been in Cairo a week" prior to the beginning of the adventure. Johnny had been in Egypt "three weeks" before that. He was in *The Three Devils*, so this adventure must follow that one by at least that length of time.

"All of them except Monk spoke Arabic to varying degrees. Doc and Long Tom handled the language fluently, while ... Ham Brooks, knew just a little".

The Man Who Was Scared (4 days) occurs during a "wartime" "June". An April 15, 1944 LPO precludes a placement in that year, so it is placed in June 1943. *The Pharaoh's Ghost* occurred "last month", at least "twenty-eight days" earlier, and the villain of this adventure is the brother of the villain in that adventure, seeking revenge. This means that with *The Pharaoh's Ghost* in late May, *The Three Devils* occurred in late April, following *Death Had Yellow Eyes*.

Doc has published "A Short Pamphlet On Practical Criminal Psychology". Yet again, there is no mention of the "gland" theory of criminality. Gaines, a neurologist, and Doc "studied neurology in Vienna together". Did they study under Lestzky, mentioned in *The Golden Man*?

The police description of Doc reads: "height about six-four, weight around two-ten or -twenty". This can probably be taken to be more accurate than those descriptions of Doc suggesting he is 6'6" or taller.

"Doc's father, about the time Doc was born, evidently received some sort of shock which completely warped his outlook on life – made him devote the rest of his days to raising a son who would follow the career of righting wrongs and punishing criminals who seemed to be outside the law. Doc never knew what happened to his father to give him such an idea". This is the most complete description of Doc's father's motivation we have thus far (it also suggests that Doc's father was absent because he was raising money to pay for Doc's training, as alluded to in *Waves of Death*). It will be discussed in greater detail at length.

"Ham lived in [a] club". This is probably still the Midas Club, often mentioned in earlier adventures, as previously discussed. "It was the custom of Ham ... to arise at ... about ten o'clock in the morning". Of Doc's two hour exercise regimen, it is said: "Sometimes ... he let it slide. But not too often". Doc still has "the special license number on his car". According to Murray, following this story is an unrecorded adventure involving Elma Champion, the female lead of this story, at her ranch.

In *The Shape of Terror* (3 days), a haystack and grazing cattle are mentioned, for a likely late summer or early fall placement. Its LPO precludes a 1944 placement (despite a reference to the November 1943 Teheran Conference), so it is tentatively placed in Summer 1943, following *The Man Who Was Scared* (June) and preceding *The Derelict of Skull Shoal* (September).

Doc claims to speak Czech only "fair", and "Doc wasn't too skilled at lip-reading German", both of which contradict numerous statements in early adventures (including one scene where Doc lip reads Chinese, where the **tone** of the word is important to its meaning – and even then, there may be numerous homophones).

Doc "had never taken a life in cold blood, not even, as far as he knew by accident". Did Doc kill in the first two adventures, as it is described, or not? If Doc did kill, as was his supposed "code", why would he have had the college, its only purpose the rehabilitation of criminals, which was around prior to *The Man of Bronze*, as we learn in *The Purple Dragon*? I believe that Doc has **not** killed, making the statement in this adventure true, and the scenes in *The Man of Bronze* and *The Land of Terror* are therefore actually in error. Doc likely complained of this untrue portrayal of himself shortly after their publication, explaining the change in the tone of the series after those first two published adventures (although the violence would continue for a short period thereafter, Doc was not portrayed as killing after the first two adventures).

Weird Valley (3 days) seems to occur during the spring or fall due to sparse weather information, and 1944 based upon the ages of the "old men" in this story. "Fog" suggests it is Spring rather than Fall, so it likely begins the Spring 1944 sequence.

Monk had been "turned green [for] several months" in Doc's headquarters lab, due to a chemical mishap, sometime in the past. Looking back over the chronology, the only two stretches of "several months" are the winters of 1943 and 1944. Because this incident is not referred to as having just occurred, it must have happened Winter 1943 (actually December 1942 through March 1943).

Pat is again described as Doc's "only living relative". Doc, unusually, does not wear his special vest in this adventure. Both Monk and Ham speak Spanish. At the end of this adventure, Doc tells virtually the same lie he had Monk tell in *Meteor Menace* – he tells the daughter of the villain her father was innocent and was killed by the villain.

Jiu San (33 days) takes place when "there was not much night-time at this period of the year" in Alaska, so it is summer, near the longest day of the year, which occurs in late June. Its LPO of July 21, 1944 will just allow it to be squeezed into that year and it also seems unlikely that the Allies would be planning for the occupation of Japan in early 1943, more than two years before the war ends, as they are doing in this story. Also, Spring of 1943 is rather full, confirming the placement of this adventure and the last. Doc has been on the case "six weeks" prior to the adventure (by distancing himself from his aides and making pro-Japanese statements), probably beginning about mid-April, because this adventure can end no later than July 21, and probably ends a short time before that date. *Weird Valley* must therefore occur in early April, which agrees with what we know about it. *The Shape of Terror* (late Summer 1943) occurred "a few months ago", confirming its placement.

Doc "was on the inactive list, in a special way ... but he was still a Brigadier General", according to another officer (Monk seems to confirm Doc's rank). What the "special way" is not explained. Is this a polite way of saying "honorary"? When did Doc receive this rank? This is the first time it is referred to (and the last, by the way).

Although Doc has not been acting superhuman for the past two dozen (published) adventures or so, he knocks Monk out with one blow so quickly that a woman watching the two of them doesn't even see the blow. Later, "Doc was having trouble with ... a master of ... Judo", but then "hit him hard enough to make him temporarily unconscious". Apparently the man was a better Judo master than Doc.

Monk "had been born in Tulsa", Oklahoma and "had no memory whatever for names, but he could remember a face as if it was a photograph". He worked in Japan for "four months", apparently shortly "before the war", because he "could see Pearl Harbor coming", and sabotages the chemical plant he is supposed to be supervising. This occurred almost certainly from the last part of 1939 to early 1940, the most recent time "before the war" Monk has had "four months" free, according to this chronology. This also means that *Devils of the Deep* therefore probably occurred shortly after this period, beginning in early March of 1940.

Ham "believed fear affected him much worse than it affected other men. It got hold of every nerve with a clawing, sick frenzy, a panic that made him weakly ill. Always it was thus". This is the first time we have heard about this. Because he is obviously brave enough to adventure with Doc, it can be deduced that Ham does not become frightened easily, but when he does, it is paralytic. In this instance, in fact, he believes he is about to be killed. Since Ham is in danger and probably comes close to being killed several times a year, it must be that he rarely **believes** himself close to death, and when this realization sinks in (only "on a few occasions", according to this adventure), he experiences the sensation being described here (one might also add that Ham has chosen an odd past-time for someone who can be paralyzed by fear). He "had been studying [the Japanese language] since before Pearl Harbor" and Doc coached [him] a lot on writing Japanese". Although Monk says he "can't ... speak Japanese", he seems to know quite a few words, probably learned during his earlier work there.

At the end of this adventure, Doc asks Carlta Trotter on a dinner date (!) thereby losing Monk and Ham a thousand dollars because they bet her Doc wouldn't go.

Satan Black (4 days) occurs during "war-time" in "early summer", and can follow *Jiu San* in July 1944. Further, it is after "the invasion" (presumably D-Day, June 6, 1944). The "moonshadows were thick" on the first night. This is probably due to the full moon of July 5. Doc has been on the case about six days at the beginning of this adventure, or since about June 29, putting the beginning of *Jiu San* no later than May 27, and quite probably a little earlier since there is no mention of this adventure beginning the same day that one ended.

Doc threatens Nola Morgan with violence in this adventure, in order to get her to be quiet (and they end up going on a date at the end of the adventure, which Monk finds "most unsatisfactory"). Doc's skin is a "natural deep bronze" color. No reference is made to "tropical suns". We are told that the safe in Doc's reception room is "forty years" old, putting its manufacture date at about 1905. "Monk's bank account was currently slightly below zero". Doc "ran toward the dam" and "exhausted his wind before he reached the dam, and arrived puffing for air". Gone are the days of, for example, Doc taking a person on his back and making his way through the treetops effortlessly.

Renny (who snores) is "nearly as tall as Doc Savage, and somewhat heavier". Renny has been routinely described as 6'4", 250 lbs. "Ordinarily he was a taciturn and somewhat sour fellow, but excitement seemed to make him drunk. Afterward he would look back on the emotional binge with pleasure".

The Lost Giant (4 days) occurs in "winter"; spring is at least "a few months" away, so it is likely November or more likely December, which actually could be "winter". Its LPO precludes a 1944 placement. This fits because Doc was in "Cairo, about six months ago". This is probably a reference to *The Pharaoh's Ghost* (May 1943). Doc met General Gaines at that time, although he does not appear in that adventure. Oddly, a "Gaines" **does** appear in the following adventure, *The Man Who Was Scared* (June 1943), the sequel to *The Pharaoh's Ghost*. He is not a general, but a neurologist; Dent may not have known the general's name, and recalled the minor "Gaines" character, or, more likely, mis-remembered it.

Unusually, Doc goes to a make-up artist for help at the beginning of this adventure. Monk "was continually broke. He was in the habit of thinking fifty dollars was a comfortable sum". "Ham Brooks had a weakness for blondes". He also speaks German. Doc "had learned not to depend implicitly on [Monk and Ham] where [women] were involved". "One of the telephones in his headquarters" "was listed as a sporting goods house". Doc "had as much appreciation as any other man for fine worldly things".

Doc is "upset" and "physically ill" from "fears and anxiety", but is "still able to" shove "them back into his mind where they wouldn't interfere". "It wasn't like him to be so nervous, and that frightened him. He had always taken pride in his amazing self-control". Is this a long term effect from the concussion he received in *The Derelict of Skull Shoal*, only two months ago?

Violent Night (2 days) seems to take place during one of the warm months of the year and occurs after Italy's surrender on September 3, 1943, so it probably occurs Summer 1944, following *Satan Black*, continuing the sequence, which was interrupted by *The Lost Giant*.

In this adventure, Hitler (using the name of "Hans Berkshire") is captured. Neither Monk nor Ham "could speak Portugese to any extent", though Ham did back in *The Golden Man* (Fall 1940). There, he spoke just a little, which fits with this comment. Doc still has "a commission in the New York police department". He "had never lied to Monk or Pat or Ham. Not exactly. He had shaved the truth a few times, and always regretted it".

Pat claims she is Doc's "third or fourth cousin" (the text says she is "a distant" "cousin of Doc Savage"). Was "uncle" Alex actually a second cousin whom Doc **thought** of as an "uncle", due to the differences in their ages? If so, this would make Pat's and Doc's **grand**fathers, rather than their **fathers**, brothers. Pat is now "a war correspondent" "of some magazine", though she still has her "beauty parlor in New York". She was "born in Canada" and has "been to Switzerland". Her "six shooter" "that [her] grandfather used to fight Indians with" "was made before the day of Jesse James" (which was circa 1870). The "gun was [her] Dad's" and is a "forty-four calibre". I can find no Colt Frontier Single Action, which seems to be a fictitious model (or one exclusive to the universe which Doc Savage inhabits). So what is it? It is not the obvious choice, an 1873 Colt Model P, the "Peacemaker", the most popular handgun of the old West, because that was .45 and too new a model to be Pat's grandfather's gun, as well. The gun is probably an 1863 Remington, 1860 Colt Army or 1849 Colt Dragoon.

Pat says: "Doc, you're scared. This is, I think, the first time I ever saw you" scared. She also says that Doc's explanation of not getting involved with a woman because "an enemy would ...strike at him through her" is "just talk. The real reason is that" "he doesn't understand them, and so he's scared of them". Doc has confirmed this himself in past stories. In this adventure, he tells Barni Cuadrado she's "as pretty as Christmas morning".

Strange Fish (5 days) takes place more than "two months" after the invasion of Normandy (June 1944), and "most of the summer" had passed, but it is still "hot" and there are still "green leaves". It likely occurs late August or early September 1944 following *Violent Night*.

Doc has, for the past few adventures, taken to "guessing" out loud and openly complaining about Monk and Ham's arguing. According to Murray, following this adventure is an unrecorded adventure involving a plane crash at a nearby Wyoming ranch, although he suspects this might have become *The Lost Giant*, which also featured a plane crash.

The Ten Ton Snakes (5 days) gives very little seasonal data. A "lawn was cut" and shrubs are "wild and untrimmed" and it seems to be warm, so it is no earlier than late Spring. "The war [is] near its end".

Renny "had an office in a ponderous building two blocks from Grand Central Station on Fortieth street. The office was not quite seedy, but it had no floss". There is "an adjoining room which" Renny seems to use "as living quarters"; it has "a cot and a dresser". This appears to be a temporary set-up and may not necessarily mean he has moved out of his penthouse mentioned in earlier adventures. However, he tells a visiting acquaintance that he can't help him with money, so Renny may be nearly broke himself. This is odd, because in the very early adventures (at least twice), it is said that Renny doesn't have to work because he has nearly enough money to retire on, and he doesn't seem to be an extravagant spender like Monk (he is probably "puritanical" in his spending). So what has happened? Was his wealth overstated in the earlier accounts? Or, did he make bad investments in the 1930s, losing his fortune (which **had** been accurately reported in early adventures)?

"Doc Savage was a taller man than Renny Renwick, and probably as heavy". Renny is described as "more than six feet [tall], more than two hundred pounds". These measurements are somewhat less than previous descriptions. Is this part of de-superhumanizing Doc (and his milieu, by extension), or are these measurements closer to the truth? And Monk describes himself as "height five feet four, weight two hundred", also about fifty pounds lighter than earlier descriptions. His car "was a second-hand job which had belonged to a Balkan dictator who had been chased out of his country by another dictator" (this seems not to refer to World War II). "He always wears the same suit a week at a time". "He has been thrown out of" "one of the fashionable buildings close to Radio City ... for being unable to pay his rent". It is unclear when this took place. This obviously is not his Wall Street penthouse, which he owns.

Perhaps significantly, when telling a friend of meeting Doc, Renny does not mention World War I. Doc flies an "amphibian" with "two motors"; this has apparently replaced the big tri-motors of the preceding decade.

"Doc Savage finally talked a little about himself. It was the first time Renny had heard him do that". "He had never known just what had happened to his father to cause him to put his small son, Doc, in the hands of scientists for training". Earlier adventures have stated that Doc does not know why, so this statement may well be true. Farmer suggests that his father had done a great wrong, and was trying to atone for it. I believe he was instead the **victim** of a crime. Considering that Doc's father didn't push him to be a policeman or a lawyer (criminal prosecutor), but instead had him molded into the ultimate Nemesis of crime (as Doc is often referred to in the earlier novels), it may be inferred that the events surrounding this crime were somewhat fantastic, like Doc's adventures themselves. What this crime may actually have been, I will disclose shortly.

Doc's "methods probably meant he needed psychoanalysis, he reflected". This is a telling statement. More and more, Doc's life mission is made light of, that it sounds silly. And Doc frequently reflects that he still has some of the emotional maturity of a child since he didn't have the chance to outgrow it because of his childhood training.

In *Cargo Unknown* (12 days) it is "hot" and there are "concealing rows" of "sweet corn", placing it at summer's end 1944. All references to "after the war" and "peacetime" must be ignored, as the adventure's LPO precludes any placement in 1945.

"Mayan was one of several languages Renny spoke". Renny has been in London for "quite a while" at the beginning of the adventure, and he and Monk and Ham greet each other as if they have been apart for some time, so this adventure likely follows the last by some time, perhaps a few weeks. "Doc Savage ... had no family [except] ... a cousin named Patricia Savage".

We are told more about Doc's training than in any other novel: "The scientists ... had been paid for their work. The elder Savage had paid them. Doc had never known his mother; she had died when he was less than a year old. The elder Savage had died about the time Doc's unusual training had been finished", about "twenty years of training", which strongly suggests that Doc is about twenty in *The Man of Bronze*. This passage does not state that Doc's mother died in childbirth, so we may conclude that she did not. I believe the crime mentioned in the previous entry that caused Doc's father to train Doc for his life's work to be the murder of his wife, while Doc was still a baby. Since Doc's training has been stated to have begun when he was fourteen months old, we can deduce that it took Doc's father's the months between "less than a year old" and "fourteen months" to decide on his son's profession and get the scientist-tutors gathered and instructed. Presumably, Doc's father was wealthy at this time.

"He had amassed a tremendous fortune", "early in life", according to *The Man of Bronze*. We might also wonder, at this point, that the elder Savage pushed his son into medicine – it is always referred to as the subject Doc studied most intensively and learned best – did Doc's mother die because of lack of adequate medical attention? Or, perhaps sensing the possible long-term ramifications of his son as punisher, Clark Sr. sought to give Doc balance as healer. Or is it as mundane as medicine being Doc's favorite subject? And was Doc's code of not taking a life an extension of his Hippocratic oath?

There is a reference to Doc being "about thirty-eight" that is made by Renny, in the Bantam paperback edition. However, in the original Street & Smith pulp edition, this statement is made about "Clark" -- who is a member of the villain's gang and **not** Doc, as Julian Puga V. pointed out to me. The editor of the paperback edition mistakenly "corrected" this unclear passage.

"Doc slept at headquarters more often than not when he was in the city". Where else he might sleep is not mentioned, but the secret apartment (mentioned in *The Man Who Fell Up*) he keeps a "dozen" floors down in the same building seems likely; he would be able to monitor his headquarters rather easily that way. Or perhaps the "residences" mentioned, but not specified, in *The Giggling Ghosts* (December 1937).

Renny, while in Doc's reception room, is shot at from "the Mercator Automotive Building" which "was three blocks over and a short drive north", actually north-by-northeast (from "above the twenty-fifth floor", Doc notes). This matches the location of the Chrysler Building from the Empire State Building. It is not mentioned that this is the building described in both *The Man of Bronze* and *The Terror in the Navy*, but the similarity is striking. We are left to consider once again that the reception room is visible from the Chrysler Building. If it is, it cannot be in the "west" corner as Dent states in *The Man of Bronze*. This is the only corner that is **not** visible from the Chrysler Building. Flip-flopping my floor plan of the 86th floor would fit some of the descriptions but not others. Once again, it comes down to which account you want to believe, the "west corner" or "the Mercator Automotive Building"? I stand by my original floor plan, keeping the reception room in the "west" corner. Numerous comments about the location of the rooms, discussed in previous comments, all support the reception room being in the west corner, contradicting the two – almost only – references suggesting it is not in the west corner. Also, we have seen previously that an error is sometimes repeated by a following author who didn't check his facts, and relied only upon the earlier, erroneous account.

Rock Sinister (5 days) seems to end the seasonal sequence. There is "frost" and "chilly" air in New York, and it seems to be the rainy season (summer) in South America, so it is probably winter. Its LPO of February 16, 1945 allows it to be placed in Winter 1945, following the last adventure by several months.

Monk still has his "laboratory-penthouse-home establishment which he maintained far downtown in Manhattan, in the Wall Street section", so the comments about him being thrown out of residences must have occurred before *The Man of Bronze*. After a long absence, Habeas makes an appearance.

"Ham Brooks had picked up his nickname of Ham because he had once, in a fit of temper and because he could not find anything else to fuss about, howled that he did not like pork in any form. Ham was Brigadier General Theodore Marley Brooks and his statement about his tastes had been made in a mess hall he was inspecting, so ever after he had been 'Ham' Brooks to his outfit". This is a quite different version of how he got his nickname than the one we have been told up until now, the one about Monk framing him for the theft of ham. Monk is not mentioned at all in this version. Is this the true cause of his nickname? Or is it the way Ham Peck, the real-life inspiration for Ham Brooks, got **his** nickname?

Monk "got some false teeth" "a couple of months ago" and "without them" he lisps. This probably does not refer to the events of *Cargo Unknown*, likely more than "a couple of months ago".

It is said that the South American nation of "Blanca Grande had been the center of Inca civilization", leading us to identify it with Peru; the Incas were centered at Cuzco, Peru. However, every other description of the country, including the mention of the "pampas", the flight plan Doc uses, and the reference to "the Blanca Grande army [being] equipped with German weapons" fits only one country: Argentina.

The Terrible Stork (3 days) takes place during "spring"; and "sixty days ago" was still "wintertime", so it is April or May, which matches constant talk of rain and the rainy season. Its LPO rules out a 1945 placement, so it must occur in 1944, probably prior to the seasonal sequence begun with *Weird Valley* (April 1944).

"Doc's father, now deceased, had sunk some money in the [Empire State] building and in the process had acquired a permanent lease on the eighty-sixth floor". "The eighty-sixth floor of the building was exclusively Doc Savage's premises, but this did not mean he had all the space in the building at that level. The normal layout of the building had not been disturbed to accommodate him. The hall, for instance, was like the halls on the other floors, except that [only] one door had a name on it". This confirms earlier deductions I presented as to the arrangement of Doc's headquarters around the building mechanicals, using existing hallways. It also invalidates comments in earlier adventures that windows are at the end of at least one hallway; they are not.

The safe in the reception room is "big enough to hold a jeep". The "laboratory ... occupied over half the floorspace", and there is a "shower in a corner of the laboratory". This is undoubtedly a chemical wash shower, and not a personal hygiene shower (though Ham uses it as such in this adventure).

"Ham was always complaining about Monk being a pushover for anything in skirts, but in Doc's opinion Ham was a more ready victim". A woman attacks Doc: "she had hold of

Doc's hair with both fists". While it is always referred to as being short or close-cropped, Doc's hair is not crewcut, and there is never any mention of a widow's peak. It is not the style depicted by Bama on the excellent Bantam covers, and is probably not the style – with the long forelocks – shown in the Baumhofer covers in the 1930s (which is not "close-cropped"). Hair gels, such as pomade, were popular in the 1930s and 40s and it is quite possible Doc's hair is slicked back.

In *King Joe Cay* (2 days), Doc works without the help of his aides, the first time he has done so (that is recorded) since *The Man of Bronze*. "All of them were out of town". "Farmers were harvesting their oats", placing it in the first half of July. Its LPO will not allow a July 1945 placement, so the reference to "Yuletide 1944" must be a typo for "1943" (or editorial change). This adventure occurs between *Satan Black* and *Violent Night* in mid July 1944, where it disturbs neither the sequence ending with *Satan Black* nor the one beginning with *Violent Night*.

The Wee Ones (3 days) takes place during "the season of ... hail storms", late May, June or July. Its LPO of May 18, 1945 rules out a placement in that year. Further, a reference to cut "clover hay" places it no later than July, so it is likely June; it is "pleasantly warm" during the adventure, not hot, and "the night was not particularly warm for the season", causing men "to turn up their coat collars and yank down their hats" (but there is "warmth" in a "night breeze" on a following night). "The occupancy of France" has apparently ended. Paris was regained August 1944, but this is at odds with the other evidence, so it is likely July 1944 when this adventure occurs, following *King Joe Cay*, because *Jiu San* occupies June.

Doc's "screening room [is] on the twelfth floor where the cranks were sorted from those who had legitimate business". Monk "didn't speak [French] too well"; "he had learned it long ago from a French chemistry student". The two may have studied together in Leipzig.

Doc "did his living at his laboratory-office. This included his sleeping. He had a folding bed arrangement in a cubicle off the laboratory, and there was also a bath and a clothes locker and a kitchenette", although "Doc was an awful cook". If the arrangement of these rooms hasn't changed since they were mentioned in *The Land of Fear* (September 1935), the first room is likely the bedroom-"kitchenette" and the inner room the "bath"-"dressing room". If, in fact, Doc's apartment does abut the reception room, his dressing room may be the one mentioned in *The Headless Men* (September 1939) and *Bequest of Evil* (August 1940), which connects to the reception room (and the outside corridor). At the very least, the two dressing-bathrooms are back-to-back (it doesn't seem likely that Doc would want visitors in his private dressing room).

Terror Takes 7 (2 days) takes place after Germany has been "occupied", and it is rainy. Its LPO of June 15, 1945 places it in May 1945, after the fall of Berlin on May 8, which fits with the weather. It begins the warm month seasonal sequence for 1945.

Monk still has his "place downtown, and he was getting almost tired of its [ultra modernistic] flash as he was of the mortgages he had on the place". Ham uses a "one-fingered system" to type. Doc has had "an impulse to eliminate [his] private lift to cut expenses". This is the first suggestion that Doc's enormous fortune is dwindling, and of the ways he could cut expenses, this seems an unlikely first step. Could this be part of the de-superhumanizing edict, to give Doc money problems? Doc and his aides have police commissions which "nobody but the Commissioner can cancel". He almost does, due to pressure from the district attorney's office, but has faith in Doc. Doc's "silk line ... would hold half a ton". Oddly, when he wants possible eavesdroppers not to understand what he is saying to Pat, Doc speaks French, rather than Mayan. This implies that Pat may not actually speak Mayan, despite earlier accounts.

The Hidalgo warehouse has "boarded-over windows"; in as much as it does not have windows, this must be literal window dressing to make it less conspicuous, if not dramatic license. The place contains "a seaplane, a helicopter equipped with floats, a speedboat and a larger express cruiser". Note that no mention is made of Doc's normal large amphibian plane, his smaller single-engine speedplane or the *Helldiver* sub. No explanation is given for these three notable absences. As suggested earlier, he may have retired the big tri-motors in favor of two-engine seaplanes.

The Thing That Pursued (2 days) takes place during "the present war", but Germany has been "occupied". There is also "a corn field". Its LPO of July 20, 1945 allows it to be placed following *Terror Takes 7*, probably no earlier than late June or early July, because the corn in the field is tall enough to provide cover for men.

Doc "did not like to think of himself the way the newspapers referred to him, as a man who went around righting wrongs and punishing evildoers". This is a rather odd comment, considering that it is for **exactly** this that Doc was trained.

The gadget of this adventure is a Nazi machine that projects ball lightning. These were referred to as "foo fighters" during the war. There is some evidence that the Nazis actually had such devices, known as *feuerballs* ("fireballs"). This conclusion was reported in the December 13, 1944 "South Wales Argus" by Marshall Yarrow, the Reuters special correspondent to Supreme Headquarters, and in the January 2, 1945 New York "Herald Tribune", in connection with an Associated Press release, for example. Further, in late December 1944, stories were leaked to the "American Legion Magazine" which reported that it was the opinion of several U.S. Intelligence officers that the foo fighters were radio-controlled devices of the Nazis.

Trouble on Parade (2 days) occurs during "August". An LPO of August 17, 1945 just allows it to occur in that year, continuing the seasonal sequence. The adventure begins on a "Wednesday", and that night there is "crystalline moonlight". Because this adventure occurs so close to its LPO, there are only two Wednesdays that this adventure could begin on: August 1 and August 8. August 8 is the first night of the new moon, and there would be no moonlight, so the adventure must begin on August 1.

At the beginning of the adventure, Doc is on his way to Nova Scotia "to make some money" by buying then re-selling some "war surplus ships". Later, seeing an "express cruiser" costing "about thirty five thousand dollars", Doc's "thought was that he probably couldn't afford to rent" it. Is Doc broke now?

Monk's telephone number is CEntral 0-9000.

The Screaming Man (6 days) ends the seasonal sequence. Johnny entered Japan "about six months" earlier, sometime after late November 1944, when Allied bombing began, so the earliest placement for this adventure would be late May 1945, which fits with the remark that it occurs after "Germany fell". This adventure surely begins before the dropping of the A-bomb, because there is no reference to that momentous event. It can follow *Trouble on Parade* in August, beginning before the first A-bomb was dropped on August 6, which actually must take place **during** the adventure.

Doc "can't dance". Johnny became known in Japan as "the Screaming Man" because he "is a man of many words, none small". He is on the trail of Jonas Sown, who was responsible for the "last ten years" of war. He completes the triumvirate of greatest Doc villains, alongside John Sunlight and Dr. Madren. Sown may have used a machine to manipulate people into war, according to Johnny, but if so, the evidence has been dumped over the side of a ship and is now lost. Sown may have been based on Karl Haushofer, one of Hitler's political advisors who devised the strategy of a German alliance with Japan so that it would have access to the Pacific. Haushofer, who loved Japanese culture, committed *seppuku* (Japanese ritual suicide) at the end of the war.

Measures for a Coffin (4 days) occurs in "December". Although it is said to be "after the end of the war" in Europe, the story's LPO will not allow a December 1945 placement, so this story must occur December 1944. Monk returns from "occupied Germany", where he has been for "the past six weeks" prior to this story. We might consider that since this issue would have been on the newsstands in December 1945, "December" could be an editorial insertion, but there is a "blizzard" and numerous other meteorological references to suggest it **is** a "December" story. Alternately, the latest this adventure could have taken place in 1945 is early October, because of its LPO. If this is the case, Monk would have leave for Germany almost immediately after *The Screaming Man*, which can end no earlier than June 1945, more likely August. Ultimately, it is not central to the story that the war has ended or that Monk has been in Germany; therefore this adventure receives a December 1944 placement.

"Ham carries a gimmick to pick locks", which he has obviously learned to do since *Mystery on Happy Bones* (Summer 1942).

Doc uses "an interviewing office on the fourth floor" which belonged to "a private detective agency office", "the Durwell Agency". "The owner, Mike Durwell ... had been associated with Doc Savage for a considerable period of time", although Doc has not previously used his agency to screen visitors, according to accounts in other novels (or perhaps he did, off-screen, when Doc's aides haven't been available to do so). Durwell is described as "honest" but is not described as a graduate and his agency is certainly not the worldwide graduate detective agency. His agency is doubtless one of those referred to *Resurrection Day* (Spring 1935). Durwell "sold his agency" "two weeks" prior to the beginning of the story, to some criminals who kidnap Doc, unbeknownst to Durwell.

Se-Pah-Poo (6 days) takes place during "the summer" and likely follows *The Screaming Man* in Summer 1945.

Monk is living "at the Forty-First Street Hotel", which has "a willingness to extend Monk ... credit". Apparently, his sentiments about his mortgages in *Terror Takes 7*, just four months ago, were more serious than they seemed. For at least the third time in the series, a (native) Indian who acts like a stereotypical Indian, but actually is not, appears. Oddly, a character by the name of "Kissel" appears in this story, as in the last, although there is no connection between them.

For an unexplained reason, Monk and Ham take a commercial flight to Arizona (during which they meet a major character in the story) rather than using one of Doc's planes. This may be a case of plot contrivance. On the other hand, there is no mention of Doc's tri-motor in the warehouse months earlier (in *Terror Takes 7*), so perhaps Doc doesn't have a large cross-country plane at this time. Perhaps he has been selling them off to raise cash for his crime fighting operation, but this seems unlikely.

Terror and The Lonely Widow (3 days) begins after "the war was over" but it is still "blistering hot". It can follow *Se-Pah-Poo*.

"Doc Savage ... owns a large share of [an air]line", which he has acquired during the last "ten years". This contradicts earlier comments that suggest that Doc is broke (unless the airline itself is faltering).

"Renny Renwick probably came nearer than any other one of Doc Savage's group of five associates to looking like what he was – an internationally known engineer". What about Ham, with his often-described orator's mouth, or Long Tom, who looks like he spends all of his time indoors? "He had one foppish habit, which was smearing his hair, dark and uncontrollable hair, with some kind of pomade. He was touchy about this", which may explain why it's never been mentioned before. But this habit is confirmed by information in Dent's notebook.

During the adventure, Doc works with the "Office of Special Investigation" (which is run by Brigadier General Theodore Lowell), which may be the O.S.S. (Office of Strategic Services), the U.S.'s war-time spy corps. Disbanded in September 1945, it was virtually reconstituted in 1947 as the C.I.A.

Five Fathoms Dead (8 days) begins in "late March" "1946". But this cannot be, because of its January 18, 1946 LPO. The gang in the story stole two subs "after the end of the war", and then spent "five months" training, then they began "operating". A newspaper editor says that ships have been disappearing for "the last six months" – apparently the length of time the gang has been "operating", so on the face of it, this adventure occurs late summer 1946, which we know cannot be the case. This issue would have been on the newsstands in March 1946 and "late March" may be an editorial insertion, which may explain why the history of the gang doesn't make chronological sense. In a one-day prologue (the part that supposedly occurs in "late March"), a Nazi sub, now in New York, is stolen; "the sub put into a South American port after the war ended". In fact, U-977, a Nazi U-boat, arrived at Mar del Plata, Argentina on August 17, 1945. A few weeks later, an Anglo-American commission went to Argentina to investigate, suspecting that the sub had been used to transport Hitler and Bormann. Later, the sub was taken to America. Using this real-life event as a guide, the prologue probably actually occurs in late September. "About ten days" later, the adventure proper begins, in "early, very early April", which is therefore **October**.

Doc is using "an office on the fifth floor for screening [visitors] ... of what seemed to be a private detective agency". This is undoubtedly the office mentioned in earlier novels.

Death is a Round Black Spot (2 days) takes place after "the end of the war" (by at least "two months") and "sleet" "is a big change in the weather" (it was "warm" before it), so this must be Fall 1945, following *Five Fathoms Dead*, no earlier than mid October. This seasonal information supports keeping *Five Fathoms Dead* where it's placed, in sequence. If we consider "the end of the war" to be the formal surrender of Japan (on September 2), this adventure would occur in November. But "shade trees" still have their leaves, so it must be no later than mid October in this adventure, with "the end of the war" referring to the informal surrender of Japan on August 17, 1945. "The moon" casts "shadow[s]" dark enough to hide in, so it must in fact be near the full moon of October 21. This also fits with the placement of *Five Fathoms Dead* in early October.

170

It is said that Pat is "in her twenties" in this story. The oldest she could be is 29, with a birthday in late Fall, after this adventure. This would put her birth date late Fall 1915 (after October 21), making her 16 (very nearly 17) in *Brand of The Werewolf*, where she appears to be "about eighteen" years old.

According to Murray in his Afterword in *Omnibus* #13, this story was written over a non-Doc Savage story.

Colors for Murder (2 days) seems to occur in fall "after the war" (its LPO precludes a 1946 placement): "early summer" was "less than ... a year" earlier; "a gas heater was singing softly", and, "the rain was coming down hard". It is probably November – the rainy season in New York – when this adventure takes place.

The idea for this story was originally proposed in a letter by Dent dated "Dec. 21, 1934".

During *Fire and Ice* (4 days), it is "warm" in Alaska, and there are "crickets", so it must be summer. It is also "after the war". But it cannot be Summer 1946 because of its LPO. The only place this adventure can occur without disturbing a sequence is between *The Screaming Man* and *Se-Pah-Poo*, no earlier than late August, after the informal surrender of Japan on August 17. Because of the "moon" in *Se-Pah-Poo*, that adventure must occur in late August before the new moon of September 6, or in mid September, after the new moon. Since there is a reference to "the moon" in this adventure (and no more, such as it being "bright" or "round"), these two adventures likely straddle the September 6 new moon.

Doc is the "director" of an "airline", and is looking for an air route for postwar vacationers to Alaska at the beginning of this adventure, suggesting that he expects -- hopes – to derive income from it. This is doubtless the airline mentioned in *Terror and The Lonely Widow*, which occurs only a couple of weeks after this adventure. It is unclear whether the "Sparton Executive", a "speedy single-engine plane ... a cabin job with ample room for six passengers", is Doc's plane or one which belongs to the airline, and would be used in this run once established.

Three Times a Corpse (2 days) takes place "several months following the end of the war". Doc is vacationing in Miami, a winter resort spot, and it is "cold" at night off the coast of Florida, so it is likely December 1945. He has been in Miami for some time (he has an observable pattern, which the villains use to draw him into the affair), "for a vacation", "wondering if he might not be losing a zest for excitement". Perhaps Doc is outgrowing the "kid stuff" which has been referred to over the past few years as the motivation for Doc's life work (as opposed to its **purpose**).

"Apparently [Monk] had gone to considerable trouble to dress as sloppily, and also as loudly, as possible". There is a reference that "the champ won [a boxing match] at Chicago tonight", in "the sixth" round. Unfortunately, this does not help us place this adventure because Joe Louis, the heavyweight boxing champ at the time, did not have a bout in 1945, or 1946 until June 9, beyond this story's LPO of May 17, 1946 (and that match was in New York City, and he won in the eighth round).

In *The Exploding Lake* (18 days), it is "winter in New York". This must be Winter 1946, as the "atom bomb" is common knowledge, and follows *Three Times a Corpse,* in sequence.

On "the seventh floor, Room 710", specifically, is "a detective agency, a private outfit, which is kept on retainer to see that Doc isn't bothered too much" (Ham is there, working with them). Renny lives in a "shabby hotel on Twenty-eighth Street"; apparently he's nearly broke, like Monk and perhaps Doc. There is mention of "many mysterious submarine stories after the Nazis fell", one of which was U-977, which was discussed in the comments for *Five Fathoms Dead*. U-530 similarly docked in South America months after the end of the war, prior to U-977's arrival.

Death in Little Houses (3 days) takes place in "July" "1946". An LPO of July 15, 1946 will just allow placement in early July of that year.

In *The Devil is Jones* (2 days), the war is "not-so-long-ago" and it is summer ("the night ... was soft and warm"; a woman is wearing a "bathing suit" and frolicking in the water outdoors), probably Summer 1946, following *Death in Little Houses*. Hazard, who brings Doc (and so Monk and Ham) into the affair, "got ahold of [Doc] a week" prior to the beginning of the adventure.

"Ham Brooks was most irritated when slicked in small things" by Monk, who knows this. Monk speaks "Mayan ... understandably ... not fluently"; Doc speaks "the Mayan tongue ... slowly so that Monk would understand". Johnny makes his last contemporary appearance – via telephone – in this story. According to Murray in his Afterword to *Omnibus* #13, this story was originally a non-Doc Savage.

The Disappearing Lady (2 days) takes place in "late October", "postwar". Its LPO precludes a 1946 placement, so it falls between *Death is a Round Black Spot* and *Colors for Murder* in late October 1945.

Ernest Green, a bank director who knows Doc, mentions Doc's "unusual organization with its facilities for unearthing things in a hurry". Is he referring to Doc's worldwide detective agency composed of graduates, as it is described in *The Red Terrors*? Or is he referring to the mysterious organization alluded to in *The King Maker* and *The Fiery Menace*? How does he know of either, as they are probably supposed to be secret?

"Women, as a rule, did not interest Doc Savage". This was true in the early years of Doc's career, but lately he has taken to dating, as noted in the comments for several recent adventures. He seems to be outgrowing the adolescent part of his personality, the part that loves excitement and is afraid of women. "There was no place for a woman in ... [a] life" "in which there was always real danger". This, too, is a throwback to earlier years. Pat has contradicted this, stating that Doc's fear of women is behind his disinterest of them, and this has been supported somewhat by Doc himself, although he has never backed down entirely from the original claim.

Doc is lost in thought while visualizing the woman who sings a song he is listening to, and generally seems to have trouble concentrating during the adventure. Is this a long term effect of the concussion he suffered in *The Derelict of Skull Shoal*, two years earlier? This adventure was written by Bogart, which may explain some of the slight aberrations in this story.

Target for Death (9 days) occurs after "the war years" so it's 1946. It could follow *The Devil is Jones* in Summer 1946, occurring as late as early October (the month of its LPO) in the year.

Pat once states Renny's name is "Henry". Did she make a mistake? Or did Bogart? Or were they, perhaps, thinking of his **middle** name?

The Death Lady (11 days) seems to occur in the summer; "it had started to rain. The night had been humid and sultry, but now there was a threat of a storm blowing up". "Four years ago" was "during the war", so it is Summer 1946 (its LPO precludes a Summer 1947 placement and it cannot be 1945 because "four years" earlier, 1941, was not fully "during the war").

We learn that Long Tom is friends with fellow adventurer Happy Halliday; they are apparently contemporaries, and Long Tom may have gone adventuring with him in the 1920s prior to joining Doc's group in 1931.

Monk deduces the identity of the villainess of the story by recognizing her legs!

Danger Lies East (3 days) occurs after "[19]45"; World War II was "finished a few months ago". "It was chilly and the sidewalks were wet" from rain and "it was cold in Washington [D.C.]", but warm in Cairo so it is probably not winter, but rather spring. Its LPO precludes a 1947 placement so it is Spring 1946, probably April.

There "was a rather Galahadian motivation for what [Doc Savage] did, and he usually denied such high ideals if they were mentioned to him, and certainly never expressed it that way himself". In fact, Doc usually refers to it as excitement-chasing, and this is explicitly stated – in more than one adventure – to be the bond that holds the group together.

Doc's father "had possibly been a little cracked on the subject of crooks, particularly of the international sort"; this seems to support the idea that Doc's father was victimized by criminals, rather than attempting to atone for his own misdeeds. Doc describes himself as "about six feet two, weigh[ing] over two hundred" pounds. We can therefore probably take this to be an accurate description of Doc. "Unexpected head blows had always held unique terror for [Doc] than almost anything", probably because of his medical knowledge. This opinion was almost certainly reinforced by the concussion he received in *The Derelict of Skull Shoal*, more than two years earlier.

No Light to Die By (2 days) begins on a "Friday" in "February", and that night, "there was no moon", although it is not cloudy (and therefore a new moon). World War II is "just finished", which implies 1946. Although its LPO will just allow a February 1947 placement, there is a lengthy exchange of messages – primarily cablegrams – between Doc and the author "Robeson" which rules out a 1947 placement. Further, the new moon mentioned matches the Friday mentioned, in 1946: The new moon was February 2, 1946, Saturday.

This adventure is written first-person by "Sammy Wales", and we might consider that it may be a truer account than others published in the series for that reason. Doc writes: "Kenneth Robeson has written ... fictionalized versions" "around the adventures of our group". There is therefore the possibility that Doc was a licensed product of the publisher, and none of the stories are "true", such as episodes of television show "Seinfield"; Jerry portrays himself, yet none of it is actually real, though some situations are undoubtedly based on real events. Each adventure may be totally fictional, but is more likely based on an incident that happened to Doc, as "fictionalized versions" suggests. Each adventure may be factually based upon notes supplied by one of Doc's aides, as Farmer speculates in his book. Obviously, most (if not all) of the dialogue would not be communicated in this manner, and would therefore be dramatized. Plots could be summarized in a few sentences, covering the key points of the adventure. *The*

Man of Bronze might have been summarized thusly: "Doc returned to the city from his secret Fortress of Solitude, shortly after his father had been killed by a mysterious plague. A sniper shot at us while Doc learned of his inheritance – gold in a small valley in Central America. The trail led there. The mastermind of the plot to rob Doc of his inheritance was a corrupt Hidalgo government official, who had the help of disgruntled warriors of the valley culture. They unleashed the plague on the valley to undermine Doc's popularity but Doc found the cure to the plague. We were all made honorary members of the village as a result. Doc and Princess Monja were attracted to each other, but Doc doesn't get involved with women. King Chaac put the valley's gold at Doc's disposal for use in righting wrongs. We stayed for a vacation then returned to New York."

I acknowledge that the stories are not docudramas of Doc's adventures, but I accept as much of them as "factual" as possible. Actual vegetation and weather would probably not be supplied by the author of the notes, unless the weather was particularly violent or unusual for the season; knowing when an adventure occurred would allow an author to insert appropriate vegetation and seasonal weather, even if it was not strictly accurate. Phases of the moon would almost always be at least as relevant, as a new moon provides cover while a full moon eliminates it; this actually happened in the series, which is why I believe it is relevant, and worth considering.

Doc also states: "My father [was] victimized by criminals", referring to the elder Savage's motivation for Doc's training, which lasted, according to Doc, "from the time I was fourteen months old until I was twenty years old". This statement has three significances. First, Doc knows more about his father's reasons for his training than has previously been (explicitly) stated, and we can therefore deduce that either Dent did not have access to this information, or was prevented by Doc from revealing it. Second, it confirms earlier comments that suggest that Doc was about twenty at the time of *The Man of Bronze*, if not exactly twenty, as his words suggest.

Lastly, it confirms that Doc's father being the victim of crime was his motivation, not trying to atone for one of his own past sins (as Farmer claims). It also explains the type of training Doc received, to battle "international" criminals.

Dent – as "Robeson" – mentions the notation in his notebook about the writing of the first Doc Savage adventure: "This thing started Nov. 12, 1932". However, the actual entry reads "Dec. 10, 1932" (this information is available from the Western Historical Manuscript Collection at the University of Missouri-Columbia, by the way). I believe Dent, trusting his memory, was actually thinking of the date *The Man of Bronze*, the **adventure**, began on, and what we know about that date does indeed fit with a beginning date of November 12 (albeit a year earlier in 1931; Dent did, of course, remember the **year** that he began writing the series correctly). **Everything** in *The Man of Bronze*, from weather data to lunar data to which days of the adventure are likely weekdays and which are weekend days, fits with a Nov. 12 start date for that adventure. So in a real sense, "this thing" – Doc's career – **did begin** on "Nov. 12".

There is no mention by Wales of the terrific speed of Doc's private express elevator. Has Doc removed this special feature? Or, did Wales use Doc's "public" private elevator? Or, are we finally getting something closer to the truth – Doc never appropriated a public elevator for his use, and his private express elevator wasn't quite as fast as described in the early tales? There's not enough information to conclusively decide, in my opinion. My best guess is that Doc never appropriated one of the public elevators; a public elevator brought visitors to a screening room (or detective agency). The single elevator that runs above the 80th floor was gimmicked for anybody who bypassed the room, and intended to cause trouble.

Doc says his anaesthetic gas "becomes ineffective" "in about forty seconds". Is this closer to the true length of its effectiveness? Or a modification of the longer length mentioned in previous stories?

In the library in Doc's headquarters, there is a small case in one corner that contains Doc's military awards, including four "purple hearts". It is implied that these were received in World War II, but the details are not mentioned. Additionally, Purple Hearts were not given out in World War I; this honor was reactivated by Hoover in 1932, but it was not retroactive, so the awards must be for service in World War II.

The Monkey Suit (2 days) occurs while it is "raining" and "not hot". Further, "March" is in the past but not referred to as "last month", so it is likely May 1946, following *Danger Lies East*. And, "first-of-the-month bills" are still unpaid, so it is actually early May.

This story is told from the point of view of Henry Jones. Although there is a short note at the beginning of the adventure explaining this, there is no mention of (or hoopla about) him actually writing the story, as there was in *No Light to Die By*.

Although *Let's Kill Ames* (3 days) appears to follow *The Monkey Suit* in Spring or Summer 1946 (there is mention of a "beautiful afternoon" and "sparrows"), it is also "1947", starting a new seasonal sequence. This story is told from the point of view of Travice Ames.

In *Once Over Lightly* (7 days), "the temperature ... [was] past a hundred" degrees "in Southern California", so it is summer. Doc and Monk have been at a resort "for days" prior to the story, more than two days but less than two weeks, according to the comings and goings of other characters.

Doc is "not quite seven feet tall", according to "Mote" Trunnels, from whose point of view the story is told. If his height is closer to 6'2", as he describes himself, Doc must have made a big – no pun intended – impression on Mote. She works for the "Metro Detective Agency" in New York. She also appears in "The Mystery of The Immodest Mouse", an uncompleted novella by Dent, which may or may not predate this adventure. Murray believes that story may actually have been adapted to become **this** adventure.

Monk tells her, "In new acquaintances can lie danger, whereas old friends can be trusted, or at least you know which one of them is a stinker".

It also seems to be warm (and there are "green trees") in *I Died Yesterday* (1 day), which is narrated by Pat. "It has been some time since" she has had an adventure (apparently since *Target for Death*, July 1946, a year earlier according to this chronology).

She claims she "hadn't been keeping up [her] reputation as a hair-raising adventuress", and this is what draws her customers (she also mentions her salon's exclusivity, though). Pat now has "a collection" of "a couple of hundred of" Doc's gadgets (this is apparently her first adventure using them), gotten by "Monk Mayfair, but the other [aides] had helped". She has been doing this "a few months", since Doc had "concluded" that his belief about a gun crippling a man's initiative also applies to his gadgets, which "he no longer used ... as much" (this coincided, by the way, with an editorial decree from Street & Smith). Pat thinks he's "trying to live down" that "phase of his life" (this seems to echo Doc's own feelings mentioned in *Three Times a Corpse*). She also believes that Monk "didn't include modesty in his vices", and that he "would accept the most preposterous lie for gospel, if a woman told it to him".

Doc's anaesthetic gas is "nullified ... in approximately forty seconds", according to Pat. "A private detective agency [had been] hired to monitor and screen all calls on [Doc's] listed [telephone] number".

Pat's heirloom gun is a "single-action six-shooter", weighing "a little more than four pounds". I have been unable to find a gun weighing that much in my research. Of the guns I put forth as possibilities earlier, the 1849 Colt Dragoon is by far the heaviest, and thus is probably the model Pat owns.

In this adventure, Pat says "our grandfather", referring to her and Doc, meaning that she and Doc share a common grandfather; if so, this would make them first cousins. However, she also claims in *Violent Night* that she and Doc are "third or fourth cousin[s]". This would mean that Doc and Pat share a **great**-grandfather, and that her father Alex and Doc's father were first cousins, as previously noted. So it may very well be that the two share a common great-grandfather, as the narrative in *Violent Night* agrees that she is a "distant" cousin of Doc's. I tend to believe that to be the case, although the evidence is by no means conclusive. The majority of accounts do agree, however, that she is Doc's only living relative, so we can probably take this to be true by this time – 1947.

And we learn more about Pat's grandfather, the Indian fighter (as she describes him in *Violent Night*): He lived in a "log cabin" (she believes), and "there were villages named after him all over the northwest". This seems to suggest that Alex himself was born in the area (whether the area was Canadian or American is in some question, however), and Clark, Sr., Doc's father, as well. Clark, Sr., probably born with the traveling bug, perhaps did not settle down until his son's birth. Or maybe he felt there was less opportunity for him at the Savage homestead as a younger son. Whatever the case, he almost certainly was not born in England, as Farmer claims.

Pat describes herself, referring to Doc's wealth, as one "who didn't have a tribe of grateful Mayans to keep us in spending money", implying that she is not – or wasn't raised – opulently wealthy. Her opinion of wealth seems to differ from others, as she did go to boarding school in Switzerland, not a cheap education, and the residence in the northwest was not the main Savage household.

In *The Pure Evil* (2 days), it is "winter", and "last January 18" was "more than a year ago". Its LPO precludes a 1948 placement so it is placed in Winter 1947.

Doc uses a "jet ship" which he seems to keep at La Guardia airport (the former North Beach airport that Doc used early in his career before the Hidalgo Trading Company warehouse had been built; it was expanded and re-named in 1937. It is interesting to speculate that Doc kept a hangar out there all those years, as a back-up. Could this have been kept under the same false name he keeps the secret apartment a dozen floors down from the "86th floor", mentioned in *The Man Who Fell Up*?). Undoubtedly, the jet plane needs a runway, which his warehouse hangar doesn't possess, explaining why he doesn't keep it there.

Monk says: "We usually have a private detective agency sift ... [telephone] calls". Renny is now described as being "near seven feet" tall, so perhaps we can gather that Doc and Renny are about the same height, 6'4".

This story was inspired by the "zany" (in Dent's words) stories of UFOs circulating at the time, particularly the one by Kenneth Arnold, the man credited with the first modern UFO sighting in June 1947. The incident at Roswell – whatever it was – followed in July of that year.

In *Terror Wears No Shoes* (5 days), peaches (and pears) are "in bloom", so it is almost certainly April. Its LPO precludes a 1948 placement, and it can follow *The Pure Evil* in 1947. Doc, Monk and Ham have been on the case "a month". Following the story, Doc and his crew must spend "several weeks" in quarantine. *Let's Kill Ames* probably does not occur before this adventure, because of Doc's pre-adventure activities here, so this tells us it occurred in the first half of June, the latest it can occur in the year because of its LPO – meaning *Terror Wears No Shoes* probably occurs no later than mid April, leaving five weeks between the two adventures.

This story contains the statement that Long Tom had "vanished ... early in 1942 ... and reappeared a few weeks ago", spending "more than five years" working for the U.S. government, placing this adventure in 1947. Let's examine this claim.

Looking back over the chronology, Long Tom appears in several adventures in 1942, and *The Pharaoh's Ghost* (May 1943), then doesn't appear again until *The Death Lady* (August 1946). He is also said much of the time to be in Russia, China, etc., during the war. These references can be dismissed as a cover story for his work for the government. His appearances in the other aforementioned adventures during this same time period cannot so easily be dismissed. If we are to believe the statement, these adventures would have to be moved to 1941 or earlier. This is unlikely, if not impossible, especially for the seven 1942 adventures. *The Pharaoh's Ghost* should probably not be moved, for it would take *The Man Who Was Scared*

(June 1943), and probably *The Lost Giant* (December 1943) with it, as well.

What about *The Death Lady*? It could be moved, without much fuss, to early July 1942, prior to *The Running Skeletons* (July 1942). We could then amend the statement to "vanished ... early in 1943 ... and reappeared a few weeks ago", taking the "1942" as a typo for "1943". It may be helpful to consider that *The Death Lady* was written by Bogart, and this adventure (and statement) is by Dent, who presumably had the more accurate information about Doc and his group. Also consider that in *The Death Lady*, Long Tom has his usual looks. In this story, he is "twenty pounds heavier, tanned" (to his detriment: "he'd developed a stomach ulcer"). It seems as though – and would be logical to conclude – Dent had access to information that Bogart did not.

We are left with two choices: *The Death Lady* actually occurred nearly four years (at the minimum) earlier than it was published, or, Bogart did not report the physical changes in Long Tom in *The Death Lady*, **and** Dent made a serious error in his accounting of Long Tom's time and whereabouts during the war years. In the latter case, the statement would have to be amended to "vanished ... early in 1943 ... and reappeared a few months ago", shortly before *The Death Lady* (August 1946).

We have one clue suggesting when *The Death Lady* actually occurred, if not in 1946: According to Murray, the idea for *The Death Lady* (originally called *The Lost Safari*) was proposed in June 1940, well before Long Tom's disappearance. While this alone is not to enough to justify the movement of a placement of an adventure, it supports the theory that *The Death Lady* did not occur when it at first seemed to – Summer 1946. Neither one of these two choices is satisfactory, but a decision must be made.

Begrudgingly, *The Death Lady* receives a placement of Summer before 1943, because I take Dent's word over Bogart's, and because references to the war in that adventure are not essential to the story (and can therefore be considered topical). *The Lost Safari* being proposed when it was suggests that it occurred about Summer 1940, and Bogart probably wrote *The Magic Forest* instead, which had an LPO of December 19, 1941, so *The Death Lady* is placed in July 1939 (which is wide open), because Summer 1940 is rather full. If you recall, *The Magic Forest* occurred a year earlier than it at first seemed to, as well, suggesting the same for *The Death Lady*. But it is also possible that *The Death Lady*, given its probable LPO, could be placed in early July 1941, preceding the three-adventure sequence which begins with *The Time Terror*.

The Angry Canary (4 days) occurs during spring: "The odor of ... [a] mountain flower ... was rampant at this time of year ... [and] at this altitude, the desert didn't mean heat", so it is spring. "Pakistan was a ... nation just born" and India has "self-government". Both of these events happened in August 1947, so it is Spring 1948 here. The latest the adventure can occur in 1948 is during the first half of April, due to its LPO.

Monk mentions the college to a couple of characters; there have been rumors of it for years, and this may explain Monk's willingness to mention it here.

"The private detective agency downstairs" which Doc uses "did nothing but screen and investigate the people who wished to see Doc". "Monk took the private elevator to the eighty-sixth floor" from this office. This must be Doc's **public** "private elevator", because his private express lift makes no stops between the ground floor and the eighty-sixth floor. This seems to confirm that the elevator labeled "Doc Savage" goes to the detective agency, if Doc did indeed appropriate an elevator, and also to the 86th floor (probably actually the 80th, where the transfer must occur), when the detective agency is not open.

"Brigadier General C. E. Caspell ... was second in charge" "of the government intelligence [agency] that applied itself to the ferreting out of any new discoveries that might be dangerous to the safety of the nation". It is also referred to as "the new department the government set up for science espionage". This may be the "Office of Special Investigation", which also used military personnel, with whom Doc worked in *Terror and The Lonely Widow* (Summer 1945). This sounds very similar to the agency run by Oscar Goldman, **also** O.S.I. – although the "S" there stood for "Science" – from THE SIX MILLION DOLLAR MAN television show/ *Cyborg* novel by Martin Caidin (actually, this is only the most well-known name; in the novel it operated under another name and in the TV show, it had three different names).

The anger-making gadget used in this adventure – which is the cause of India's recent "troubles" – is "a combination of supersonics ... and high-frequency electrical fields", like Long Tom's bug-zapper. "Supersonics" is used incorrectly here; that word pertains to the velocity of a moving object. The correct term is "**ultra**sonics".

The Swooning Lady (1 day) takes place in "late June", after World War II. Its LPO will allow a 1948 placement, and it probably belongs there following *The Angry Canary*.

Monk says he weighs "two hundred and thirteen pounds" and stands "five foot five" inches tall; weight changes we may expect during a lifetime, but not changes in **height**, particularly not growth in an old man.

"Doc owned the [Empire State] building" (the first time such a claim has been made), and, in addition to his headquarters, "maintained ... a smaller suite of two rooms on a lower floor ... occupied by a private detective agency which did nothing but screen visitors". Previously, the detective agency has been said to have been "hired" by Doc, so it is unclear whether this is the same agency as before, and "maintained" is being used loosely here, or this agency is a new one, which Doc controls. Could this be the worldwide detective agency composed of graduates?

The Red Spider (12 days) seems to occur during the early spring or late fall; "the rain had changed suddenly to sleet", and there is enough of it that Monk "slipped on the ice and he fell". "Monk had been in Russia since early last summer, and Ham almost as long", which has been "several months" now.

Because *The Angry Canary* is a Spring 1948 adventure, this tale must take place before that one, in order for Monk and Ham to have returned from the Soviet Union. This means Monk and Ham would have to leave shortly after *I Died Yesterday* (June 1947). We will temporarily leave this adventure unplaced. Interestingly, although Long Tom appears briefly in the adventure, he is not described. We are therefore unable to confirm the physical changes described in *Terror Wears No Shoes*. This adventure is his Tom's and Renny's last contemporary appearances (even though the novel was not published until 1979).

Seryi Mitroff, to whom Doc is greatly attracted, is described as "Madonnalike", as was Rhoda Haven, in *The Freckled Shark*, the first woman after Princess Monja to whom Doc was greatly attracted. Interestingly, Monja is Spanish for "nun", so Doc's attraction to these three women having this similarity is probably not a coincidence. It almost certainly says something about Doc's opinion of the ideal woman.

In *The Green Master* (5 days), it "was late spring down here", "in Peru", south of the equator, so it is late Fall in New York, December. If *The Red Spider* occurs in Spring 1948, this adventure would then have to be placed in 1946, because of Monk and Ham's long absence, rather than 1947 as we would expect, so *The Red Spider* probably occurs in late November or early December 1947, shortly before this adventure. This is exactly what we would expect – the later-submitted adventure following the former. We can now see that *The Swooning Lady* could occur in 1947, prior to *The Red Spider*, preserving the sequence, or in 1948, where it would preserve a sequence following *The Angry Canary*, based on Submission Order and internal evidence. But a reference in *The Swooning Lady* to "a blonde [who] had nearly been the finish of all of them" – who appeared in *The Angry Canary* – suggests that the former adventure properly follows the latter.

Monk uses "a small pocket radio", similar to a walkie-talkie.

Doc's private elevator now has a surveillance camera in it, which can be monitored from the lab. It is also "using pneumatic power rather than the conventional cable mechanism". It is not revealed when this change occurred. Although it is fast-moving, it seems to be noticeably slower than in the early years; this may the result of the changeover to pneumatic power, or perhaps, Doc's express elevator was never quite as fast as described in those early adventures. Did the changeover take place shortly before *No Light to Die By* (February 1946), wherein Sammy Wales rode in the elevator but made no mention of its unusual speed? Or is this Doc's public elevator, the one that goes to the private detective agency before going to the 86th floor?

A comment is made that "the regular elevators did not rise to this floor", the 86th, Doc's headquarters; a transfer occurs on the 80th floor (unspecified in this adventure). Farmer, in his biography of Doc, spends some time discussing on which floor Doc's headquarters was found, as it could not actually be the 86th, informing us that no elevator goes above the 80th floor; a transfer is required. This transfer that occurs in this tale is never mentioned in any other story. This seems to confirm that Doc's headquarters was above the 80th floor, likely the 85th, the highest possible floor, and these transfers were left out of stories for dramatic purposes. If no transfer was necessary, there would be no reason to include it here; however, if a transfer was always necessary, there would be more than sufficient reason to leave it out, in order to speed the story along.

"The reception room was ... about forty by twenty feet". However, a room of this size located in any corner of the Empire State Building would not be reachable without changing or extending a corridor, which contradicts the comments in *The Terrible Stork*. The size of the reception room, according to my floor plan, is approximately fifty-five feet by twenty feet.

This story is a return to the pre-war Doc Savage, gadgets and all, by the editorial decision of William de Grouchy. It might have begun a second golden age of Doc Savage adventures, but for the fact that the DOC SAVAGE magazine was cancelled within a year.

Return From Cormoral (5 days) occurs during "spring". As its LPO will not allow a 1949 placement, it must occur with *The Angry Canary* in Spring 1948, following *The Green Master*. Because a man in Canada still considers it "winter", it must be no later than April, where it fits nicely preceding *The Angry Canary* (leaving it and *The Swooning Lady* in sequence). There is mention of "the moon" which seems not be a full moon, so this adventure probably begins in early April, at least a few days later than the full moon of March 25.

Doc "is tops as a psychiatrist", according to Macbeth Williams. This is the first reference to Doc being a psychiatrist, and considering Doc's lack of understanding (and fear) of women, it seems as though Williams is in error.

Williams himself is an interesting look at what Doc might have been, had his training gone awry: His "youth [consisted of] lots of books and tutors, but not too many playmates"; his "father was very busy being a tycoon. Quite a remarkable man, though". Williams says he didn't "tak[e] over the management of my father's estate", adding, "I'm simply not a man of sound judgment. I can't make plans that work out".

"Monk Mayfair was somewhat more than three feet wide". Doc trills in this adventure, after a long time (since 1945). Doc uses "a jet job of a new type, partly experimental". It uses moveable airfoils to help turning and braking. Doc still has his "Federal commission", which is "old". As Doc has several Federal commissions, this one likely refers to his F.B.I., or Secret Service one.

"Doc Savage changed motels frequently as a matter of common-sense precaution". Why he does not use the secret apartment a "dozen floors" below his headquarters or any of the safe-house "residences" throughout the city is not explained. And in *The Angry Canary*, which must follow this adventure by no more than a week, Doc is back at headquarters. However, Doc still **uses** his headquarters in this adventure, but does not **sleep** there. This is probably also the case in *The Angry Canary* although no mention of this situation is made (another clue that this tale precedes that one? By the time of that adventure, the situation had already been described to the public, at least in submission order). This change seems to have been made since *The Green Master*, four months earlier. It is also worth mentioning that it is in that adventure that Doc first uses security cameras in his elevator. Is this because of the new threat of Soviet assassination?

The final contemporary recorded adventure, *Up From Earth's Center* (6 days), occurs during "early winter", which is likely 1949.

Renny is said to be in the area where the adventure begins, doing engineering work, but makes no appearance. Doc has accompanied him for some unexplained reason. This adventure is without question the strangest of Doc's career; he apparently battles demons of Hell in caverns beneath Maine. I can't accept this claim at face value.

First, the original ending planned by Dent exposed the whole situation as a hoax. Editorial direction by (new) Daisy Bacon changed this to leave some room for doubt on the part of the reader. And greater hoaxes have been perpetrated in the series.

Second, nothing happens that cannot be explained without invoking the Supernatural. Linninger's explanation can almost be accepted at face value, with the possible exception of the cause of Doc and Monk sharing the same hallucination; nearly everyone they meet during the adventure says something to reinforce the supernatural angle, and it is probably this, rather than their "long association" that causes similar hallucinations. It is not unreasonable to think that each, semi-conscious, reacting aloud, fed the other's hallucination.

But this theory can be delved into further. Consider:

Williams and Wails are "in cahoots", plain and simple, according to the police. This is true, even with Wails' spin on the situation. Neither are searched at any time for unusual gadgets or chemicals.

Before going into the Cavern, both Monk and Doc, our only independent observers, are "doped" (by an unknown substance in their food), according to their professional assessments as physician and chemist, and as very experienced adventurers.

While in the Cavern, there is an odd scent, slightly reminiscent of flowers. No one can identify it. Doc's chemical analysis reveals "not even what the odor was", only that Doc cannot identify it as any dangerous gas known by him. This gas comes from the crevice that was opened several months earlier; whether it actually originates there – or was planted – is not addressed.

This gas may be an hallucinogenic, or may render the victim susceptible to suggestion (or both). Clancy, Leona, Gilmore, Wails and Williams have all discussed "devils" and "Hell" with Doc and Monk. This gas also seems to make its victims sluggish: Doc has trouble catching the short, pudgy Wails. And "Monk had much the same experience as Doc Savage earlier – his quarry began showing signs of speed and endurance beyond the human". It is worth mentioning that neither Wails nor Williams exhibit these particular traits while **outside** the Cavern, where this gas is not present.

Later, deeper into the Cavern, at the crevice where the gas is coming from, the scent is stronger, and it is here that Doc sees stones come to life. Gilmore was exposed to this gas for "two weeks". No wonder he believes "a devil was chasing him"! Gilmore's mental state prior to inhaling this gas is never addressed. The possibility that he received a head injury while spelunking is never mentioned. Gilmore's sister Leona even calls Gilmore's episodes "hallucinations". Obviously, she nor her servants ever saw anything amiss, that is, Supernatural.

Linninger and the Sullivans, who accompany the others into the Cavern, do not go deep into it, near the crevice, where the gas is strongest. And they do not experience any of the things Doc and Monk do. This seems to suggest that the gas is responsible for the things Doc and Monk experience, whether this is a question of perception or true, strange activity.

There is another gas here, as well, on the other side of the crevice. It has a "dead scent". This seems to induce panic in Doc: "he ran ... as he had never run before", and "excitement caused him to throw the grenade much too hard". And, to cap it all off, "Doc screamed [in] terror", for "the first [occasion] ... in his lifetime".

Both Monk and Doc encounter living "toadstools". Yet these are nearly identical to the plants in *Land of Always-Night*.

The two most difficult episodes to explain are the ability of both Wails' and Williams' to see in the dark, and Wails' ability to enter and leave locked rooms without being seen. Yet the title characters of both *The Evil Gnome* and *The Vanisher* do the latter. And in Wails' case, there is no one watching the door in either instance of his doing so, as there was in both other adventures. He is simply in a locked room in one case (not there when the room was being locked), and simply not in a locked room in the other (although it is implied he would have been seen entering or leaving an area near the doors, it is not stated as fact). The possibility of something as mundane as lockpick being used is not even considered, much less something more fantastic like the amazing gadgets of some of Doc's foes.

Lastly, if the references to "devils" and "Hell" are removed, this adventure would no more suggest the Supernatural than *Murder Melody*, *The Red Terrors* or *The Mental Wizard*, to name but three of Doc's fantastic adventures.

The Frightened Fish (9 days), written by Will Murray, takes place during "early-winter" "of 1949". This is said to be "almost a year" after *The Red Spider*. But this is "almost a year" in Murray's chronology, with *The Red Spider* in Spring 1948, and *The Frightened Fish* in Winter 1949 (the former is

190

even referred to as having occurred "last year"). Moving *The Red Spider* to Spring 1948 would mean moving *The Green Master* to 1946, a full year earlier, because of Monk and Ham's activities in the two adventures. So it seems to be "winter" "1949" in this adventure, which would have been the next following *Up From Earth's Center*, had DOC SAVAGE magazine continued publication. "There was no moon" "about two weeks ago" at the beginning of the story; this would seem to have been due to the new moon of December 30, 1948, putting the beginning of the adventure in mid January, about January 13. Although this story would have been submitted after *Up From Earth's Center*, and there is no internal evidence to contradict such a placement, Murray has stated – in print – that none of his adventures occurs outside *The Man of Bronze-Up From Earth's Center* time frame, so the latter tale actually follows this one in late January (probably not February, as it is "early winter" in that story).

Remember, just because one story was **submitted** after another doesn't necessarily mean it **occurred** after it. While placing this adventure in January 1949 pushes *Up From Earth's Center* out of "early winter", the eighth day of this story is January 23: the surrender of Peiping, China on Jan. 23 is mentioned in the following day's paper (thanks to Julian Puga V. for spotting this).

In the reception room, there is "a long bank of windows through which the Hudson River was visible", confirming the west location of that room. Doc's "plane was a twin-engine experimental jet". Ham doesn't speak Japanese well enough to follow a conversation, although he apparently trained intensively for the *Jiu San* case. Doc studied philosophy under the Chinese scholar Wo To Sei-Gei (as did Jonas Sown). This "philosophy" was apparently a form of sociology or mass psychology, because Sown uses his knowledge to manipulate people into violence (using a machine he had built). Wo To Sei-Gei is probably the "Chinese philosopher" mentioned in *The Fiery Menace*.

Flight Into Fear (14 days), adapted by Will Murray, occurs during a "fall" after *The Red Spider*. Doc assumes his "Banner" identity three months prior to the story, and "even before he had assumed the identity of ... Banner, he had taken to residing in hotels, changing accommodations frequently. This was to foil Soviet-inspired attempts on his life", which is Murray's explanation of the comment in *Return From Cormoral* (April 1948). Although there are a couple of comments which seem to rule out a 1948 placement (such as a reference to the United Nations buildings; construction did not begin on the permanent buildings until 1949), this adventure belongs in 1948, which was Murray's intent.

The aforementioned comments were meant to have been edited out of Dent's original draft (a non-Doc Savage story), as Murray stated in a telephone conversation. Murray's **intent** outweighs an editorial oversight. Fall-blooming asters are in bloom, which happens from September 1 until the first hard freeze, so this adventure begins no later than November, and probably in October. On the first night "there was no moon" (this is said twice) and near a full moon at the end of the story. The first night is probably the night of the new moon on October 2 and the following full moon of October 18. Since this is a span of 16 days, and the adventure only 14 days, the adventure must begin on October 2 – or the day after – and end just before October 18. "A full moon" is mentioned on that same first night as "no moon", but this occurs in a chapter that Murray added, the one which gives Doc's bio, and so can – and **must** – be considered a mistake.

Doc works with "Mr. Dryden [who] is chief of the Special Security section, and Mr. Breckinridge [who] is his executive officer". This "agency" may be affiliated with (or renamed from) the Office of Special Investigations with whom Doc has worked in the past (particularly *Terror and the Lonely Widow* and probably *The Angry Canary*); it may, in fact, actually be a "section" of that organization. It is also entirely possible that it, or **both**, may be affiliated with the spy corps from *Red Snow*.

Doc must have moved out of the skyscraper shortly after *The Green Master* (December 1947), as noted earlier, assuming the "Banner" identity in late June or early July, shortly after *The Swooning Lady* (late June 1948). As Doc is undercover for this length of time ("three months"), there can be no adventures between early July and *Flight Into Fear* in the Fall.

Part II

The Unknown Adventures

In 1934, Doc Savage had 26 adventures that were not published. They were instead performed as fifteen minute radio plays. Of the 26, all written by Dent himself, only two appear to be adaptations of existing novels (a two-part *The Man of Bronze*; other scripts exist, which were not aired, including adaptations of *Quest of the Spider* and *The Polar Treasure*, also perhaps two parts; there is some confusion over the early episodes which version was actually aired, since no record of this exists). All of these adventures were very short, lasting a day (frequently it took Doc longer to get where he was going than it did for him to solve the mystery and catch the villain). They are, as Murray says of them, "much like what one would expect Doc to deal with in the spaces between his great pulp adventures". Monk appears in the adventures (with the exception of #4) with Doc. Ham appears in two of them. Long Tom, Johnny and Renny only appear in *The Man of Bronze* adaptation (in that adaptation, Long Tom is noted to have a "southern drawl". Since no mention of this is made in **any** novel, it is likely a slight fiction to help distinguish the character voices. But it also bolsters his possible connection to Thomas Jefferson).

Using the same methodology as with the novels, I've placed the radio adventures in the chronology as noted. The radio adventures were numbered by Dent, and remain in that order except where there is a glaring difference of season, and of course, they fit LPO guidelines; the first adventure had to finish before January 19, 1934 and the last of them had to finish before July 20, 1934.

Will Murray, in discussing the scripts in his two-volume book about them (*The Incredible Radio Exploits of Doc Savage*), named each of them. As he is an official Kenneth Robeson, and submitted alternate titles to Bantam for their reprints (such as *The Magic Island* for *Ost*), these titles are used in the chronology.

The first original radio adventure, "The Red Lake Quest" (#3), takes place in winter. Ham also appears. Doc uses the chemical used in *The Polar Treasure* (to track Victor Vail) to find the villain.

#4 through #14 seem to occur during the spring or fall.

In "The Sinister Sleep" (#9), a woman chemist gives to Doc an anaesthetic virtually identical to the one he uses in his small glass grenades, first used in *The Polar Treasure* (Spring 1932). With one exception: It does not dissipate. Remember, in its first appearance in the novels, Doc's gas did not dissipate. In its second appearance, in *Pirate of the Pacific* (Spring 1932), it dissipated after two or three minutes. Did Doc originally get the gas from this chemist, then refine it, adding the dissipation element? A couple of the early adventures state that Doc created the gas, but usually it's said that he "perfected" it, which may mean that he did not create it, as this adventure suggests.

This seems to indicate that #3-#9, at least, occur prior to *The Polar Treasure*, from Winter to Spring 1932. Because that period is time is very full, #10-#14, which also seem to have similar weather, probably occur the following Fall.

"The Sniper in The Sky" (#4) has a sniper shooting at Doc from a unfinished skyscraper, in a scene very similar to the one in *The Man of Bronze*, with two important differences: The characters involved are not the same, and the glass in the windows is now bulletproof, which didn't happen until after *The Man of Bronze*. Doc replaced them specifically **because** of that shooting.

"The Impossible Bullet" (#11) shares with *The Squeaking Goblin* the impossible missing bullet.

In "The Box of Fear" (#15), Doc and Monk have just finished gathering evidence against racketeers, who strike back in "The Phantom Terror" (#16), which occurs "a few weeks" later on a surprisingly "warmish ... evening", probably in Spring 1933. The warm weather wouldn't be much of a surprise, probably, if it had been warm previously.

In "Needle in a Chinese Haystack" (#19), the two are in China, and it probably takes ten days longer than the one day script covers. By virtue of the length of this trip, this adventure must occur in early 1934.

"Monk Called It Justice" (#20) states that "Doc ... is ... young".

Doc and Monk are in Germany for "The Fainting Lady" (#23); including the sea voyage, the length is likely fourteen days or more. It seems to be "spring". This adventure, though not identical to *The Swooning Lady* (June 1948), shares with it a cache of diamonds, two thugs after them and a lady who pretends to faint to attract the attention of a confederate. If *The Swooning Lady* is indeed an expansion of this earlier episode, the former adventure should be placed in Spring 1934, just before *The Spook Legion* (April 1934), or perhaps "late June" 1932.

In "Poison Cargo" (#24), Monk says that Doc has "a file of the known crooks of this town", New York City. Doc's telephone number is EMpire 1-7900.

"The Growing Wizard" (#26) seems to take place in the spring, or possibly the early summer, and deals with a new rubber plant which can be grown in the arid regions of the U.S. Although the names are different, this same idea is used in *The Land of Fear* (September 1935) and *The Flaming Falcons* (August 1938).

It is clear that Dent had several ideas that he held over for years before using them in novel form (in addition to the ones noted here, Dent came up with the idea for *Colors for Murder* (1945) in 1934, and Bogart's *The Lost Safari*, from 1940, didn't see print until after World War II as *The Death Lady*). This brings up the question: Are the adventures which share details with earlier story ideas merely expansions of the ideas, or share common, coincidental details?

Murray's belief is that two similar stories that share common details are indeed two separate adventures, that, for example, *The Swooning Lady* – perhaps the most obvious case of similarity – is not just an expanded version of "The Fainting Lady", despite their many identical details, but another adventure altogether. I remain skeptical, but the radio plays are placed as entirely different adventures of Doc and his group.

Other Appearances

Doc Savage has appeared in other media – not to mention internet fan fiction, which has sprung up since the first edition of this book (one piece of which I myself am guilty of) -- and while some of these are authorized, none can definitively be considered part of the canon.

In addition to the 1934 radio program, Doc appeared in a 1942 or 1943 version, which Dent had nothing to do with; Doc had a gem-covered hood which gave him mystic powers. Will Murray adapted *The Thousand-Headed Man* for radio in 1985.

Doc, and his aides, have appeared in licensed comic books starting in 1942. This series was written by Ed Gruskin, who wrote the aforementioned contemporary radio series as well. A couple of years later, Doc appeared in a back-up strip in THE SHADOW comic book, written by Bruce Elliott, one of the Shadow's ghost writers. In personal correspondence, Murray says of them: "The Elliott comics might as well have been about a P[rivate] I[nvestigator] coincidentally named D[oc] S[avage]". In the 1960s, Gold Key published a one-shot adaptation of *The Thousand-Headed Man*, which was mostly notable for its Bama cover. Later, Doc starred in series by Marvel in 1972, DC in 1987, Millennium in 1992, and Dark Horse in 1997. All had the bad habit of using their own visual interpretations of Doc and his aides, ignoring Dent's descriptions of them. The DC version was particularly bad: it was set in the present and co-starred Doc's grandson. The newer "First Wave" version is no better. Doc, Monk and Ham appear in "The Untold Origin of Ms Victory #1", a World War II adventure published by Americomics, 1989; "Doctor Kent Feral, Junior" instructs the superheroine in hand-to-hand combat. These three also appear – unnamed – in the first Rocketeer adventure by Dave Stevens (collected into a self-titled graphic album by Eclipse Comics in 1985); Doc is the inventor of the Rocketeer's rocket pack (this connection was dropped from the film version).

Doc, Monk and Ham appear, under other names, in Farmer's "Doc Caliban" stories, particularly *A Feast Unknown* (in which Monk and Ham are killed) and *The Mad Goblin* (in which Monk and Ham's sons help Doc). Monk appears under his own name in the 1968 Captain America novel *The Great Gold Steal*, by Ted White. He is a minor thug ("a West Coast trigger-man with a long record") who is killed, by laser beam, early in the book trying to warn Captain America of the Red Skull's plot. Even given that Monk somehow has turned to evil in the years since *Up From Earth's Center* (not very likely in itself), he would have been in his eighties in the 1960s. So if the name is not a "coincidence", it's not unlikely that one of Monk's Mayfair relatives has assumed his identity (or was named after him). We know the Mayfairs are usually homely, and it wouldn't be to surprising that one of Monk's nephews or cousins resembled him. Or perhaps an illegitimate son, as Farmer gives him in his *The Mad Goblin*. And, of course, there is Philip Jose Farmer's *Escape From Loki*, which tells the story of how Doc met his aids during World War I, as suggested by comments in *The Man of Bronze* and *The Land of Terror*. Farmer first put forth his theory in his *Doc Savage: His Apocalyptic Life*, first published in 1973. Although a fount of information about Doc, his aides, his headquarters, etc., there is quite a bit of speculation, which is made without much basis in evidence found in the Doc Savage novels.

Doc **might** appear in "Who Goes There?" by Ramsey Campbell, according to Albert Tonik, a Doc Savage scholar. The similarities between the lead in the story McReady, and Doc, are striking, as Tonik points out. I would place this adventure in 1930, in September because of the references to the season. Doc seems to be busy during the summer of 1931 for it to occur then (I believe he was in the Guyanas that summer). Despite the comment that the events of the story take place twelve years after McReady began interning (which would suggest a year of 1933 or so), there is very little room in any of the years after *The Man of Bronze*. If Doc **is** McReady, then comments referring to historical events must be considered topical, and references to new technology mean this expedition **pioneered** such technology, as these comments suggest a 1935 or later occurrence, which is not possible, according to this chronology.

The Man of Bronze was filmed by George Pal and released in 1975. A planned sequel was never filmed. During the 1960s, *The Thousand-Headed Man* was almost filmed, with Chuck Connors as Doc.

Part III

The Chronology

1907

~May 26

Clark Savage, Jr. ("Doc") is probably born.

1911

Clark Savage, Sr. and Hubert Robertson discover the Valley of the Vanished; Doc's father returns a short time later with Secret Stevens (possibly the following year).

1919

Doc probably begins college-level course learning (from his special tutors).

1923

Doc probably receives his M.D. He goes on to study neurology in Vienna.

1925

Doc begins research on the Resurrection Process, probably at the Fortress of Solitude.

1926

Doc begins travelling the world, undertaking specialized training under many native experts.

1929

Doc captures Joe Mavrick in Chicago; the College is already in operation.

1930

late summer

Doc is probably in Antarctica, using the name "McReady", as told in the short story "Who Goes There?". He meets Richard Henry Benson, who is going by the name Norris, there.

1931

summer

Doc is in the Guyanas in South America.

late October

Doc's father dies.

October to November 12

Doc is at the Fortress of Solitude.

November 12 to December 6

The Man of Bronze (25 days)

1932

January	Doc releases information about a brain surgery innovation he's developed.
February	"The Red Lake Quest" (1 day)
March 4-24	*The Land of Terror* (21 days)
late March	"The Sniper in the Sky" (1 day)
late March	"The Evil Extortionists" (1 day)
late March	"Black-Light Magic" (1 day)
late March	"Radium Scramble" (1 day)
early April	"Death Had Blue Hands" (1 day)
early April	"The Sinister Sleep" (1 day); Doc is given a powerful new anaesthetic gas.
early April to early May	*The Polar Treasure* (30 days)
early to mid May	voyage back to New York City following *The Polar Treasure*
mid to late May	*Pirate of the Pacific* (16 days)
early June	*The Red Skull* (4 days)

early June to June 20	Doc is at the Fortress of Solitude; adds dissipation factor to anaesthetic gas?
June 20-25	*Quest of the Spider* (6 days)
~ June 26 to July 1	Doc is at the Fortress of Solitude; creates "mercy" bullets as well as "single-fire"option for super-firers
~ July 2-14	*The Lost Oasis* (13 days)
~ July 15 to ~ August 16	*The Sargasso Ogre* (about 32 days)
~ August 17-20	*The Czar of Fear* (4 days)
	Unrecorded Death Valley adventure? This would have to be short, a day or two at most, beginning immediately after *The Czar of Fear* and ending immediately before *The Phantom City*. There seems to be no other time for this adventure to occur.
~ August 22 to ~ September 15	*The Phantom City* (24 days)
~September 16 to late September	voyage back to New York City following *The Phantom City*
~ October 5	Alex Savage, Doc's "uncle", is killed.

~ October 13-16	*Brand of The Werewolf* (4 days)
November?	Doc and his aides return to the Luzon Union for the cornerstone ceremony of "The Savage Memorial Hospital"?
November	"The Southern Star Mystery" (1 day)
November	"The Impossible Bullet" (1 day)
November	"The Too-Talkative Parrot" (1 day)
December	"The Blue Angel" (1 day)
December	"The Green Ghost" (1 day)
December	Doc and Monk go to Chicago to trap racketeers.

1933

early January	"The Box of Fear" (1 day)
January 15-22	*The Monsters* prologue; first appearance of the Monsters
~ February 9-14	*The Man Who Shook the Earth* (6 days)
~ February 14-27	Doc and his aides stay in Chile to oversee

	construction of a charity hospital.
~ February 28 to ~ April 6	*Meteor Menace* (about 38 days)
late April	*The Mystery on the Snow* (3 days)
May	"The Phantom Terror" (1 day)
May 30 to June 1	*World's Fair Goblin* (2 days)
early to mid June	*The King Maker* (13 days)
mid June to July 2	Doc and his aides vacation in Calbia.
~ July 3-7	*The Thousand-Headed Man* (5 days)
~ August 3-7	*The Squeaking Goblin* (5 days)
early September	*Fear Cay* (3 days); Doc and his aides spend a few days on the island afterward.
mid September	Pat moves to New York, buys "The Park Avenue Beautician" salon.
September 29 to October 10	*The Monsters* (12 days)
mid October	*Death in Silver* (2 days)
mid October	Doc is at the Fortress of Solitude; creates

	silencers for super-firers.
October 19 to November 3	*Python Isle* (16 days)
~ November 5-8	*The Sea Magician* (4 days)
	Unrecorded adventure beginning with Long Tom in Europe
November 16, 17	*The Annihilist* (2 days)
late November	"Mantrap Mesa" (1 day)
late November	"Fast Workers" (1 day)
November 28 to December 2	*The Mystic Mullah* (5 days)
December 17-19	*Red Snow* (3 days)
late December	Doc stays in Miami to conduct experiments following *Red Snow.*

1934

early January	*Land of Always-Night* (5 days); debut of first dirigible.
rest of January	Doc and his crew stay in Land of Always-Night.
February	"Needle in a Chinese Haystack" (1 day)
March?	"Monk Called It Justice" (1 day)
March?	"The White Haired Devils" (1 day)

210

March?	"The Oilfield Ogres" (1 day)
late March	"The Fainting Lady" (1 day)
early April	*The Spook Legion* (5 days)
mid April	*The Secret in the Sky* (2 days)
mid to late April	*Spook Hole* (5 days)
late April	Doc and crew stay at Spook Hole
May	"Poison Cargo" (1 day)
May	"Find Curly Morgan" (1 day)
May	"The Growing Wizard" (1 day)
late May	*The Roar Devil* (2 days)
early to mid June	*Quest of Qui* (about 7 days)
mid June	*Cold Death* (3 days)
late June	*Land of Long Juju* (6 days)
June 29 to July 27	*The Majii* (29 days)
July 4-8	*Murder Mirage* (5 days); destruction of first dirigible.
July 16-17	*Murder Melody* (2 days)

August	Doc's HQ is remodeled, giving the reception room an ultra-modernistic look; he may also have the outside corridor done at this time.
August 12-25	*The Jade Ogre* (14 days)
September 1-14	*Mystery Under the Sea* (14 days)
September 14 to October 13	Doc and crew remain at Taz to study it.
mid or late October	second Viking ship arrives from Qui; Johnny is consulted.
late October	Johnny leaves for Galapagos expedition, prior to *The Fantastic Island*.
mid November	*The Fantastic Island* (3 days)

1935

January	*Haunted Ocean* (4 days)
January	*Dust of Death* (3 days); debut of second ("stratospheric") dirigible.
March	*The Seven Agate Devils* (4 days)
early April	*The Midas Man* (4 days)
early April	*The Black Spot* (4 days)

mid April	*The Men Who Smiled No More* (4 days)
April 17-20	*The Terror in the Navy* (4 days)
late April	*Mad Eyes* (3 days)
April 28 to very late June	*Resurrection Day* (about 60 days)
very late June to early August	*Repel* (40 days)
early to mid August	Doc is at the Fortress of Solitude.
mid August	*The Derrick Devil* (6 days)
early September	*He Could Stop the World* prologue (2 days); Johnny is apparently killed.
early September	*The Vanisher* (8 days)
mid to late September	*The Motion Menace* (9 days)
September 26-28	*The Land of Fear* (3 days)
mid October	*He Could Stop the World* (2 days)
October 15-28	*The Whistling Wraith* (14 days)
October 29 to November 8	Long Tom is undercover as "Punning Parker" in Cuba prior to *The Metal Master.*
November 8-10	*The Metal Master* (3 days)

mid November	*White Eyes* (5 days)
November 21 to ~ February 7, 1936	*The South Pole Terror* (about 78 days)

1936

~ February 14 to ~ February 28	*The Infernal Buddha* (about two weeks)
~ March 1 to ~ March 10	*The Mental Wizard* (about 10 days)
mid to late March	*Devil on the Moon* (13 days)
April	*The Golden Peril* (4 days)
early to mid May	*The Feathered Octopus* (11 days)
mid May to early July	Doc is at the Fortress of Solitude.
early July	*The Living Fire Menace* (3 days)
July 8-15	*The Mountain Monster* (8 days)
July	John Sunlight finds the Fortress of Solitude.
August 1-4	*Tunnel Terror* (4 days)
~ August 11-16	*Horror in Gold* (6 days)
~ August 17 to August 29	*The Desert Demons* (about 13 days); Doc gets involved on Aug. 24; second dirigible is destroyed.

~ August 31 to ~ September 17	*The Forgotten Realm* (about 18 days)
August 14 to ~ December 27	*Ost* (about 137 days); Doc gets involved ~ September 26; debut of third "demountable" dirigible.

1937

~ January 12-28	*The Sea Angel* (about 17 days); a small dirigible is in the warehouse – may or may not be the third from *Ost*, or perhaps a mistake.
early February to early March	*Fortress of Solitude* (33 days)
March 15 to April 3	*The Pirate's Ghost* (20 days)
early April to late August	*The Red Terrors* (143 days); Doc is on vacation for the first "nine weeks"
~ August 28 to ~ September 27	*Mad Mesa* (about 30 days)
October 7 to ~ October 27	*The Devil Genghis* (about 21 days)
late October to early November	*The Munitions Master* (6 days)
early November to mid December	*The Submarine Mystery* (33 days)
mid to late December	*The Giggling Ghosts* (9 days)

1938

~ February 4-16	*The Green Death* (13 days): debut of fourth ("big") dirigible.
Spring?	*Merchants of Disaster* (8 days)
~ June 6-12	*The Yellow Cloud* (about 7 days)
June 22-27	*Hex* (6 days)
~ July 3-23	*The Gold Ogre* (21 days)
~ August 4-11	*The Freckled Shark* (about 8 days)
August 12-30	*The Flaming Falcons* (19 days)
September 4-7	*Poison Island* prologue (4 days)
early September	*The Crimson Serpent* (4 days)
mid September	*The Angry Ghost* (7 days)
September 16	*The Stone Man* prologue (1 day)
~ September 24-26	*The Headless Men* (3 days); fourth dirigible destroyed.
~ October 14 to ~ October 21	*Poison Island* (8 days)
November 7-13	*The Stone Man* (7 days)

December 9-20	*The Dagger in the Sky* (12 days)
late December to late January, 1939	Doc is on vacation.

1939

late January	*The Dagger in the Sky* epilogue (2 days)
mid to late March	*The Other World* (7 days)
~ April 1 to May 4	*The Magic Forest* (about 34 days)
~ May 4 to early June?	Doc stays in Alaska following *The Magic Forest.*
July	*The Death Lady* (11 days)
early August	*The Spotted Men* (3 days)
August 12-16	*The Purple Dragon* (5 days)
mid August to early September	*The Awful Egg* (18 days)
mid to late September	*The Flying Goblin* (10 days)
early October	*The Mindless Monsters* (2 days); debut of fifth ("small") dirigible.
mid October to November 3	Doc is at the Fortress of Solitude?
October 30 to November 5	*The Evil Gnome* (7 days)
~ November 12-14	*The Boss of Terror* (3 days)

| mid November to early March, 1940 | Monk works in Japan, sabotages a chemical plant, foreseeing the day when the U.S. would be at war with Japan. |

1940

mid February to early March	Doc is investigating events leading to *Devils of the Deep* (two weeks).
early to late March	*Devils of The Deep* (about 21 days)
April 10 to ~ May 15	*The Awful Dynasty* (about 36 days)
~ June 5-7	*The Pink Lady* (3 days)
~ June 15-18	Doc is investigating *The Green Eagle* case (4 days).
~ June 19-27	*The Green Eagle* (9 days)
early to mid July	*The Men Vanished* (about 10 days)
mid July to August 2	Doc is at the Fortress of Solitude while Monk and Ham investigate *The Devil's Playground*.
August 2-4	*The Devil's Playground* (3 days)
August 12-28	*Bequest of Evil* (17 days)
early September	*The All-White Elf* (4 days)
September 17-19	*The Too-Wise Owl* (3 days)

late September to mid January, 1941	*The Golden Man* (about 116 days); Doc gets involved in mid January.
October 23-29	*The Stone Death* (7 days) [if you consider it canonical]

1941

	Unrecorded adventure ending in Charleston, SC?
April	*Mystery Island* (3 days)
April	*Birds of Death* (6 days)
May 8-11	*The Rustling Death* (4 days); last mention of fifth dirigible.
~ May 25-27	*Peril in The North* (3 days); Doc's birthday is probably May 26.
June	Doc is investigating *The Invisible-Box Murders* (about 3 days).
June	*The Invisible-Box Murders* (4 days)
July	*The Time Terror* (6 days)
July	*The Talking Devil* (6 days)
August 12-14	*Waves of Death* (3 days)
mid August	Doc is at the Fortress of Solitude.

mid to late August	*The Laugh of Death* (8 days)
August 26 to October 20	*The Devil's Black Rock* (56 days); Doc gets involved on October 19.
~ September 3-7	*Men of Fear* (5 days)
mid September	*The Three Wild Men* (2 days)
early October	*The Fiery Menace* (3 days)
October 7-16	*They Died Twice* (10 days)
late October	*The Man Who Fell Up* (3 days)
late October	Johnny disappears prior while on his way to China to *Pirate Isle.*
November	Monk is in England, meets Winston Churchill.
November to early January, 1942	Doc is at the Fortress of Solitude?

1942

January 8-22	*Pirate Isle* (15 days)
~ January 24-26	*The Speaking Stone* (3 days)
~ January 26 to late February?	Doc stays in Arriba to study the culture.
late February or early March	Doc tries to get involved in the war

	effort (as described in *The Fiery Menace*).
March 7-15	*The King of Terror* (9 days)
June	*The Running Skeletons* (2 days)
mid July	*Mystery on Happy Bones* (2 days)
mid to late July	*The Goblins* (3 days)
late July	*The Mental Monster* (1 day)
~ July 27-31	*Hell Below* (5 days)
~ August 23-25	*The Whisker of Hercules* (3 days)
~ August 27-31	*The Secret of the Su* (5 days)
~ September 1-7	Doc and crew stay with the Su (about a week).
September 11-24	Doc is investigating *The Spook of Grandpa Eben* (two weeks).
September 24-26	*The Spook of Grandpa Eben* (3 days)
October 1-5	*According to Plan of a One-Eyed Mystic* (5 days)
November 18-22	*The Black, Black Witch* (5 days)
December to April, 1943	Monk's skin is turned green due to a chemical accident in Doc's lab.

1943

April	*Death Had Yellow Eyes* (3 days)
late April	*The Three Devils* (2 days)
late May	*The Pharaoh's Ghost* (4 days)
late June	*The Man Who Was Scared* (4 days)
	Unrecorded adventure beginning with Elma Champion at her ranch?
July or August	*The Shape of Terror* (3 days)
mid or late September	Doc is investigating *The Derelict of Skull Shoal* (about 3 days).
late September	*The Derelict of Skull Shoal* (5 days)
December	*The Lost Giant* (4 days)

1944

early April	*The Terrible Stork* (3 days)
early April	*Weird Valley* (3 days)
~ April 10 to May 18	Doc is undercover working on the *Jiu San* case (six weeks).
May 19 to June 20	*Jiu San* (33 days)
~ June 29 to ~ July 4	Doc is investigating *Satan Black* (about five days).

222

~ July 5-8	*Satan Black* (4 days)
mid July	*King Joe Cay* (2 days)
late July	*The Wee Ones* (3 days)
August	*Violent Night* (2 days)
mid to late August	*Strange Fish* (5 days)
	Unrecorded adventure involving plane crash at nearby ranch (possibly became *The Lost Giant*).
late August	*The Ten Ton Snakes* (5 days)
mid to late September	*Cargo Unknown* (12 days)
October	Monk and Ham go to Europe prior to *Measures for a Coffin.*
early December	*Measures for a Coffin* (4 days)

1945

January	*Rock Sinister* (5 days)
mid or late May	*Terror Takes 7* (2 days)
first half of July	*The Thing That Pursued* (2 days)
August 1- 2	*Trouble on Parade* (2 days)
early August	*The Screaming Man* (6 days)
~ August 28-31	*Fire and Ice* (4 days)

~ September 13-17	*Se-Pah-Poo* (5 days)
mid September	*Terror and the Lonely Widow* (3 days)
late September	*Five Fathoms Dead* prologue (1 day)
early October	*Five Fathoms Dead* (8 days)
~ October 20-21	*Death is a Round Black Spot* (2 days)
late October	*The Disappearing Lady* (2 days)
November	*Colors for Murder* (2 days)
December	Doc is on vacation in Miami prior to *Three Times a Corpse.*
December	*Three Times a Corpse* (2 days)

1946

January	*The Exploding Lake* (18 days)
February 1- 2	*No Light to Die By* (2 days)
April	*Danger Lies East* (3 days)
early May	*The Monkey Suit* (2 days)
early July	*Death in Little Houses* (3 days)
early July to mid July	Doc is investigating *The Devil is Jones* (a week).

mid July	*The Devil is Jones* (2 days)
late July	*Target for Death* (9 days)

1947

February	*The Pure Evil* (2 days)
early March	Doc and crew begin investigations leading to *Terror Wears No Shoes.*
mid April	*Terror Wears No Shoes* (4 days)
mid April to early June	Doc and crew are quarantined due to the events of *Terror Wears No Shoes.*
early June	*Let's Kill Ames* (3 days)
June	Doc is investigating *Once Over Lightly* (about a week).
June	*Once Over Lightly* (4 days)
June	*I Died Yesterday* (1 day)
early July	Monk goes to Russia in preparation for *The Red Spider*; Ham follows a short time later.
late November to early December	*The Red Spider* (12 days)
mid December	*The Green Master* (5 days)

1948

Winter

Doc moves out of his 86th floor headquarters, sleeping at motels, due to the threat of Soviet assassination attempts

~ April 1-5

Return From Cormoral (5 days)

early to mid April

The Angry Canary (4 days)

June 10-19

Doomsday (10 days)

late June

The Swooning Lady (1 day)

late June or early July

Doc assumes "Banner" identity, spends "three months" undercover in Scandinavia and northwest Russia in preparation for *Flight Into Fear*.

October 2-5

Flight Into Fear (14 days)

1949

January 16-24

The Frightened Fish (9 days)

~ January 25-February 2

voyage back to New York City following *The Frightened Fish*.

mid February

Up From Earth's Center (6 days)

Part IV

Conclusions

Although Doc Savage was active prior to *The Man of Bronze* (Fall 1931) – probably adventuring by himself – it was with this adventure that his career truly began. Doc was likely adventuring part-time – perhaps as part of his latter training – because it is during Winter 1932 that he really gears up for his career, installing his private express elevator and developing the bulletproof vests. Doc puts his aides through a Mayan language crash course. He purchases the warehouse that will become his "Hidalgo Trading Company" hangar and begins its renovations, including the installation of the "flea run". That none of this was ready by the time of *The Man of Bronze* suggests that Doc's adventuring prior to this novel was done while traveling the world as part of his training (he was already becoming famous throughout the world by the time of *The Man of Bronze* and his tri-motor is "years old").

Contrary to popular images of Doc and his crew, they dressed in clothing normal for the period (Monk albeit a little gaudier and shabbier, and Ham quite a bit more fashionably), including suit coats, vests and hats. Dress was so uniform in the 1930s that it wasn't necessary to state this, unlike today, when what a person wears can reveal quite a lot about them. Doc himself is usually found in "dark" or "brown" business suits (the few times his attire is mentioned at all), underneath which he wears his famous vest of gadgets. *The Pirate's Ghost* states: "The contents of the vest, of course, rarely remained the same for any two engagements. He changed the gadgets in the pockets to fit situations". But he does stock some standard devices; these include a nose clip, a miniature periscope/telescope/microscope, an infra-red lantern and goggles, smoke bombs, firecrackers, anaesthetic grenades, a spring-generator flashlight, explosive and a variety of other types of grenades, a silk line and grapnel, and ultraviolet chalk. "The vest was padded, so that its presence under the bronze man's clothing [was] not ... noticeable", according to *The Metal Master*.

None of Doc's aides seem to have grown up wealthy. Both Johnny and Monk probably grew up on farms, based on comments on the series. Renny, we are told in more than one early adventure, made his fortune, while Ham must have done the same in order to be able to live at the Midas Club. Long Tom's miserliness suggests depravation when young.

Dent, in *Death in Silver* (August 1933), tells us that Pat's salon, "The Park Avenue Beautician", is located on Park Avenue. Donovan states that the salon is not on Park Avenue, but near it (*Land of Long Juju*, June 1934). The next reference by Dent, in *The Feathered Octopus* (May 1936), puts the salon off Park Avenue, agreeing with Donovan. Later, its name is "Patricia, Inc." (*The Yellow Cloud*, June 1938), the first contemporary reference to its name since *Death in Silver*. This suggests that she has moved the salon and renamed it, probably prior to June 1935. Dent, without naming it, puts it back on Park Avenue in *The Men Vanished* (June 1940), though, so it probably never changed locations, only names.

The first mention of Doc employing his graduates is in *Cold Death* (June 1934), where they are working at the Hidalgo Trading Company hangar. They are employed there in a variety of tasks throughout the 1930s (as well as working elsewhere in other occupations). The last mention of them in that capacity is in *The Red Terrors* (Summer 1937), where they are crewing Doc's yacht.

But the graduates are more importantly working as a worldwide detective agency, gathering information for Doc, first mentioned in *Fortress of Solitude* (January 1937). Some of them work part-time, having regular jobs and living otherwise normal lives; but maybe **all** of Doc's graduates keep an eye out for trouble around the world for Doc, whether they work for the detective agency or not. This is suggested by the "scores" of them that are in U.S. alone (mentioned in *The Flaming Falcons*). This worldwide detective agency may be the one mentioned in *The Disappearing Lady* (October 1945), though it does not specifically state that organization is composed of graduates. That comment may be a reference to the mysterious organization mentioned in only one adventure, *The King Maker* (June 1933), and hinted at in another (*The Three Wild Men*, October 1941). The men of this organization may be contacts

Doc developed in his world travels prior to *The Man of Bronze*, men who shared the same goals as Doc, men whom he could trust; he surely would have foreseen the usefulness – almost the necessity – of such informants in his career (and he probably could not have foreseen the success of his crime college so early in his career). These men may be the "special correspondents" mentioned in *The Time Terror* (July 1941); they are not referred to as graduates, or as belonging to a detective agency.

Doc first (apparently) appropriates an elevator in the Empire State Building for his use by the time of *Dust of Death* (January 1935). This seems to be a normal elevator, certainly not his "express" model (alternately, it may have been a normal elevator in every respect, with those wishing to see Doc referred to the screening room by the building's directory). A year later (in *The Feathered Octopus*, May 1936), Doc has a screening room in place, on the second floor of the building. A ground floor screening room weeding out those who seek financial assistance is added later (by the time of *The Other World*, March 1939), but the other screening room is still used (primarily by Monk and Ham, the two aides who appear most often in the series), but it is now on the twentieth floor (*The Awful Egg*, August 1939). It moves to its permanent location on the fifth floor, mentioned in several novels, by April 1941 (*Birds of Death*). In *The Wee Ones* (July 1944) this floor is mistakenly called "the twelfth". But by December of that year (*Measures for a Coffin*), the screening is done by a private detective agency on the fourth floor; Doc's aides no longer seem to be involved in the process. Although Doc has been using the agency for some time (and has been using numerous agencies since long before *Resurrection Day* (Spring 1935), according to that adventure), it is not stated this agency has been screening visitors for Doc long, and has probably taken over the job since *The Wee Ones*, only months earlier. This doesn't work out and the next mention of the screening room is in *Five Fathoms Dead* (October 1945), again located on the fifth floor, in what "seemed" to be a private detective agency. Have Monk and Ham reopened the office they had used for a few years? No mention is made of them, yet it seems likely they have done so while Doc looks for another detective agency to do the screening. By the time of *The Exploding Lake* (January 1946), he has done so; it is located in Room 710 (on the seventh floor) of the building. At least four more references to a private detective agency doing Doc's screening are made in the series, but its location nor his aides' involvement with it are ever mentioned (Ham was at the one in *The Exploding Lake*). We may assume that this is Doc's final agency. It is interesting to speculate that this agency is manned by his graduates, though there is no evidence of this whatever (the only hint that this **might** be the case is that Doc "maintained" this last detective agency, which he would not do if it were privately owned like Durwell's; the owner would naturally "maintain" it). Why Doc does not employ them in this fashion, although they belong to a detective agency, is never addressed in the series; it is certain that the first (named) agency Doc uses, Durwell, is not composed of graduates.

No mention is ever made of the ages of Doc or his aides, at least directly. The closest we get to the aides' ages is a reference in *Quest of the Spider* that one of Ham's college buddies started his business thirty years earlier, putting his age (and Ham's) at fifty, at least, in 1932. We do know that all the aides served in World War I (even though Johnny has no rank), according to comments in both *The Man of Bronze* and *The Land of Terror*, and their ubiquitous ranks, so we can make some educated guesses as to their ages. Because advancement through the ranks during the peacetime following the war was almost nonexistent, it is almost certain that they had attained their military ranks during the war (we are told that Ham did). Based on their ranks, all of the aides must have been in their thirties by the end of World War I, at least, making their birth years no later than 1885 (roughly), and quite probably earlier. For example, Major Greg "Pappy" Boyington, the **highest ranking Allied ace** in World War II was 29 when he became a major – and he pulled a slick maneuver to do so (he should have been a captain). So almost certainly none were under thirty when the war ended in 1918 (this means that all were established in their professions **prior to** World War I). This makes them 50ish in *The Man of Bronze*, which fits with the comment in *Quest of the Spider*. Ham, with the highest rank, is undoubtedly older (and we can speculate that, given Monk's temperament, he was probably passed over for promotion or demoted at least once in his military career, making him older than the others, as well; Farmer estimates Monk was born in 1899, making him fifteen when the war broke out in 1914 – while working as a chemist in Italy! I have to wonder if this is actually a typo for "1889". In *Tarzan Alive*, Farmer states, "Monk was born circa 1890".). And there were no true generals under the age of thirty-five in World War I, also suggesting that Ham's age at the time of *The Man of Bronze* was more likely fifty-five. They are therefore at least 60ish (with Ham a decade older) at the end of the adventures, which may account for the diminished participation of Renny, Long Tom and Johnny (whom I always thought of as the oldest for some reason) in the later tales.

There are numerous comments to suggest that Doc is about twenty-one when his training is completed, and some state that this was shortly before *The Man of Bronze*, particularly those in *No Light to Die By*, in a letter written by Doc himself. We know that Doc was working on the resurrection process used in *Resurrection Day* no later than 1925. This is probably after his training had been completed, but we cannot be sure; he must at least have had his M.D. If he is twenty then, he is twenty-six in *The Man of Bronze*. We know Doc was likely born no earlier than 1904, based on comments from *Devil on the Moon*, and before 1911 based on comments in *They Died Twice*. I strongly believe his birth year is in the 1905-1907 range ... but I could be talked into 1908.

What about that comment in *The Man of Bronze*, made by Doc himself, that Doc met his aides during World War I? The comments in *The Land of Terror* seem to exclude him: Doc's "five friends ... had first assembled during the Great War".

Oddly, it does not say "Doc **and** his five friends". Doc's military rank in that war is never mentioned, and during World War II, he is said to have an honorary rank of Brigadier General. Why? The ranks of the others are often commented upon (with the exception of Johnny, as previously noted). Perhaps Dent did not know how Doc met each of his aides, and fudged the account to include Doc, creating an easy explanation (remember that Doc is portrayed as violent, out of character, particularly in those first two published stories; obviously, Dent did not have all the facts concerning Doc at that time). If we are to believe Doc did meet his aides during the war, he would then likely be at least in his middle thirties, in *The Man of Bronze*, a far cry from "about twenty" (even Farmer's estimate puts him at 29). There may be a good reason the explanation of Doc meeting his aides from *The Man of Bronze* is **never repeated**: It may not be correct. In reference to Doc and his aides, Dent's notebook contains the statement: "The others were his companions in the World War". No further information is given, and although there are references to each of the aides' participation in World War I, there is not a **single** reference to Doc's role in the war in the **forty pages** of notes about him.

Further, in *The Man of Bronze*, Doc says, "Tonight we begin carrying out the ideals of my father". Why couldn't they have begun doing so before he was killed? Was it because Doc was too young? Doc's father, who had planned from his son's birth for Doc to lead the life he did, did not have a private aerodrome built for him. Remember, he'd had the Fortress, the college and the 86th floor built and/or equipped starting in 1929, at the latest (more likely 1925, when Doc began work on the resurrection process). But no aerodrome. Is this a further clue that Doc undertook his lifelong mission early?

The evidence suggests that Doc was born about 1906, and did not serve in World War I. It is clear that Doc was very near to "inheriting" the Valley of the Vanished from his father at the time of the latter's death in Fall 1931, and would therefore undertake his life's work shortly thereafter. I believe that Doc was born in Spring (late May) 1907, and **would have** started his career near his twenty-fifth birthday in Spring 1932, if not for the murder of his father.

Doc was surely a child prodigy, years ahead of other children his age. It would have been possible for him to have begun college-level courses (taught by his special tutors, of course) at age twelve (circa 1919, I believe), and become an M.D. by age sixteen (circa 1923; even with Doc's brilliance and his father's money, there is no way around four years of medical school to become a doctor). The "Boards" and the residency program of today were not so formalized in the early part of the twentieth century, and Doc could have opted out of an apprenticeship following medical school. Conceivably, he could have practiced medicine, as a General Practitioner, following graduation.

I believe – but cannot prove – that Doc met his aides through his father, and that Dent was not privy to this information (at least when he wrote the early adventures). It is obvious from comments in *The Man of Bronze* that they all knew the elder Savage. "Moved by mutual admiration for" him, they "decided to take up his work of good". Note that it is not their admiration for **Doc**, whom they supposedly have known for more than ten years, but for his **father**, with whom they were peers in both age and accomplishment.

And there are a couple of curious incidents that suggest that perhaps Doc's aides are not as old as I've deduced. Ham, in *According to Plan of a One-Eyed Mystic* (October 1942), is worried that the wrinkles in his make-up will stay on his face. Yet he must be more than sixty-five years old at the time. Why is his hair "prematurely" gray in *The Man of Bronze* when he's at least fifty-five? One could **expect** a man in his middle fifties to have gray hair. Monk, in *Hell Below*, calls a man "old-timer" and "pop" even though he must be at least sixty years old himself. Does any reader really think of Monk and Ham as being in their fifties during the heyday of Doc's adventures (in the 1930s)? There is **not one** disparaging comment about two old men chasing women in their twenties (sometimes even younger) in all the novels. It may also be of note that outside of the story concerning Monk and Ham getting each other into trouble during World War I, there are no virtually no references to the wartime activities of any of the aides after *The Land of Terror*, the second adventure (and what few there were have been noted in the comments for the adventures). Is this because Dent found out that his account of their wartime service was incorrect? Did Dent, in fact, **invent** prestigious backgrounds for them, either out of ignorance or in order to bolster Doc's reputation? Lastly, if Doc's aides were all experts in their fields, virtually unchallenged but for Doc himself, why weren't any of them his tutors in the years prior to World War I, when they were all apparently in their late twenties, at least, and presumably established in their fields? It is just possible that Doc's aides were young men during World War I, not having the described ranks attributed to them, and not yet established in their professions; this would make them in their early thirties at the beginning of the series, and explain some of the oddities I've mentioned. However, I'm not suggesting that this is enough evidence to ignore the references to the aides' war service. But it is kind of interesting, isn't it?

Although no mention is made of it, I believe Doc retired to the Valley of the Vanished, marrying Princess Monja, some time after *Up From Earth's Center* (Winter 1949), perhaps directing the actions of his graduates' detective agency from behind the scenes. Doc probably turned forty-two that year. Comments in later novels – both textual and character by both Doc and Pat – suggest he is maturing out of the "kid stuff" part of his personality, the part that was afraid of women and loved excitement. In 1950, the floors above the 80th (that is, 81-85) were converted into television broadcasting facilities. This probably coincided with Doc moving out of his headquarters permanently.

Perhaps Doc felt as though he had become too easy a target for too many criminals, as evidenced by the comments in *Return From Cormoral*. Perhaps he felt his Herculean physique beginning to fade with age (no one else would have noticed, probably). Perhaps he decided that his vocation **was** silly -- in the way he practiced it, at least, as he reflects in more than one later novel. Perhaps he felt, as the later adventures show, that there weren't that many world-threatening villains anymore, and his time would be better spent as scientist than as adventurer. Perhaps he was humbled by his experience in the Maine caverns in *Up From Earth's Center*, his first real defeat (I like to believe he returned to the caverns and emerged victorious, supernatural menace or not). Or maybe he just realized he had no place in a world of atomic weapons and cold war.

Afterword

My first DOC SAVAGE book was *The Red Skull*, which I found at a shoe repair/used book shop in 1970, mistaking it for a book about Captain America and **his** foe, the Red Skull. I was nine years old and I was hooked. The fantastic gadgets. Doc's stoicism and code against killing. The rapid-fire pace of the story. The weird, cool, **crisp** names. Doc's brilliant foresight. Monk and Ham (especially Monk).

I began buying every "Doc" I could get my hands on. Within a few months, I purchased *The Pirate's Ghost* (published July 1971) new (for a whopping 75 cents; the last few I bought secondhand in the mid-90s cost quite a bit more, as many of you probably already know).

Many of the ones I read back then and loved so much are still my favorites today. These include *The Red Skull*, *The Czar of Fear*, *The Fantastic Island*, *The Secret in the Sky*, *Mystery Under the Sea*, *He Could Stop the World*, *Land of Always-Night*, *The Pirate's Ghost*, *The Freckled Shark*, *The Other World*, and *The Purple Dragon*.

My reading of ones collected later in life, or re-reading of the ones collected earlier, left me with more favorites, such as *The Polar Treasure*, *Python Isle*, *The Spook Legion*, *White Eyes*, *The Mental Wizard*, *The Terror in the Navy*, *Death in Silver*, *Danger Lies East*, *Fortress of Solitude*, *Pirate Isle*, *The Three Wild Men* and *The Living-Fire Menace*.

My two favorites would have to be *The Red Skull* and *The Freckled Shark*. If you've ever wondered how Doc has managed to stay alive for so long in his dangerous occupation, read *The Red Skull*. *The Freckled Shark* is probably the funniest of the novels. *The Fantastic Island*, in particular, would make a good movie. Can you see The Rock as Doc? How about Jessica Biel as Pat?

Lester Dent, of course, was the best "Kenneth Robeson". Of the other contemporary "Kenneth Robesons", I liked Johnson best – whose style most closely approximated Dent's, in my opinion – followed by Donovan. Davis' are kind of hit-or-miss for me. Some are very good, making my "favorites" list, but others leave me cold (*The Living-Fire Menace* contains probably the best single scene in the entire series: Doc believes he is going to die in attempting an escape, and having been in disguise, removes it so that the last image his men have of him alive will be that of his true face and form). Hathway's leave no impression on me, but they are quite similar to Davis', according to Murray. The worst Docs were written by Bogart, in my opinion (although I enjoyed *The Flying Goblin*, for instance). *Death in Little Houses*, despite its title and a couple of interesting ideas, is my nomination for the single worst Doc novel (followed closely by *The Disappearing Lady*, also by Bogart). My lack of affection about Bogart may be due to the fact that I liked his **type** of story less, although he turned in a few really enjoyable ones. I like the latter adventures (even Dent's) less than I like the earlier adventures, with the superhuman Doc, and his colorful world-beating villains and their fantastic "infernal machines". This phase began with *The Men Vanished* (published December 1940), the first adventure wherein there was no "fantastic element", although it didn't gain its full force until Moran took over as editor in 1943.

Farmer made *Escape From Loki* too much his own for me to consider it canonical, which was why it was not discussed. The first rule, to my mind, of a Doc Savage story is that it must be "Dent-esque". The style and tone of *Escape From Loki* are simply too different from Dent's (and the story is not based on an unfinished work by Dent, as Murray's are). And just as importantly – perhaps even more so – the novel is based upon speculations Farmer made in his biography of Doc, *Doc Savage: His Apocalyptic Life* (which I recommend, despite the slanted perspective and unwarranted speculations therein). It gave me a lifelong love of "behind-the-scenes" books; I've since branched out to the Shadow, Sherlock Holmes, John Carter of Mars, Tarzan, etc. As of 2011, I've written one myself: *The Way They Were: the Histories of Some of Adventure*

Fiction's Most Famous Heroes and Villains, which includes a section of Doc Savage.

Will Murray does such a brilliant job of writing as a "Kenneth Robeson" that my first reaction is to say that no other writer could do it. This may not literally be true, of course, but it is hard for me to imagine anyone else writing as genuine a "Doc Savage" novel forty years after the fact. I could usually tell when one of Dent's contemporary ghost writers wrote a story; I'm not sure I could with Murray. He uses authentic 1930s and, more importantly, **Dent** language in his narration, not just in dialogue (as other novelists have done for effect). Murray writes of his novels, in his Afterword in *Omnibus* #13: "Every effort will be made to make them as authentic as possible". He keeps his word.

My own *The Stone Death*, based on a short synopsis by Davis, Dent's first ghost writer, was published as a serial at The Hidalgo Trading Company website ("www.docsavage.org") in 1999, and is still there. It occurs during the time that Monk and Ham are in a South American jail in *The Golden Man* (Fall 1940), and has been placed in the chronology for those of you who consider canonical.

Each story was read twice in preparation for this chronology. About 80% were read a third time, upon purchase (whenever that may have been), years before I constructed a chronology. Parts of a dozen or so were re-read, for clarification about a specific point. Three hundred pages of notes in a three-ring binder notebook were compiled. The first edition of this book is the result of more than seven hundred man-hours of labor, and, in addition to being a lot of work, was a lot of fun. I hope you enjoyed it.

I welcome your comments.

Jeff Deischer
Ikonoklast61@juno.com

January, 1999

PS (2002) After this book first went to press I received the submission **dates** for the novels, and planned a revision based on those dates, using it for my LPO rather than the publishing date. I found thirty-eight adventures would have to be moved. Some of these could be moved without much trouble, but in many cases, the submission-based LPO contradicted internal evidence. *The Pure Evil* is just such an example. The internal evidence clearly points to early 1947 – but this is beyond the submission date LPO! Central to the story are events that occurred in India and Pakistan. Placing this in early 1946, to fit the weather as well as the submission LPO therefore doesn't work. My feeling is that if I need to ignore internal evidence such as weather, et al., then my entire chronology could be considered invalid. Therefore, I have chosen not to revise the chronology based on submission dates, as it would invalidate too many placements, and by extension, the whole work.

APPENDIX A
Doc Savage Adventures in Order of Submission
with publishing order and cover dates

The Man of Bronze	1	March 1933
The Land of Terror	2	April 1933
Quest of the Spider	3	May 1933
The Polar Treasure	4	June 1933
Pirate of the Pacific	5	July 1933
The Red Skull	6	August 1933
The Lost Oasis	7	September 1933
The Sargasso Ogre	8	October 1933
The Czar of Fear	9	November 1933
The Phantom City	10	December 1933
Brand of the Werewolf	11	January 1934
The Man Who Shook the Earth	12	February 1934
Meteor Menace	13	March 1934
The Monsters	14	April 1934
The Mystery on the Snow	15	May 1934
The King Maker	16	June 1934
The Thousand-Headed Man	17	July 1934
The Squeaking Goblin	18	August 1934
Fear Cay	19	September 1934
Death in Silver	20	October 1934
Python Isle	183	October 1991
The Sea Magician	21	November 1934
The Annihilist	22	December 1934
The Mystic Mullah	23	January 1935
Red Snow	24	February 1935
Land of Always-Night	25	March 1935
The Spook Legion	26	April 1935
The Secret in the Sky	27	May 1935
Spook Hole	30	August 1935
The Roar Devil	28	June 1935
Quest of Qui	29	July 1935
Cold Death	43	September 1936
The Majii	31	September 1935
Mystery Under the Sea	36	February 1936
Murder Melody	33	November 1935
The Fantastic Island	34	December 1935
Dust of Death	32	October 1935
The Seven Agate Devils	39	May 1936
Murder Mirage	35	January 1936
The Midas Man	42	August 1936

244

246

APPENDIX B
Ghost Writers Author List

It should be noted that almost every one of the following adventures written by Dent's ghost writers were collaborations between the ghost writer and Dent, to varying degrees. In some cases, the adventure was heavily re-written by Dent. Donovan and Hathway (and Bogart, in at least some later cases) wrote directly for Street & Smith, and Dent did not edit their work. See Murray's article "The Secret Kenneth Robesons", which was reprised as the Afterword in *The Frightened Fish*, for more information.

William Bogart
The Angry Ghost
The Awful Dynasty
Bequest of Evil
Death in Little Houses
The Death Lady
The Disappearing Lady
Fire and Ice
The Flying Goblin
Hex
The Magic Forest
The Spotted Men
Target for Death
Tunnel Terror
World's Fair Goblin

Evelyn Coulson
The Yellow Cloud

Harold Davis
The Crimson Serpent
Devils of the Deep
Dust of Death
The Exploding Lake

The Golden Peril
The Green Death
The King Maker
The Land of Fear
The Living-Fire Menace
Merchants of Disaster
The Mountain Monster
The Munitions Master
The Purple Dragon

Laurence Donovan
The Black Spot
Cold Death
Haunted Ocean
He Could Stop the World
Land of Long Juju
Mad Eyes
The Men Who Smiled No More
Murder Melody
Murder Mirage

Alan Hathway
The Devil's Playground
The Headless Men
The Mindless Monsters
The Rustling Death

Ryerson Johnson
The Fantastic Island
Land of Always-Night
The Motion Menace

Will Murray
The Desert Demons
Flight Into Fear
The Forgotten Realm
The Frightened Fish
Horror in Gold

250
The Infernal Buddha
The Jade Ogre
Python Isle
The Whistling Wraith
White Eyes

APPENDIX C
Mapping Doc Savage's "86th" Floor Headquarters

The perimeter of the Empire State Building, where Doc Savage has his headquarters, is rectangular, the long side being roughly one and a half times as long as the short side. The corners of the building are nearly aligned with the points of the compass; the long sides of the rectangle are the northeast and the southwest walls. An inner rectangle of approximately the same proportions is at the center of the 85th floor, the highest floor that Doc Savage could have lived on; the 86th floor has always been the Observation deck. This inner rectangle houses the building mechanicals: elevators, ventilation, stairs, restrooms and fire-fighting areas.

As stated in *The Terrible Stork*, Doc arranged his headquarters around the existing building mechanicals, changing not even the hallways; this comment, along with others throughout the series, invalidates a minority of scenes that put windows at the end of one hall, among other things.

Doc's private express elevator lies in the alcove at (1), beyond the only bank of elevators – the freight elevators (F) – on the floor, according to *The Magic Forest*. Comments in *The Man of Bronze*, *The Land of Terror* and *Pirate of Pacific* – wherein it is revealed that Doc does not occupy the entire 86th floor at the time – to name but three references, also suggest this.

The reception room (REC), we know, is in the west corner of the floor, according to virtually every account in the series. *The Man of Bronze*, for example, actually calls it the "west" corner. Virtually the only information that disputes this is scenes wherein Doc is shot at from a neighboring building, supposedly the Chrysler Building ("Mercator Automotive Building", although it goes unnamed in two of its three mentions).

There is one door (2) visible from the (single) passenger (P) elevator that goes to the 86th floor, and it is not in the opposite direction from the door to the reception room, according to *The Green Death*. This is an entrance to the operating room (3). This room would naturally be the size of an ER operating room, or approximately so. The door to this room is also probably the door from which Ham emerges in *The Evil Gnome*; that door is said to be "at the side of" the elevator.

Although Doc has not re-arranged the standard layout of the floor (as previously described), the door to the reception room must face NW, as a small washroom (4) next to the reception room has access to the hallway outside (described in both *The Headless Men* and *Bequest of Evil*).

Despite Farmer's detailed map of Doc's 86th floor headquarters in *Doc Savage: His Apocalyptic Life*, there is not enough evidence in the adventures to place Doc's many items of furniture and various devices and equipment. The large safe in the reception room is likely against an inside wall, and the inlaid table, into which are built several controls, seems to be in front of the door to the library, but there isn't enough information to be certain.

Comments in *The King Maker* seem to place the library (LIB) on the northwest side of the building; in *Fortress of Solitude*, we're told the windows face north. *The Mystery on the Snow* tells us that the doors to the reception room and the lab are visible to one another, and in fact, the bookcases are so arranged as to form a "corridor" (5), which is said to be filled with traps, although some people, such as Sammy Wales, in *No Light to Die By*, have managed to wander around in the library without setting them off. (6) seems to be a logical location for the hidden niche that Doc sometimes uses to observe those in the reception room. It is large enough to comfortably hold a chair and more than one person, and so is deep; the size of the pillar next to this location would suggest this depth (about five feet). A case, which Sammy finds, that holds Doc's awards, is in one corner, and seems not be against the windows; the location of the niche therefore leaves this corner (7), the only one available. The location of the northern wall between the library and lab would seem to be determined by the existing building mechanicals wall.

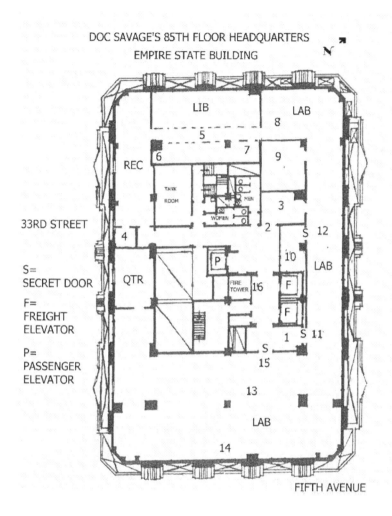

DOC SAVAGE'S 85TH FLOOR HEADQUARTERS
EMPIRE STATE BUILDING

N

LIB

LAB

8

5

REC

6

7

9

TANK
ROOM

MEN

3

WOMEN

33RD STREET

2

4

S   12

P

10

S=
SECRET DOOR

QTR

FIRE
TOWER

16

LAB

F

F=
FREIGHT
ELEVATOR

F

P=
PASSENGER
ELEVATOR

1   S   11

S

15

13

LAB

14

FIFTH AVENUE

The lab (LAB) is fully a block long, according to *Python Isle*, and on the east side of the building, according to *The Mystery on the Snow*. By the time of *Quest of Qui*, the lab has windows on three sides, indicating that Doc has expanded it since *Pirate of the Pacific*. The chemical lab (8) is always (or nearly so) the room mentioned when someone enters the lab from the library. With the placement of the chemical lab and the operating room, (9) would therefore be a logical location for the great storeroom, which is near the chemical lab. A secret room (10) that is virtually undetectable would surely use existing walls to disguise its presence. It is large enough to house a couch, where Doc stashes Nan Tester in *The Metal Master*. This room could conceivably have an exit to the outside hallway, but why? With fewer entrances, it would be less detectable, and there is a normal door just around the corner in the operating room.

Since the Empire State Building had been completed some time before the first use of the "flea run" (unnamed in *The Midas Man*) and a new elevator shaft would be a difficult thing to install after completion, the entrance to that conveyance realistically probably does not come all the way up to the 86th floor, and it is Doc's private express elevator Doc and his aides use to get to the basement garage where the true entrance to the flea run lies. But conceivably, the two elevators share the same shaft. Either way, the entrance lies behind a secret wall panel, which must therefore be at (11), originally a doorway.

It is probably Doc's biological-forensics lab (12) that lies along the northeast wall of the lab, a somewhat narrow space (by the way, Doc's lab is never described as being split up into different sections, but it is reasonable to assume that he has grouped *equipment* by use and field. And there is no indication that the lab itself has walls; some rooms, like the storage room and the operating room, are described in such a way that they are separate rooms from the lab itself). It is here that the bird cage secret passage and the poisonous fish bowl secret exit lie, if they are not, in fact, one and the same. I suspect they are; both are mentioned only one time apiece (the fish bowl in *Spook Hole*, and the bird cage in *He Could Stop the World*; although the fish bowl was mentioned in *The Men Who Smiled No More*, the secret exit was not). Did Donovan, the author of *He Could Stop the World*, mis-remember the fish bowl, as an exit which is disguised by a container of animals? This lab is both related to the chemical one just to the west, and it wouldn't require the large machines of Doc's remaining lab, the physics lab (13), which contains equipment for both electronics and atomic works. It also has a machine shop. The southeast wall (14), facing lower New York Bay, opens, and it is from here that Doc fired the ray-repeller in *The Flying Goblin*. It is this and the fact that large machines are necessary for this type of work that suggests this end of the building, a very large area, is probably the physics lab, which reinforces the idea that the biology lab lies to the north, next to the chemistry lab.

There is a secret door that leads directly from the lab to the outside corridor. This undoubtedly lies at (15), because there could be no better place to locate it: There would be little use for one on the other (biological-chemical) side of the lab, since the operating room door is not far away from that location, and, also, this was originally a normal doorway. A secret staircase (16) which leads to the fire cabinet on the floor below, must also be nearby, as the Fire Tower Court lies just on the other side. This is mentioned in *The Spook Legion*.

Doc's living quarters (QTR) lie at the back of the lab; they are small, consisting of two rooms. The first room, which is reached from the lab, is a buffet apartment; the other is a dressing room, as described in *The Land of Fear* and *The Wee Ones*. Because of its location and plumbing concerns, it undoubtedly abuts the reception room's dressing room.

APPENDIX D
The Men Who Made Doc Savage

Much has been written about the men who co-created Doc Savage and the authors who wrote the semi-biographical adventures about him. But what about the scientists and other experts who trained Doc Savage to become the Man of Bronze, the "supreme adventurer", as he was conceived? We are told very little in the way of specifics about the men who tutored Clark Savage, Jr. over the course of the (original) 181 DOC SAVAGE novels. Usually, they are referred to as a group, "the scientists" who trained Doc from the time he was a young child until he was twenty. Only one of them is ever named, definitively, in the original novels: Jerome Coffern. Doc's chemistry tutor, he is killed in the opening pages of *The Land of Terror*, the second novel in the series.

To call Coffern merely a "chemistry teacher" would be to do a disservice to him. Like each of us, Doc probably had a single teacher for the early years of his education, teaching him several basic subjects. Unlike most of us, young Clark Savage, Jr. whizzed through this period – due likely to a combination of Doc's innate genius and his father's experimental teaching methods. Playtime for young Clark, for example, consisted of roughhousing with other boys – older and bigger boys. So Coffern was probably a later specialist who taught young Doc – he had acquired the nickname while still a child (by 1911, according to *They Died Twice*) – the subject of *college-level* chemistry, which Doc must have studied in his early teens. Based on the whole of information in the series, I believe Doc started college-level courses when he was twelve and became an M.D. after four years of medical school at age sixteen, as a General Practitioner.

It is obvious by the grief that Doc experiences in *The Land of Terror* over Coffern's death that he has a deep affection for his former tutor. That Doc does not keep in contact with *any* of his other teachers (as far as we are told) suggests a special bond between him and Coffern, perhaps a unique one. With the elder Savage apparently absent for much of Doc's upbringing, on expeditions (he made at least two trips to Central America in the early 1910s), Coffern might well have been a substitute father figure.

Doc's medical tutor was the head of a large psychiatric hospital in New York City (which seems to be Bellevue Hospital) at the time of *The Majii* (mid 1934). He is apparently murdered during the course of the adventure. I say "apparently" because Doc barely acknowledges this man's death, which is somewhat surprising considering that we are told over and over that medicine was the subject that Doc studied most and best. So it seems quite possible that a subordinate took over the case for Doc's tutor, and it was this man who was actually murdered. Either way, it seems odd that this tutor was never named.

Following his graduation from medical school, Doc studied neurology in Vienna with a classmate named Gaines, according to *The Man Who Was Scared* (*Hell Below* adds that Josef Goebbels – named as "Vogel Plattenheber" in the story -- also attended this university with Doc). *The Golden Man* tells us of a Baron Orrest Karl Lestzky, a "friend" of Doc's who is about to be killed in Vienna. He is a great surgeon, one of the few in the world who understands Doc's brain surgery technique. Was Lestzky in fact Doc's surgical tutor?

Doc had another tutor from Vienna, an elderly man (at the time of *Repel*, 1935) who goes unnamed. He taught electrochemical-astronomy – although one must wonder if in fact this isn't Dent's vague and inaccurate way of saying "astrophysics", the study of the functioning of stars. This otherwise seems an odd combination of sciences, and we already know that Doc's chemistry tutor was Jerome Coffern.

Wo To Sei-Gei is a Chinese philosopher mentioned in *The Fiery Menace* and named by Will Murray in *The Frightened Fish*, where it is revealed that he also taught Jonas Sown, one of Doc's more dangerous adversaries. Sown uses this knowledge to manipulate mass opinion, causing World War

II eventually (as revealed in *The Screaming Man*) – though he has the help of an "infernal machine".

Doc Savage had at least two African tutors – probably rather late in his training, though this is not altogether clear. He seems to have traveled the globe between becoming a surgeon (circa 1925) and the murder of his father in *The Man of Bronze* (1931). For example, the tri-motor he flies in that adventure is "years old". Doc does probably not fly used planes, and likely purchased it new. Also, the men who raised Doc seem to have been scientists, not experts located around the globe, suggesting that this type of training occurred after the tutoring of the scientists (circa 1923, I believe; we know, for example, that Doc had his M.D. no later than 1925, when he started researching the resurrection process seen in *Resurrection Day* (1935)).

And Doc, according to *The Derelict of Skull Shoal*, spent "many months exploring the jungle of northern Brazil, and in the" Guyanas. The only time that Doc had "many months" free to do this was prior to *The Man of Bronze*. This must surely have occurred after his formal tutoring. And let us not forget that Doc's skin is repeatedly said to be bronzed by "tropical suns". Is this a result of his time in South America? And does this mean that this period immediately preceded *The Man of Bronze*? I believe so.

One of these African tutors is an old Ubangi hunter who taught Doc the trick of remaining awake even while sleeping (as described in *Mystery on Happy Bones*). The other, mentioned in *The Fiery Menace*, is a voodoo expert. As voodoo originated in western Africa (actually, the religion from which voodoo came) and the Ubangi people inhabit central Africa, these are likely not the same man. The African "jungle chief" who taught Doc tracking (as told in *Waves of Death*) is probably the Ubangi (since he was a "hunter"), and his people are the "jungle natives in Africa" who taught Doc "the art of silent movement" (as described in *The Goblins*).

But Doc did do *some* globetrotting as a child. "Early in life", a Hindu yogi taught Doc his habit of trilling, according to *The Mental Monster* and *Waves of Death*; *The Laugh of Death* states that the yogi taught Doc emotional control. *The Mental Wizard* adds that Doc learned hypnotism in "India and elsewhere", presumably while under the tutelage of the yogi. And as a child, Doc met the Khedive of Egypt, who gave him an expensive carpet (we are told in *Mystery Under the Sea*). This occurred no later than 1914, when the last Khedive ruled. The title was changed that year for political reasons.

Waves of Death also mentions a Yale expert on atomic phenomena and the unnamed-but-unmistakable Edgar Cayce, the famous "Sleeping Prophet", who is described here as the "Virginia experimenter" in E.S.P.

The Boss of Terror tells us that "the ventriloquist known as the Great Lander had taught the bronze man ... the art of 'throwing' the voice; he had taught Doc to imitate other voices, and to make them seem to come from very far away.

And that is all we are told about the men who made Doc Savage. The Man of Bronze must have had a number of other tutors, but thus far they remain unidentified.

APPENDIX E
What Dent Wrote, What Dent Knew, What Dent Meant
The Final Word on Doc Savage's Age

At first glance, Lester Dent, one of the co-creators and the main writer of the DOC SAVAGE series, seems to have been careless in his facts regarding Clark Savage Jr.'s background. In *The Man of Bronze*, the first novel of the series, Dent tells us that Doc met his five aides during the Great War – World War I. In later novels, Dent makes comments regarding Doc's age that indicate that he was too young to have served in the war.

For example, *Devil on the Moon* (which occurred in 1936, according to my chronology of the series) states that Doc Savage is "a young man". This almost certainly indicates that his life is not yet half over at the time; based on the life expectancy of a man of his era, this means that he was born no earlier than 1904. But we know that he *was* born by 1911, when, according to *They Died Twice*, he had already acquired his nickname.

Cargo Unknown states that "the elder Savage had died about the time Doc's unusual training had been finished", "about twenty years of training". This strongly suggests that Doc's birth year was about 1911, since *The Man of Bronze* takes place in 1931. So how could Doc have possibly served in World War I if he was born in 1911 (or even 1904)? There is some evidence that when Dent wrote *The Man of Bronze*, he did not have all the facts.

In *The Ten Tons Snakes* (written in late 1944), Dent stated that Doc "had never known just what had happened to his father to cause him to put his small son, Doc, in the hands of scientists for training". However, in *No Light to Die By* (which occurred in 1946), Doc himself writes, "My father [was] victimized by criminals", referring to the motivation of the elder Savage for Doc's unusual training, which, Doc writes, lasted "from the time I was fourteen months old until I was twenty years old". These comments have several significances, the most obvious of which is that it confirms that Doc was indeed about twenty in *The Man of Bronze*.

Second, in 1944 Dent did not know – or was prevented from saying – that Doc knew what had caused his father to have Doc trained as he was. Almost exactly two years later, Doc reveals this himself to the public. So Dent did not reveal everything there was to reveal about Doc, whether from lack of knowledge or by Doc himself preventing it. So it is possible that the same circumstance applies to Doc's war service – or lack of it.

Third, the motivation for Clark Savage Sr. having his son trained to fight crime was because he had been victimized by criminals, not because he was trying to atone for any sins he might have committed previous to Doc's birth. We may infer that the victimization caused the elder Savage a devastating loss, for him to go to such extremes to prevent something similar happening to others; one does not devote the life of one's son to fighting crime because of a common mugging.

The introduction to *No Light to Die By* is the subject of some controversy: "Robeson" [Dent] wrote, referring to the writing of *The Man of Bronze*, "This thing started Nov. 12, 1932". But Dent was relying on his memory when he wrote this, and he was wrong. In fact, the actual notation in his famous notebook reads "Dec. 10, 1932". Philip Jose Farmer concluded that Dent was thinking of Doc's birthday. He was not.

Information in *Peril in the North* conclusively puts Doc's birthday in late May. In this story, Doc celebrates his birthday. At that time, the midnight sun is visible near Greenland. This occurs between May 25 and July 25. Due to the realities of publishing (which we know apply in Doc's universe because of the introduction to *No Light to Die By*), the adventure could have occurred no later than May. The intersection of these two facts leaves only very late May for Doc's birthday.

I believe that Dent was thinking of the date that the events that he would "novelize" as *The Man of Bronze* began when he wrote "Nov. 12" in *No Light to Die By* (he of course correctly remembered the *year* that he began writing). Evidence in the novel points to a placement late in the year (1931, to be exact). The date of November 12 does not disagree with any information in the novel. It in fact matches the weather and lunar data and the days of the week that seem to be weekdays and weekend days. But this is beside the point.

As I have written elsewhere, I believe the crime that befell Clark Savage Sr. was the murder of his wife. *Cargo Unknown* tells us that "Doc had never known his mother; she had died when he was less than a year old." So between this time and when Doc turned fourteen months old, Clark Sr. decided to have his son trained as the Nemesis of crime. *The Man Who Was Scared* tells us: "Doc's father, about the time Doc was born, evidently received some sort of shock which completely warped his outlook on life – made him devote the rest of his days to raising a son who would follow the career of righting wrongs and punishing criminals who seemed to be outside the law" (*Danger Lies East* calls them "the international sort"). This links the two events – the death of Doc's mother and his father's decision to train Doc to fight crime (chronologically, at least), leading to the not unreasonable conclusion that she was in fact murdered by criminals – and, based on the nature of Doc's training, quite possibly by a fantastic mastermind such as those Doc himself would later face in his career. Not conclusive, I'll grant, but very persuasive, I believe.

Dent may have known very early that Doc did not actually meet his aides in World War I. In *The Land of Terror* (the second novel in the series), he wrote that Doc's "five friends ... had first assembled during the Great War". Note that it does not read "Doc *and* his five friends ...". Why no mention of Doc? Had Dent learned by this time that he had been in error in thinking that Doc had met his future aides during the war? Or had he been instructed by Doc to drop this fiction? In fact, the comment in *The Man of Bronze* is the *only one* in the *entire series* to refer to Doc being in World War I. Why? And although Dent's notebook states that "the others were his companions in the World War", there is not a *single* reference to Doc's war service in the *forty pages* of notes about him – unlike that of each of the five aides. This seems a glaring omission if Doc had indeed served in the war.

What about Doc's war medals, also described in *No Light to Die By*? These are four Purple Hearts. This type of medal had been discontinued before World War I and was not given out for service in that war. President Hoover reinstated it in 1932, so these awards had to have been for service during World War *II*. These are the only military awards of Doc's ever mentioned in the series.

In the aforementioned *Cargo Unknown*, when Renny tells a friend about meeting Doc, he does not mention World War I (but he does not go into specifics). So Dent seems to have learned by 1944 that Doc had not met his future aides during the war, if he did not know earlier. Doubtless he made this aspect about Doc up because he did not know how the bronze man acquired his aides in the beginning, and it would seem awkward not to explain their relationship. By the second novel, he seems to have known that this was inaccurate, even if he did not know the true facts. If Dent ever knew the truth, he never revealed it. That Renny doesn't reveal in *Cargo Unknown* how he met Doc suggests that Dent himself did not know even at this late date. But there is a clue, in – ironically -- *The Man of Bronze*: "Motivated by their mutual admiration for" the elder Savage, the five men "decided to take up his work of good". If they have known Doc for more than twelve years at this point, why aren't they motivated by *him?*

Doc, in *The Man of Bronze*, says, "Tonight we begin carrying out the ideals of my father". Why weren't they doing this *before* his death? Because Doc had not yet begun his career, and, it should be obvious by now, was too young to have done so. And the others were not yet *his* comrades; they seem to have been friends or colleagues of Doc's father prior to *The Man of Bronze*, and knew Doc through him. This, too, is inconclusive, but very suggestive.

Because Clark Savage, Sr. was in Central America on two separate expeditions in 1911, it seems that his son would have been born "fourteen months" prior to this; certainly young Doc was in the care of scientists by this time. So Doc could have been born no later than 1910, if his father's expeditions both occurred late in 1911.

What can we conclude? There can be no doubt that Doc Savage was born in late May, between 1904 and 1910 (inclusive). The preponderance of evidence suggests closer to 1910. I myself chose 1907, which is nothing more – and nothing less -- than a good deduction. But I could probably be talked in to either 1908 or 1909; any later than that, and I believe we have problems with Doc being a doctor by 1925, the time when he began the life-restoring process described in *Resurrection Day* (Doc had been working on the process for a full decade by the time of this adventure, 1935). By my reckoning, Doc became an M.D. in 1923 at the age of sixteen, after which he studied neurology.

Now that you have all the evidence, you can decide for yourself.

The truth is probably much more mundane: Dent, like later comic book writers, probably gave no real thought to the age of his hero initially, and soon found that his creation was aging much too rapidly for all the adventures he was having (Superman, for example, met President John Kennedy as both Superboy *and* Superman, due to this phenomenon!). So Dent simply dropped references that suggested that Doc was old enough to have served in World War I. Such is the "life" of an action hero

But that shouldn't stop us from enjoying the stories.

APPENDIX F
The French Connection:
in Search of Doc Savage's Parentage

Readers of Philip Jose Farmer are likely familiar with his Wold Newton genealogy. If you are one of them, you will possibly wonder, why another genealogy?

At the risk of offending the many Wold Newtonians out there, I must confess I put no stock in the WN genealogy. Before you throw rotten tomatoes – or worse, stop reading right here – let me say that Farmer's Wold Newton universe is an amazing body of work, and I have great respect (and love) for Farmer's writings. However, his genealogy is flawed. The dates he ascribes to at least some events in at least some novels and/or the histories of at least some characters are incorrect, and seemingly fudged in order to make certain marriages/births work. The error in the age of Professor Challenger's daughter (pointed out to me by Rick Lai) comes to mind, along with his more well-known assertion that Captain Nemo and Professor Moriarty were one and the same – they were not. I have not read all of the necessary writings to refute Farmer's Wold Newton genealogy point by point (and have no desire to do so), but have done enough research to know that it is not completely accurate.

Also, much of the genealogy is pure speculation, for which nothing but circumstantial evidence – often less – exists to support. Beyond meager physical characteristics and temperament of characters, there is little root system to support the huge family tree Farmer offers. This, in itself, is not so bad, because that is how theories are formed, but combined with seemingly deliberate errors in dating, it is inexcusable.

Probably the average reader is unaware of these contrivances. Countless stories would have to be read to uncover them all. So we will take a fresh look at one branch of the massive Wold Newton family tree -- that of

Doc Savage -- and see where it leads us.

As is the case with many pulp heroes, we are told little about Doc Savage's parents. Wanderlust seems to have been in the Savage family genes. Doc Savage is a well-known globetrotter. Clark Savage, Sr. – Doc's father – spent a good portion of his time treasure hunting. We are told specifically of two trips to Central America in the early 1910s (according to *The Man of Bronze* and *They Died Twice*); he almost certainly discovered the Valley of the Vanished in 1911. He seems to have been absent for much of Doc's youth; there are repeated references to the "scientists" having raised Doc, not his own father. The only references to the elder Savage's "work" are in fact exploration (i.e., treasure hunting), and it is probably this that he was doing at Andros Island when Doc was born; the western Atlantic Ocean is famous for its shipwrecks. *Waves of Death* tells us that Doc's training "was the sole purpose for which Doc's father worked for a period of many years". This seems to suggest that the elder Savage was in Central America searching for treasure in 1911 to pay for his son's training.

While he had some sort of medical training – it is said in *The Man of Bronze* that he had saved the life of Carlos Avispa (due to his "medical skill") – Clark, Sr. seems to have given up that profession early on, if indeed he ever was a physician. If he was, it seems strange that he is never identified as "Dr. Clark Savage", as Doc is. He is merely "Clark Savage, Sr.".

In *I Died Yesterday*, Pat Savage mentions that "our grandfather" – referring to her and Doc – lived in a log cabin and that "there were villages named after him all over the northwest" (in *Violent Night* she describes him as an Indian fighter; these two grandfathers must be the same man, as she refers to his six shooter, an heirloom which she owns, in both stories). If Pat and Doc are indeed first cousins – and there is some contention over this – then this man is a Savage. Based on Pat's description, he, too, was a wanderer. So wanderlust is a Savage trait.

When they are introduced in *Brand of the Werewolf*, Alex

Savage and his daughter Patricia are described as Doc's "uncle" and "cousin", respectively. Taken literally, this means that Doc and Pat are first cousins. But she (again in *Violent Night*) says that she is Doc's "third or fourth cousin" (the text reads "a distant" cousin). If she and Doc are first cousins, they share a common grandfather: the father of their fathers, who are brothers. If she and Doc are second cousins, they share a common great-grandfather: the father of their grandfathers, who are brothers; her and Doc's fathers are first cousins. If she and Doc are third cousins ... you get the idea. The family tapestry begins to unravel. If she and Doc *were* first cousins, why would Pat say anything to the contrary?

When Pat spoke of her grandfather – her and Doc's grandfather – she seems to be correct; the timing fits: when Alex is described in *Brand of the Werewolf*, he is said to have settled the area "forty years" earlier, circa 1890. He must therefore be near sixty years old at the time of his death, and quite probably a few years older (Pat, oddly, is sixteen-nearly-seventeen at that time, according to information in *Death is a Round Black Spot*). Her grandfather was therefore likely born before 1850; this matches the comment that his gun "was made before the day of Jesse James" (1866). It weighs about four pounds.

Dent calls this gun a Colt Frontier Single Action .44. This seems to be a fictional label, as I have been unable to find a gun with such a name (and in this age of the internet, if it existed, it could be found). Sam Colt manufactured guns from 1836 to 1842, and, after going bankrupt, again beginning in 1847, with the Walker model. This information may help us with dates.

So possibly Pat and Doc are second cousins -- their fathers being first cousins -- and that their common "grandfather" is actually a *great*-grandfather, and she was speaking loosely when describing herself as being Doc's third or fourth cousin. Although there is simply too much contradictory information to be certain, I believe that Pat and Doc are indeed second cousins; there would be no reason for Pat to say "third or fourth cousin" if the two were first cousins, and it is possible that she mis-spoke in saying "third or fourth", whether she was in honest error or simply being careless.

So Doc and Pat's common great-grandfather would likely have been born in the 1820s, and acquired his pre-1866 six shooter possibly circa 1840 – though this could have occurred earlier, while in his teens, or much later. It is not said that it was his first gun. According to my research into six shooters, his would seem to have been the 1849 Colt Dragoon (the heaviest of the guns I could locate – unless we posit that the Colt Frontier Single Action existed in Doc Savage's universe but not our own), which he would probably have acquired in his twenties (though possibly a little earlier).

This also provides us with some further circumstantial evidence: if this Savage is Doc and Pat's grandfather, and was born in the 1840s, why would his lifelong gun be one from the time of his birth and not something more modern, say, the famous and popular Colt Peacemaker? While it could be an heirloom, it seems more reasonable that he would want the latest in gun technology. So it seems that he was in fact born a generation earlier, and is their great-grandfather.

Nowhere in *Brand of the Werewolf* is it stated that Pat is Doc's only living relative. This idea, like that of their true relationship, fluctuates over the course of the series. It is not until *The Feathered Octopus* (1936) – Pat's sixteenth appearance (according to my chronology of the series) – that it's said that Pat is Doc's only living relative. *The Time Terror* (1941) states that Pat is "one of Doc's few living relatives", not his "only" one. In *The Laugh of Death*, which occurs the month after *The Time Terror* (again, according to my chronology), she is back to being his "only living relative"; Doc himself says this, so we may take it to be true – at least by August 1941. If *The Time Terror* is not in error – and it may well be – then the last of his other (known) relatives died in the few weeks between *The Laugh of Death* and *The Time Terror.*

Pat, like Doc, has "bronze" skin. *They Died Twice* states that "nature had given [Doc] ... bronze skin – suns had helped darken" it (these are the often-mentioned "tropical suns"). So dark skin is also a Savage family trait (as is bronze-colored hair, which Pat shares in common with Doc).

There is no reason to think that Doc's father was particularly old when he was killed in 1931. He was probably 45-55 years old; if a typical father, he would be near fifty, making him a good decade younger than Alex. Doc apparently resembles him in some ways, but not overly much: though Lester Dent (via the narrative), in *The Land of Terror*, states that the portrait of Doc's father which hangs in the 86th floor reception room bears a resemblance to Doc, Sammy Wales, in *No Light to Die By*, finds none. The elder Savage may have had bronze skin, but probably not; one would think that this would have been noticed by Sammy Wales, if true. Also, since no mention is made of golden eyes, Doc's father did not possess these, either. These would surely have been mentioned if he possessed them.

It may be that the superficial Sammy looked for only these unusual traits of Doc's in the portrait, and, finding neither, found no resemblance between the two men. So Doc may have had his father's facial features – validating the reference in *The Land of Terror.* Although this isn't certain, what else are we to conclude?

Since neither Doc's father nor his cousin Pat Savage had golden eyes, it seems likely that Doc Savage inherited this trait from his mother's family, not the Savages. But wait (you protest), Pat had golden eyes as early as *The Fantastic Island* (1934). Surely, if Pat *did* have golden eyes, they would have been mentioned in her debut and in her appearances in between that story and this one, right? But they were not. Why? Ryerson Johnson, the author of *The Fantastic Island*, admitted in a later interview that he mistakenly gave Pat golden eyes in the story when they are in fact blue -- and this error was perpetuated by later authors – including Dent himself.

Of Doc's mother, nothing is known, not even her name. All we do know is that she died shortly after Doc's birth ("when he was less than a year old"), according to *Cargo Unknown*. Although Dent is silent about her identity, there may be a clue in another story -- "Who Goes There?" by John W. Campbell.

Albert Tonik, a Doc Savage scholar, persuasively argues in his article "A Doc Savage Adventure Rediscovered" that the lead character, McReady, is actually the Man of Bronze, perhaps incognito (if you've seen either film version, ignore them). Though there is no evidence to prove it, I believe Doc was using his mother's maiden name, a not unusual means of disguising one's identity. It is in fact interesting to speculate that he kept his secret apartment on the 73th or 74th floor (mentioned in *The Man Who Fell Up*) in her name – and possibly his early North Beach Airport hangar, which predated the Hidalgo Trading Company warehouse (the latter was first in operation in mid 1932). North Beach later became La Guardia Airport, where Doc kept his experimental jet in later adventures. Perhaps he kept the hangar out there all that time, over the years.

And what of the ancestry of Doc's mother? Though she may have been born to an Irish father, Doc's maternal grandmother was undoubtedly descended from Armand Chauvelin, the yellow-eyed nemesis of the Scarlet Pimpernel during the 1790s.

Why? Gold- (or yellow-) colored eyes are so rare that it does not seem unreasonable to believe that all golden-eyed characters in fiction are related, so we may deduce that Doc's mother is a descendant of Armand (whether or not you accept the Irish connection, which I admit is speculative). *His* only mentioned progeny is Fleurette, who was eighteen at the beginning of *Sir Percy Hits Back*, which occurred in 1794. If the marriage of Doc Savage's father and mother was normal for the time, his mother was probably in her early twenties in 1907, when Doc was born (according to my research), and Fleurette would be her great-great-grandmother, through her mother, likely a Frenchwoman herself. Why?

Because another famous French character had golden eyes, and our premise is that all golden-eyed characters in fiction are related. Erik (later better known as the Phantom of the Opera), a Frenchman, also had yellow eyes. They had a peculiar sheen to them that made them visible in low light, like a cat's. Born circa 1830, Erik inherited his love of masonry from his father, and so may have inherited his eyes, as well. If so, then Erik's father was probably Fleurette's son, making Erik and Doc Savage (very) distant cousins.

Since Erik was an only child, Doc's mother was not descended from Erik's father; Fleurette likely had more than one child – Erik's father and at least one other who was Doc Savage's ancestor. Male or female, we cannot guess. The trait would not seem to be sex-specific, although it may be worth noting that golden eyes are only expressed (as far as we know) in males – Armand, Erik and Doc. Are they recessive in females?

But we are not quite done yet. Following our lead of golden eyes, there are several more fictional characters we must examine. Sam Spade, the famous private detective of *The Maltese Falcon*, had yellow-gray eyes. Wolf Larsen, the infamous title character of *The Sea-Wolf*, had gray eyes with flecks of gold in them. Philip Marlowe, the protagonist of Raymond Chandler's many mystery novels, also had gold flecks in his light-brown eyes (as stated in *Trouble Is My Business*). These of course would be related to Doc through his mother.

While Spade must be related to Doc through the Chauvelins (if you accept the premise that all yellow-eyed characters are related), Larsen need not be. There may be a closer link, for Doc has Larsen's gold flecks in *his* eyes, as well. Larsen's family -- father's or mother's, we cannot say for certain – came together with Chauvelin's, to produce a union of both unique types of eyes, yellow (or gold) with gold flecks. However, we can guess that this occurred in the near past, not the distant past, for neither trait is diluted in Doc Savage. Given this timing, a Larsen may have been Doc's maternal grandmother's father; he may have moved his family to Ireland, where his daughter met and married a McReady.

The similarities between "Wolf" (his given name is never revealed) Larsen and Doc are striking: his strength is immense; he has a massive build but does not seem massive himself; he is beautiful, in a masculine way. Like Doc, Wolf is a scholar, but a self-taught one. Their only differences are their moral code – Wolf has none – and their temperament. Wolf has none of Doc's stoicism. In fact, he has an inhuman temper. So Doc would seem to have inherited many traits from Wolf's ancestors. Perhaps he would have even turned out like the brutal captain but for his father's training. Wolf claims that he is the way he is because he was the proverbial seed that fell upon inhospitable terrain.

Wolf had several brothers, only one of whom is named – or nicknamed – in the novel, "Death"; the others seemed to have died at sea while Wolf was young. Given the time frame of *The Sea-Wolf* (apparently the turn of the twentieth century), it would seem that an uncle of Wolf Larsen married Doc's maternal great-grandmother (Wolf seems to be near fifty in the story; he is "beginning to diminish and die", he says, quoting another character). Why is it likely that the connection between the two men is so close? Because the golden flecks in eyes are such a rare phenomenon that Doc's ancestor was almost certainly closely related to Wolf -- not distantly related, which would suggest many more descendants carrying the unusual trait -- descendants which do not exist. Perhaps golden-flecked eyes began with this uncle's father, Wolf's grandfather.

The Chauvelin wife of this Larsen man (or was he the brother of Wolf's *mother*?) would have been the first cousin of Erik (A.K.A. the Phantom -- and all three would have been contemporaries of Doc's and Pat's Indian-fighting great-grandfather Savage). I am supposing that Doc's maternal grandmother's *mother* is a Chauvelin, not his maternal grandmother's father, because it seems more likely to me that a foreign husband took his French bride to Ireland (or wherever) than a French husband his foreign wife – particularly if she is not Irish (she would be the "Larsen" in that case).

However, this arrangement means that Doc's mother had both the yellow eyes and the gold flecks. It may be that the gold flecks came from Doc's father's mother's side of the family, so that Doc is the only possessor of both traits. This seems likeliest to me. This means that Clark Savage, Sr.'s mother was a Larsen by birth, making her the granddaughter of Wolf's grandfather. Was she Wolf's sister? I don't think so: I believe that she was born in the New World, the daughter of Wolf's uncle, Wolf's first cousin.

It may be worth noting that both the Irish and the French established colonies in what would become eastern Canada – a country well-traveled by Doc and Pat's great-grandfather; perhaps this is where the Larsen, McReady, Chauvelin and Savage families all met up, circa 1850: a McReady and his Chauvelin wife settled in Quebec, whether or not they were born and wed there; their daughter married Clark Savage, Sr., the son of the son of a Canadian Indian fighter and the daughter of Wolf's uncle, who may or may not have settled down in Quebec (the Larsens were, in Wolf's branch, a family of sailors). Both Clark Savage, Sr.'s grandfather and first cousin Alex seemed to be Canadian, so Clark was probably Canadian-born; on the other hand, his parents may have re-located to the United States after Alex's birth (a decade or more separates their births), making him American. This puts many diverse families in one area in a logical fashion. And it also explains how the yellow-eyed Chauvelins came to the New World in order to produce Sam Spade – he would seem to be Doc's second cousin, if I am right about the gold flecks coming from Doc's paternal grandmother and all the four families coming together in Quebec circa 1850. If they

did not, then Spade could be more distantly related to Doc
– if say, Fleurette's son came to the New World and had
enough descendants to create more branches. But I think
not: this new arrangement cleans up the family tree from
earlier versions quite a bit.

Doc's father apparently took his bride from Ireland (or
wherever, if you disbelieve my speculation about her
origins), and when she died shortly after Doc's birth, lost
contact with her family (I have to wonder if they blamed
him for their daughter's death). How else are we to explain
the fact that Doc believes Pat to be his "only living
relative"? He obviously has no knowledge of these yellow-
eyed relatives from his mother's side of the family – if they
still exist when he makes this claim. Could they all have
been dead by the time of the DOC SAVAGE series?

What about Marlowe? He was certainly alive during the
entire run of the series and the gold flecks in his eyes tie him
to Larsen, and through Larsen, to Doc Savage. Again, the
relationship between these three men must be close,
because of the gold flecks. Marlowe is almost certainly
descended from Wolf Larsen's grandfather, the probable
progenitor of the gold-flecked eyes), making him and Doc
distant cousins (third cousins, to be precise). Which
ancestor was male or female, we cannot guess, nor can we
deduce how (or when) this possessor of gold-flecked eyes
came to America. We cannot even be certain that Marlowe
came by his gold-flecked eyes through his mother – perhaps
his father was descended from Wolf Larsen's grandfather,
and not Marlowe's mother.

Spade, it has been said, was killed shortly after *The
Maltese Falcon*, in the late 1920s. This could conceivably
have brought the "yellow eyes" line to an end in the Spade
family, and perhaps the entire American branch of
Chauvelin descendants – perhaps even the end of the
Chauvelins outside of Doc himself, as Doc suggests by
calling Pat his "only living relative". Wolf Larsen dies at
the end of *The Sea-Wolf*, with no known living relatives
except his brother. Given his apparent age, Death Larsen is

almost certainly dead by 1931. This leaves us with Marlowe, who is a certain relative, even if he was not known to Wolf Larsen himself.

There is one last source of golden-eyed character to examine, and a surprising one at that: the James Bond series by Ian Fleming. It gives us no less than four yellow-eyed characters. The one most obviously related to our discussion is Mr. Big, the villain from the novel *Live and Let Die*. Born in Haiti, Bounaparte Ignace Gallia is half Negro and half French. His eyes "bulged slightly and the irises were golden round black pupils". So the Chauvelin blood made it to Haiti at some point in the past; Mr. Big seems to have been born around 1915. And his ancestry strengthens the "French connection" to the lineage I have proposed for Doc Savage.

There are three periods that are most likely for a Chauvelin to have gone to Haiti: in 1792 as part of a contingent of French soldiers to put down a revolt; a soldier part of Napoleon's expedition a short time later, or as a businessman emigrant in the 1843-1912 period. The obvious choice is a soldier sent in 1792; this would have been Armand Chauvelin's brother or first cousin then. It seems unlikely that a close kinsman (as he would have had to have been in order to share Armand's yellow eyes) would have been part of Napoleon's army, despite having served in the monarchy's army in 1792 (shortly before the Revolution).

Mr. Big's first name suggests descendency from one of Napoleon's soldiers – but those had the same goal as the earlier army – to regain control of Haiti. So it seems odd that his parents would name their son after a would-be conqueror – yet, they did. Is this because they knew that one of his men was their ancestor? Even odder, they used the Italian spelling of the name, despite Italy never having a presence in Haiti. Perhaps this was because Napoleon was born in Corsica and was of Italian background himself. For the final period, Europeans were welcomed back to the island decades later, after having either been driven from

Haiti or executed circa 1804-1806 by the revolution leader Dessalines.

There does not seem to be enough evidence to decide conclusively, though a brother of Armand's – or more likely a nephew, given the timeframe, in the last decade of the eighteenth century seems most likely to me. Perhaps as a young man who witnessed the horrors of the Reign of Terror, this nephew joined Napoleon.

Whoever his French ancestor was, Gallia was alive throughout the DOC SAVAGE series, dying in 1952 in *Live and Let Die*.

The other characters are Europeans: Rosa Klebb, a Russian in *From Russia With Love*; Irma Bunt, a German, in *On Her Majesty's Secret Service* (and *You Only Live Twice*, where she is Ernst Stavro Blofeld's lover) and; Che Che, a minor character in *On Her Majesty's Secret Service* who is of French descent. Chapter Seven of *On Her Majesty's Secret Service* may explain the dispersal of the yellow-eyed strain throughout Europe from France. Blofeld, through his attorneys, uses this to explain how he, a Pole, could be related to the French Bleuvilles: "his family fled France at the time of the Revolution, settled in Germany ... and subsequently ... migrated to Poland." Although Blofeld's claim seems to a false one, this *could* explain Bunt, a German, and Klebb, who could have a Polish background. All of these characters die in the Bond series, but no doubt they have living relatives. So there may still be golden-eyed characters running around Europe, all distantly related to Doc.

Finally, Victor Frankenstein's nameless creature, who was not alive as we know it -- he did not have the identity of the man whose yellow eyes he possessed.

Victor's creature was created in 1793, coming to life in November of that year. It is probably safe to assume that the man whose body the eyes were taken from was at least twenty years of age at that time, being born no later than 1773.

Armand Chauvelin, the chronologically earliest

documented character with yellow eyes, had an eighteen year-old daughter in 1794. Armand must have been at least eighteen years older than his daughter, born no later than then than 1758.

The two men must be related in some way, and the simplest explanation, given their ages, is that they were brothers. This saves us creating an extensive family tree and complicated relationships.

Armand's brother was in Ingolstadt, Germany when he died, in order for Victor to have had access to his corpse. What was he doing in Germany? We may deduce that he fled the revolution in his native country, which began in 1792. Perhaps significantly, the infamous Reign of Terror began in April 1793.

There is already some evidence that Armand's brother had children: Mr. Big -- Buonaparte Ignace Gallia. Armand's brother would seem to be the older of the two, in that his posited son was older than Fleurette, Armand's daughter, if only by a few years. If he stayed in France while his family moved to Germany, he must have been eighteen by 1793. His father would therefore have been born no later than 1756.

Armand's brother's other child (or children) would seem to have relocated to Germany with his or her father. Irma Bunt, Ernst Stavro Blofeld's assistant and lover, had yellow eyes. Being German, she would seem to be descended from Armand's brother.

Another of his descendants is Rosa Klebb, a member of SMERSH. "Klebb" is not a Russian name, so she would seem to be from East Germany, and possibly descended from the same child (or children) of Armand's brother. At some point, one of his descendants relocated to the eastern part of Germany, which came under Soviet control after World War II.

So there are three branches of the yellow-eyed Chauvelins: the German one, which gave birth to Bunt and Klebb; the French one which gave birth to Erik, the Phantom of the Opera, Buonaparte Ignatius Gallia and Che

Che (the minor character from *On Her Majesty's Secret Service*), and; the American branch, which came from the French one when Doc Savage's maternal grandmother's father came to the New World, and gave birth to Doc and Sam Spade.

Armand's father -- "Goldeneye", shall we call him? -- would then be the progenitor of the yellow-eye strain, giving us as few yellow-eyed people as possible.

Both sets of Doc's grandparents would seem to have died by autumn 1940, when *The Golden Man* occurs. In that adventure, a government agent from a foreign nation (the Golden Man of the title) tells Doc that he knows all about him. The text reads: "this Golden Man knew the exact place of his [Doc's] birth. It was astounding. Doc himself had known of no living man who had those facts." Surely this would include all of Doc's grandparents. There were no – or few -- relatives on his father's side of his family, the Savages, at this time (Pat surely did not have knowledge of the circumstances of Doc's birth, or Doc would not have said "no living man"). But what about his mother's side of the family?

It seems quite possible that the Golden Man came by his information through them. Doc's mother's parents would surely have told their relatives of their daughter's son, and the Golden Man tracked them down and obtained the information about Doc's birth from them. How else could he have come by this supposedly secret information?

This is not to suggest that this information was widely known among Doc's maternal relatives. Doc's father, at least, seems to have tried to keep the information regarding Doc's birth a secret (for some unknown reason), although this is far from certain. But all it would take would be one relative -- one *trusted* relative -- who was told of Doc's birth by his maternal grandparents. So it is possible that Doc has at least one relative left on his mother's side (not counting Marlowe), as well as Pat. If Doc is aware of this person or persons, perhaps he/she/they died in the gap between *The Time Terror* and *The Laugh of Death*, explaining the discrepancy in references in those two tales.

However, it is also possible that the Golden Man came by his information through a source unknown to Doc, perhaps from a letter written by an eyewitness to a friend or relative. This type of record would be difficult for Doc to know of. And the information about his birth is so specific that it might not have been relayed to relatives. "We just had a grandson who was born in the Bahamas on our daughter's yacht", maybe; "in the shallow cove at the north end of Andros Island", probably not. But an eyewitness might have, in a *series* of letters, described the yacht's location as a matter of simple interest ("today, moored off the north side of Andros Island"; and later, "Savage's wife gave birth yesterday", and so on).

Further research may uncover more specific information, but for now, this is as much as we know – or can deduce -- about Doc Savage's parentage.

DOC SAVAGE'S PROBABLE

U = unknown name (?) = unknown sex

U (?)
(possible first yellow eyes)
:_____
:

Armand Chauvelin
:

FleuretteChauvelin
b 1776   :
_____:
:   :
:   :
U (M)   U (M)   "Larsen" (possible first flecked eyes)
:   :   :_____
:   :   :
Erik   U (?)   "Larsen" (M)   Savage (M)
b~1830 :   :   "Indian fighter"
_____: :   _____:
:   :   :   :
U (F)= McReady (M) "Larsen" (F)= Sav. (M) Sav. (M)
_____:_____   :   :
:   :   :   :
U (?)   McReady (F) = Clark Savage, Sr Alex Sav.
:   :   :
:   :   :
Sam Spade Clark "Doc" Savage, Jr   Pat Savage
b~1895?   b 1907   b 1915

FAMILY TREE
(?) = lineage uncertain

```
                                              :
                                   Chauvelin (?)
                                              :
                                        U (M)
                                              :
                                              :
                                              :
                                              :
                                              :
    _____                  :
    :              :        :                 :
    :              :        ?                 :
 "Larsen (?)   Larsen = U (F)                 :
    :              _____:___           :
    :              :           :              :
 U (?)  "Wolf" Larsen  "Death" Larsen         :
    :         b~1850?                          :
    :                                          :
  U (?)                                        :
    :                                          :
    :                                          :
 Philip Marlowe        Buonaparte Ignace Gallo
 b~1905                        b~1911
```

282

APPENDIX G
Coming Down Out of the Trees
A look at the Mayfair Family

In the case of the Mayfair family, referring to its various members as being part of a tree is rather appropriate because many of them have ape-like qualities. This "Mayfair gene" seems to be a strong if recessive gene -- if it can be called that. This trait -- or set of traits -- gives its possessors resemblance to the great apes: brutish face, long arms and a mighty chest -- and strength to match.

The most familiar character to readers of Doc Savage of this type is of course Lt. Colonel Andrew Blodgett Mayfair -- better known as "Monk", due to his simian features. Monk stands just over five feet tall (his height varies throughout the series), weighing in the neighborhood of 250 pounds (though this, too, changes in the later tales). Covered in coarse red hair, he was born in Oklahoma around 1890; he had seemingly gotten his PhD in chemistry prior to the outbreak of World War I in 1914.

In the series, we meet only one relative of Monk's who is positively identified as such: "Handsome" Mayfair. In *The King of Terror*, Monk meets this distant relative, a "sixteenth cousin or something". "He certainly had none of the Mayfair homeliness", indicating that it is Monk's *father's* family, the Mayfairs, who are homely and brutish looking.

But there may be another relative of Monk in the series. In *Bequest of Evil*, Monk supposedly inherits a castle and British title. Though this turns out to be a hoax, he may be legitimately related to the true heirs (this is not resolved in the story). The true "Earl of Chester" looks so much like Monk that it takes the presence of a scar on Monk to tell them apart. It seems highly unlikely that a Monk-double also named "Mayfair" would not be related to Monk. If this British connection is true, it serves us well, for there are other English characters who share the

Mayfair traits: Professor Challenger from *The Lost World* (and other tales) and Horace Holly from *She*.

Holly seems to be in his middle forties in *She*. He writes (CH 1) that he was "twenty-two" "over twenty years ago". That he did not write "twenty-five years ago" suggests that he is not yet forty-seven -- nor probably even forty-six. So we can put his age at between 43 and 45, inclusive. If *She* occurred near the time it was written (1886), then Holly was born circa 1841. He describes himself thusly: "Short, thick-set, and deep-chested almost to deformity, with long sinewy arms, heavy features, deep-set grey eyes, a low brow half overgrown with a mop of thick black hair, like a deserted clearing on which the forest had once more begun to encroach; such was my appearance nearly a quarter of a century ago, and such, with some modification, it is to this day. Like Cain, I was branded --branded by Nature with the stamp of abnormal ugliness, as I was gifted by Nature with iron and abnormal strength and considerable intellectual powers." His resemblance to Monk Mayfair is obvious. Substitute red hair for black and this describes Monk. If Holly is indeed a Mayfair by blood, then his mother (or earlier female ancestor) would have been part of the noble Mayfair family of England.

Chapter 2 of *The Lost World* describes Professor Challenger: "It was his size which took one's breath away -- his size and his imposing presence. His head was enormous, the largest I have ever seen upon a human being. I am sure that his top-hat, had I ever ventured to don it, would have slipped over me entirely and rested on my shoulders. He had the face and beard which I associate with an Assyrian bull; the former florid, the latter so black as almost to have a suspicion of blue, spade-shaped and rippling down over his chest. The hair was peculiar, plastered down in front in a long, curving wisp over his massive forehead. The eyes were blue-gray under great black tufts, very clear, very critical, and very masterful. A huge spread of shoulders and a chest like a barrel were the other parts of him which appeared above the table, save for two enormous hands covered with long black hair. This and a bellowing, roaring, rumbling voice made up my first impression of the notorious Professor Challenger."

George Edward Challenger was born in "1863" (also CH 2), making him a generation younger than Horace Holly -- who could very well be his uncle on his mother's side: that is, Holly could have a sister who was Challenger's mother (one shudders to think what her appearance might have been). This is the most direct connection we can make between the two men, which, in my opinion, is to be desired; more distant connections suggest more similar-looking relatives of which we have no record. Also, Challenger's appearance is *very* similar to Holly's, also suggesting a close relation. Challenger's features, while brutish, are not described as being particularly ape-like, as is the case with both Monk and Holly.

If this is the case, then black hair may have come from Holly's father, for red hair seems to be a Mayfair trait, seen in both Monk and the Earl of Chester. Challenger's large head (and large body) may have come from his father's family, then, for Monk has a "nubbin" of a head, while the size of Holly's is not mentioned (we may therefore assume it not to be abnormally large, as Challenger's is). It is also worth noting that both men have gray(ish) eyes. Although Monk's eyes are never described in the DOC SAVAGE series, they are blue-gray on the original pulp cover of *The Awful Egg*. So, this, too, seems to be a Mayfair family trait.

Returning to America: Dirk Peters, from *The Narrative of Arthur Gordon Pym* (and its sequels), is also probably related to Monk. Peters is half Indian (his mother was a "squaw"). His arms and legs are bowed. He stands only 4'8" but has "Herculean" strength (CH 4 of the original story). In *The Sphinx of the Ice Fields*, "ten [men] strove to control the half-breed" (CH 22), attesting to this strength. A character in *A Strange Discovery* calls him an "orang-outang" (CH 13) and he breaks the spine of a man with his bare hands. Peters was born near the turn of the century (*The Sphinx of the Ice Fields* says 1796), putting three or four generations between him and Monk.

Since his family name is Peters, neither Dirk's father nor his paternal grandfather is a Mayfair (or else his father's and his own name would be Mayfair). So the closest connection we can make is if his paternal grand*mother* was born a Mayfair. She could be Monk's great, great, great, great aunt (because Monk is a Mayfair, he had to be descended from her *brother*, who retained the Mayfair name), probably, making Dirk Peters Monk's first cousin five times removed. If this is true, then the first Mayfair came to America prior to 1796, since Peters was born and raised in the U.S. But since we are talking about a brother and sister, a Mayfair probably came to America a generation earlier than 1796, and possibly *two* -- meaning that one or more Mayfairs may have fought in the Revolutionary War.

Since the title of Earl of Chester stayed in England, it is possible that a younger brother (or son) of the reigning Earl came to America circa 1750, so that his children -- a daughter who would marry man named Peters and bear a son who would become Dirk's father, and a son who would pass the name Mayfair on to Monk in the late 1800s -- were born in the New World by 1755 or so (the siblings' children being born circa 1775).

It is also probably worth noting that three of our four examples are geniuses, or nearly so (we don't know the state of the Earl of Chester's intelligence). It's possible that Dirk, too, was quite intelligent -- but lacked the education to properly bring it to its full potential.

For all his snootiness and bragging, Ham Brooks' family tree has nothing on the Mayfair clan.

APPENDIX H
"John Sunlight" Dossier

The Devil Genghis states that "John Sunlight" may or may not be his true name; the outline for *Fortress of Solitude* says that it's a nickname given to him because of his "black moods".

"He was not a young man" in 1937, the year of his two appearances (according to this chronology); he was therefore probably born earlier than 1905 (making him slightly older than Doc, who was probably born in very late May 1907). But there is no gray in his black hair, so he may not be much older than 40 (say, born no earlier than 1892).

Although he served in the Soviet Army in the early 1930s, "John Sunlight wasn't a Russian". He "could speak English with almost no accent at all". This seems to suggest that it is not his first language, which effectively rules out Great Britain, Canada, America and Australia as his birth nation. He does, however, seem to prefer English, both in theory and practice: In *Fortress of Solitude*, he speaks it to his Russian followers and an Eskimo he meets (but it is not clear if Sunlight does this because he believes the Eskimo is near an English-speaking territory). In *The Devil Genghis*, he wants to make English Earth's official language (this idea was bandied about at the time by serious-minded people). I tend to think that English was not Sunlight's first language. So what was?

Sunlight was undeniably white, so this leaves us with the countries of middle and northern Europe. Unfortunately, we are not told what accent he did have, and there is no evidence to lead us any further in this investigation. But we may speculate that perhaps he was born in one of the Soviet-affiliated Slav countries, which would help explain how he got into the Soviet Army. With the xenophobia of Stalin, it doesn't seem likely Sunlight could have been western European.

Sunlight was convicted of blackmailing his Soviet army superiors two and a half years prior to *Fortress of Solitude*. This, according to this chronology, occurred in summer 1934. It may be of note that Stalin's infamous purges began the following December. Did Sunlight's exposure kick off a nationwide witch-hunt? Although it's stated in *Fortress of Solitude* that, more than anything, he wants control over people, surely, with his global schemes in both *Fortress of Solitude* and *The Devil Genghis*, Sunlight was not blackmailing his superiors over better food and women. No, he undoubtedly had something larger, more sinister in mind, something which shook the Soviet government to its very foundation. And recall that Sunlight was sentenced **for life** to Siberia over this incident. It was not a minor scheme, Sunlight's offense. But, unfortunately, there is no further information to be gleaned from the adventures.

We are not told how long Sunlight served in the Soviet Army. "Russia was the first government to be afraid of him"; this refers to the circumstances that resulted in him being sent to Siberia. "The world had first learned of John Sunlight when Russia had sent him to a Siberian prison". We can glean from this statement that Sunlight was unknown to the general public before his trial. However, he is known to the governments of France, Egypt, and at least one of the two Balkan nations described in *Fortress of Solitude*. This is undoubtedly because "he had worked all his evil life toward one hideous goal", according to *Fortress of Solitude*; although not explicitly stated in this tale, this must be global domination, as described in *The Devil Genghis* (he wants to eliminate all weapons, national borders and all languages except English, among other things; although he doesn't say so, it is clear that he, of course, must be declared the leader of Earth's proposed one government). This comment virtually rules out the possibility that Sunlight was blackmailing his superiors over minor conveniences. Combined with the fact that "John Sunlight had many contacts" around the world, this seems to suggest that he was some sort of international criminal, perhaps a spy. Could he have been in the G.R.U., Soviet military intelligence? Or the K.G.B. (which, for the youthful market for which he wrote, Dent would have had to have lump in with the "army")?

By the time Doc gets involved in *Fortress of Solitude*, following the murder of Serge Mafnoff, Sunlight knows quite a bit about the Man of Bronze. He knows of Doc's upbringing, the sketchy details of which are public knowledge. But he has also figured out, in the few months he has been living in the Strange Blue Dome, that the place is Doc's secret Fortress of Solitude. How Sunlight knows its name is not explained; there is at least one other incident on the series where the name of the place is known by the public. In the months he has access to the Fortress, Sunlight steals and hides a "score" (according to Doc) of death-dealing devices. Although these are said to gadgets confiscated from masterminds Doc has defeated in the past, the two that we see – the eye-paralyzer and the electron-stopper – were never featured in any adventure (this may therefore suggest two unrecorded adventures).

It is equally a mystery how Toni Lash knows, in *The Devil Genghis*, that Sunlight is supposed to be dead. Surely Doc did not let the events of *Fortress of Solitude* become public knowledge (at least not right away; or did the events of *The Horrors*, Will Murray's proposed follow-up to *Fortress of Solitude*, which deals with the missing devices, force his hand?). And surely Stalin would not have allowed word to leak out that Sunlight had escaped? We must assume that Toni was able to learn of Sunlight's supposed death because she is a spy, and no doubt has contacts in various governments (in fact, she is in France, one of the nations which knows of Sunlight, at the beginning of *The Devil Genghis*). Or maybe she was an avid reader of DOC SAVAGE magazine.

INDEX

Bold numbers indicate the novel's entry in the chronology, *italics* indicate a listing in the chronology summary.

290

D

292

294

E

Empire State Building, the

Q

308

Y

About the Author

Jeff Deischer became enamored of Heroes -- with a capital "H", for these were not ordinary men -- at a very young age. He grew up watching DANIEL BOONE (to whom he is distantly related, by marriage), TARZAN, BATMAN, THE LONE RANGER and ZORRO on television. There is a large "Z" carved into his mother's sewing machine that can attest to this fact (as you might imagine, it did not impress her the way it always did the peasants and soldiers on ZORRO). A few years later, he discovered Heroic fiction -- the Scandinavian myths and Doc Savage and comic books. These imprinted themselves on his creative view, and everything he writes has Good Guys and Bad Guys -- in capital letters.

As an adult writer, he tries to make them *human*, as well. Of his writing he says, "My natural forte is non-fiction. I am not a born writer and writing fiction is work for me."

Though Jeff had been telling stories since he was ten years old, he did not begin to write seriously until 1998, when a happy confluence of events occurred.

Jeff's first major work was the Doc Savage fan fiction novella, *The Stone Death*, which was based on a synopsis by a series ghost writer and is available at the Hidalgo Trading Company website. This was followed in 2000 by the publication of *The Adventures of Doc Savage: a Definitive Chronology*. This work was ground breaking in at least two respects: it established Doc Savage's true birthday and for the first time included Lester Dent's Doc Savage radio plays in a chronology; it also led to a number of articles about the Man of Bronze, published primarily in convention guides in 2008-2011.

The following several years produced *The Winter Wizard* (first published 2008), featuring Jeff's own Street & Smith-style pulp hero, the Challenger; the non-fiction books *Over the* *Rainbow: a User's Guide to* My *Dangyang*, about his many trips to China (2010); *The Marvel Timeline Project, Part 1,* a chronology of the stories of the early years of Marvel Comics (2011, with Murray Ward), and; *The Way They Were: the Histories of Some of Adventure Fiction's Most Famous Heroes and Villains*, a collection of chronology-minded essays about characters as diverse as Korak (Son of Tarzan), James Bond, Captain Nemo and the Phantom of the Opera -- among many others (2011); as well as a few novels published under pen names, all of which are available at Amazon, along with Jeff's newest novel, *Spook Trail*, a pulp adventure set in 1946.

Made in the USA
Lexington, KY
21 August 2013